AF478436

Palgrave Studies in Nineteenth-Century Writing and Culture

General Editor: **Joseph Bristow**, Professor of English, UCLA

Editorial Advisory Board: **Hilary Fraser**, Birkbeck College, University of London; **Josephine McDonagh**, Kings College London; **Yopie Prins**, University of Michigan; **Lindsay Smith**, University of Sussex; **Margaret D. Stetz**, University of Delaware; **Jenny Bourne Taylor**, University of Sussex

Palgrave Studies in Nineteenth-Century Writing and Culture is a new monograph series that aims to represent the most innovative research on literary works that were produced in the English-speaking world from the time of the Napoleonic Wars to the *fin de siècle*. Attentive to the historical continuities between 'Romantic' and 'Victorian', the series will feature studies that help scholarship to reassess the meaning of these terms during a century marked by diverse cultural, literary, and political movements. The main aim of the series is to look at the increasing influence of types of historicism on our understanding of literary forms and genres. It reflects the shift from critical theory to cultural history that has affected not only the period 1800–1900 but also every field within the discipline of English literature. All titles in the series seek to offer fresh critical perspectives and challenging readings of both canonical and non-canonical writings of this era.

Titles include:

Eitan Bar-Yosef and Nadia Valman (*editors*)
'THE JEW' IN LATE-VICTORIAN AND EDWARDIAN CULTURE
Between the East End and East Africa

Heike Bauer
ENGLISH LITERARY SEXOLOGY
Translations of Inversions, 1860–1930

Laurel Brake and Julie F. Codell (*editors*)
ENCOUNTERS IN THE VICTORIAN PRESS
Editors, Authors, Readers

Luisa Calè and Patrizia Di Bello (*editors*)
ILLUSTRATIONS, OPTICS AND OBJECTS IN NINETEENTH-CENTURY LITERARY AND VISUAL CULTURES

Colette Colligan
THE TRAFFIC IN OBSCENITY FROM BYRON TO BEARDSLEY
Sexuality and Exoticism in Nineteenth-Century Print Culture

Dennis Denisoff
SEXUAL VISUALITY FROM LITERATURE TO FILM, 1850–1950

Stefano Evangelista
BRITISH AESTHETICISM AND ANCIENT GREECE
Hellenism, Reception, Gods in Exile

Laura E. Franey
VICTORIAN TRAVEL WRITING AND IMPERIAL VIOLENCE

Lawrence Frank
VICTORIAN DETECTIVE FICTION AND THE NATURE OF EVIDENCE
The Scientific Investigations of Poe, Dickens and Doyle

Yvonne Ivory
THE HOMOSEXUAL REVIVAL OF RENAISSANCE STYLE, 1850–1930

Colin Jones, Josephine McDonagh and Jon Mee (*editors*)
CHARLES DICKENS, *A TALE OF TWO CITIES* AND THE FRENCH REVOLUTION

Jarlath Killeen
THE FAITHS OF OSCAR WILDE
Catholicism, Folklore and Ireland

Stephanie Kuduk Weiner
REPUBLICAN POLITICS AND ENGLISH POETRY, 1789–1874

Kirsten MacLeod
FICTIONS OF BRITISH DECADENCE
High Art, Popular Writing and the *Fin de Siècle*

Diana Maltz
BRITISH AESTHETICISM AND THE URBAN WORKING CLASSES, 1870–1900

Catherine Maxwell and Patricia Pulham (*editors*)
VERNON LEE
Decadence, Ethics, Aesthetics

Muireann O'Cinneide
ARISTOCRATIC WOMEN AND THE LITERARY NATION, 1832–1867

David Payne
THE REENCHANTMENT OF NINETEENTH-CENTURY FICTION
Dickens, Thackeray, George Eliot and Serialization

Julia Reid
ROBERT LOUIS STEVENSON, SCIENCE, AND THE *FIN DE SIÈCLE*

Anne Stiles (*editor*)
NEUROLOGY AND LITERATURE, 1860–1920

Caroline Sumpter
THE VICTORIAN PRESS AND THE FAIRY TALE

Sara Thornton
ADVERTISING, SUBJECTIVITY AND THE NINETEENTH-CENTURY NOVEL
Dickens, Balzac and the Language of the Walls

Ana Parejo Vadillo
WOMEN POETS AND URBAN AESTHETICISM
Passengers of Modernity

Phyllis Weliver
THE MUSICAL CROWD IN ENGLISH FICTION, 1840–1910
Class, Culture and Nation

Paul Young
GLOBALIZATION AND THE GREAT EXHIBITION
The Victorian New World Order

Palgrave Studies in Nineteenth-Century Writing and Culture
Series Standing Order ISBN 978–0–333–97700–2 (hardback)
(*outside North America only*)

You can receive future titles in this series as they are published by placing a standing order. Please contact your bookseller or, in case of difficulty, write to us at the address below with your name and address, the title of the series and the ISBN quoted above.

Customer Services Department, Macmillan Distribution Ltd, Houndmills, Basingstoke, Hampshire RG21 6XS, England

---

Illustrations, Optics and Objects in Nineteenth-Century Literary and Visual Cultures

Edited by

Luisa Calè
Birkbeck College, University of London

and

Patrizia Di Bello
Birkbeck College, University of London

Foreword by

Hilary Fraser

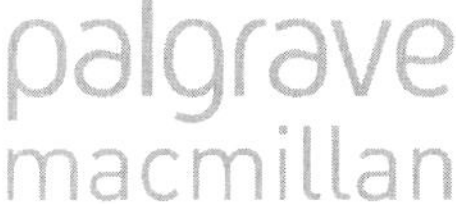

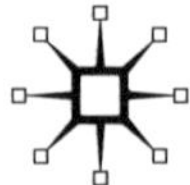

First published 2010 by
PALGRAVE MACMILLAN

Palgrave Macmillan in the UK is an imprint of Macmillan Publishers Limited,
registered in England, company number 785998, of Houndmills, Basingstoke,
Hampshire RG21 6XS.

Palgrave Macmillan in the US is a division of St Martin's Press LLC,
175 Fifth Avenue, New York, NY 10010.

Palgrave Macmillan is the global academic imprint of the above companies
and has companies and representatives throughout the world.

Palgrave® and Macmillan® are registered trademarks in the United States,
the United Kingdom, Europe and other countries.

ISBN-13: 978–0–230–22197–0 hardback

This book is printed on paper suitable for recycling and made from fully
managed and sustained forest sources. Logging, pulping and manufacturing
processes are expected to conform to the environmental regulations of the
country of origin.

A catalogue record for this book is available from the British Library.

A catalog record for this book is available from the Library of Congress.

10   9   8   7   6   5   4   3   2   1
19 18 17 16 15 14 13 12 11 10

Printed and bound in Great Britain by
CPI Antony Rowe, Chippenham and Eastbourne

Contents

Part IV   Precious Objects

List of Plates

The Plates will be found between pages 193 and 194.

Foreword

Hilary Fraser

This collection of essays, which is concerned with objects and practices of reading, viewing and collecting in the nineteenth century, focuses on material visuality and the formulation of a material aesthetic. It represents an exciting intervention into current debates about visuality inaugurated by Jonathan Crary's influential book *Techniques of the Observer* (1990). Crary's project, in writing what he proposes as the pre-history of Guy Debord's 'spectacle', is to delineate the emergence of a new corporealised observer in the nineteenth century. His account of the modernisation of vision and the new validation of the visible in that period begins by explaining how the sense of touch, which had been a crucial component of classical seventeenth and eighteenth-century theories of vision (according to the Cartesian model, the blind 'see with their hands'),[1] became dissociated from sight in the nineteenth century; and how this 'unloosening of the eye from the network of referentiality incarnated in tactility', this 'autonomisation of sight', was 'a historical condition for the rebuilding of an observer fitted for the tasks of "spectacular" consumption'.[2]

Crary's focus is, like Debord's, on visuality, and his thesis requires him to himself slough off the tactile. But what of the equivalently novel conceptualisation of touch in the visual field that might also be said to have begun to emerge in the nineteenth century? What was the pre-history of, say, Maurice Merleau-Ponty's multi-sensorial phenomenology, according to which 'Everything I see is on principle within my reach [...] The visible world and the world of my motor projects are both total parts of the same Being', and whereby the body is 'a self by confusion, narcissism, inherence of the see-er in the seen, the toucher in the touched, the feeler in the felt – a self, then, that is caught up in things, having a front and a back, a past and a future'? Where might we look for the cultural lineage of his celebrated account of the materiality and embodiment of perception: 'Visible and mobile, my body is a thing among things; it is one of them. It is caught in the fabric of the world...'?[3] This is the intriguing territory that the essays in this volume begin to map.

Merleau-Ponty's aesthetic theories were developed in three essays on painting written between 1945 ('Cézanne's Doubt') and 1960 ('Eye and

Mind'). Therefore, one area in which we might seek this pre-history is in late nineteenth-century writing on art. During the same period that Merleau-Ponty was formulating his ideas for the posthumously published 'Eye and Mind', on modern painting and philosophy, the art critic and connoisseur Bernard Berenson was producing his own last book, *Seeing and Knowing*, which was written in 1948 and published in 1953. Berenson had written his first ground-breaking studies of Renaissance art when he was in his thirties, in the 1890s, at which time he was closely identified, by contemporaries such as Roger Fry, with a fin-de-siècle school of art criticism founded on physiological aesthetics. In the mid-twentieth century, and in the teeth of modern developments in art which he deplored, Berenson was still insisting upon the artist's power to make objects 'as tangibly visible as if you could touch them' and asserting 'the psycho-physiological urge to create'.[4] Berenson's aesthetics and art criticism, developed in the context of late Victorian visual philosophy and practice, provides a way of situating the material on optics and objects in the essays here collected within an emergent theorisation of the tangibility of the visual in the nineteenth century.

'Look into your sensorium, and write. All will then go well.'[5] This was Berenson's advice in 1893 to his friend Edith Cooper, soon after she and Katharine Bradley had published, as Michael Field, a volume of exphrastic poems entitled *Sight and Song* (1892). His own way of approaching art was multi-sensorial. Kenneth Clark described his method of authenticating paintings thus: 'He would come very close to [a painting] and tap its surface and then listen attentively, as if expecting some almost inaudible voice to reply. Then, after a long pause, he would murmur a name.'[6] Berenson's most important contribution to late nineteenth-century aesthetics and art criticism, though, was his signature theory of the tactile imagination. It was first articulated in *The Florentine Painters of the Renaissance* (1896), in which he defines 'the essential in the art of painting' as being 'somehow to stimulate our consciousness of tactile values, so that the picture shall have at least as much power as the object represented, to appeal to our tactile imagination'.[7]

Berenson drew on his reading in the current psychological literature, especially the work of William James, in the development of his thesis. He wrote to Katharine Bradley ('Michael') in 1895 : 'Psychology is more & more absorbing me. Tell Field [Edith Cooper] that as she loves me & herself I urge her to get the large edition of James' Psychology & to read it diligently'.[8] In *The Florentine Painters* he notes that 'Psychology has ascertained that sight alone gives us no accurate sense of the third dimension', rather 'In our infancy long before we are conscious of the process, the sense of touch, helped on by muscular sensations of movement, teaches us to appreciate depth, the third dimension, both in objects and in space':

> In the same unconscious years we learn to make of touch, of the third dimension, the test of reality. The child is still dimly aware of the intimate connexion between touch and the third dimension. He cannot persuade himself of the unreality of Looking-Glass Land until he has touched the back of the mirror. Later, we entirely forget the connexion, although it remains true that every time our eyes recognize reality, we are, as a matter of fact, giving tactile values to retinal impressions.[9]

In the two-dimensional form of painting, the artist, in order to achieve a realistic effect, must then construct a third dimension, arousing 'the tactile sense' by means of the surface texture of the paint on the canvas, for, he writes, 'I must have the illusion of being able to touch a figure, I must have the illusion of varying muscular sensations inside my palm and fingers corresponding to the various projections of this figure, before I shall take it for granted as real, and let it affect me lastingly' (p. 63).

It was his insistence on the physical apprehension of the plastic qualities of an object represented imaginatively on a canvas, those qualities in a painting that he regarded as creating the illusion of tangibility and stimulating the sense of touch, that led to Berenson's writing about art and aesthetics being associated with physiological rather than psychological aesthetics, though the two were closely connected in their origins. His emphasis was on what he called the 'ideated sensations' of movement, energy, space, and above all touch in art, which in his view heighten our sense of reality in ways that merely visual sensations do not. He celebrates the capacity of great figurative art to stimulate, for example, 'muscular feelings of varying pressure and strain' (p. 95). Thus, of Pollaiuolo's *Battle of the Nudes* he writes:

> Look at the combatant prostrate on the ground and his assailant bending over, each intent on stabbing the other. See how the prostrate man plants his foot on the thigh of his enemy, and note the tremendous energy he exerts to keep off the foe, who, turning as upon a pivot, with his grip on the other's head, exerts no less force to keep the advantage gained. The significance of all these muscular strains and pressures is so rendered that we cannot help realizing them; we imagine ourselves imitating all the movements,

and exerting the force required for them […] while under the spell of this illusion […] we feel as if the elixir of life, not our own sluggish blood, were coursing through our veins.

(pp. 98–9)

Similarly, of the same painter's *Hercules Strangling Antaeus* he avers:

As you realize the suction of Hercules' grip on the earth, the swelling of his calves with the pressure that falls on them, the violent throwing back of his chest, the stifling force of his embrace; as you realize the supreme effort of Antaeus, with one hand crushing down upon the head and the other tearing at the arm of Hercules, you feel as if a fountain of energy had sprung up under your feet and were playing through your veins.

(p. 99)

Michael Field was especially appreciative of the tactile dimension of both Berenson's and his collaborator (eventually his wife) Mary Costelloe's writing about art. Katharine Bradley writes to the latter of a passage from her forthcoming *Guide to the Italian Pictures at Hampton Court* (1894): ' "With stuffs that tickle the eye & yet rest it" is a phrase in the Bonifazio paper – that gives one the very artist. You can give the artists […] by <u>their way of taking pleasure</u>, whether they liked the <u>feel</u> of a stuff, as well as its hue, & how it seemed to them nicest the folds shd. fall'.[10] The Hampton Court *Guide* everywhere demonstrates and elucidates this tactile imagination at work. Of Giorgione's *The Sleeping Venus*, for example, subject of one of the lusher lyrics in Michael Field's *Sight and Song*, Costelloe writes that this artist's works 'never fail' in their 'power to call up the actual physical sensations of the scenes themselves […] they speak directly to the sensations, making the beholder feel refreshed and soothed, as if actually reclining on the grass in the shade of trees, with his mind free to muse on what delights it most' (p. 13).

Other friends and associates of the Berensons, such as their neighbour in Florence, the art historian, aesthetician and fiction-writer Vernon Lee, and her companion Kit Anstruther-Thomson, pursued their own empirical experimentation to demonstrate the physiological basis of aesthetic responses, which eventuated in a series of intriguing joint publications in physiological aesthetics, beginning with the essay 'Beauty and Ugliness', which appeared in 1897. In their interestingly eccentric intervention into late nineteenth-century psychology, they elaborate an aesthetic of empathy based on Kit's recorded physiological responses to art works, arguing that the contemplation of a beautiful thing – a painting, a building or sculptural form – elicits a motor response in the viewer, who unconsciously imitates the formal properties of the object of vision and, as it were, projects their own bodily movements back onto it: 'the aesthetic seeing, the "realisation" of form, was connected' as Lee later wrote, 'with bodily conditions and motor phenomena' that included 'muscular strains', ' "sensations of direction" [...] and sensations of modification in the highly subtle apparatus for equilibrium', as well as 'sensations of altered respiration and circulation sufficient to account for massive conditions of organic well-being and the reverse'.[11] The 'Anthropomorphic Aesthetics' developed by Lee and Anstruther-Thomson depends upon a 'projection of our inner experience into the forms which we see and realise' (p. 17). Their insistence that aesthetic experience 'consists in the attribution of an individual and varying complexus of dynamic (and perhaps organic) conditions', and therefore that 'it must always, in real experience, bear the character of the individual form by which it is elicited' (p. 31), is close to Berenson's theory of the importance of the tactile imagination, and indeed he was to accuse them (unjustly) of plagiarising his ideas.[12]

Stung by these accusations, Lee's response was that they were ideas that were in the air: 'We were part of a mutually, perhaps unconsciously, collaborating band of enquirers'.[13] She, the more established cultural critic, and more-widely read in continental psychology and aesthetics, had also been more generous in her affirmation of Berenson's originality. In an interesting exchange of 1894 with Katharine Bradley, Berenson bemusedly recounts how Lee's attribution of great originality to him is a complete mystery to him:

> She has discovered that I have discovered the greatest discovery that has ever been made in aesthetics. She has told me in words what my discovery is; it seems to me like no discovery at all. She threatens therefore to take all the credit of it, unless I hasten & write a book 'on the genesis of the work of art' embodying therein these my by-myself-unrecognised discoveries. Is not this a misfortune to befall a creature so conceited as I am supposed to be – to be unconscious of his real greatness? It is like Columbus not knowing that he had discovered America.

According to Lee, he sighs, 'the only way I have of finding out what I am & what I ought to do is to read those gentlemen whom my discovery, when I become conscious of it, will cast into oblivion, or at least render archaic'.[14] He proposes to start by reading Hegel's *Aesthetics* and asks Katharine to lend him their copy.

My point is that, for all that Berenson may have, in ways seemingly unbeknown to himself, discovered and articulated new visual methods and new ideas about perception in a particular form and in relation to particular objects – in the form of art criticism, as applied to Renaissance painting, drawing and sculpture – they were methods and ideas that were recognisably, to Lee at least, located in a contemporary intellectual and cultural field that included aestheticians, psychologists and philosophers and was more broadly characteristic of nineteenth-century aesthetic theory and practice. They were, in short, part of a more general exploration of the embodied nature of vision in the nineteenth century that the essays in this volume explore.

Illustrations, Optics and Objects in Nineteenth-Century Literary and Visual Cultures finds suggestive connections between early and late nineteenth-century visual-tactile encounters in various forms of multi-sensorial aesthetic engagement that took place from Romanticism to the Victorian fin de siècle. It proposes new perspectives on nineteenth-century visuality that are driven by and speak to the 'material turn' in modern cultural studies that is itself indebted to the material aesthetics of twentieth-century philosophers such as Merleau-Ponty and Walter Benjamin. The collapse of distinctions between internal impressions and external signs of which Crary writes are evident in the physiological aesthetics of Lee and the Berenson circle. We have, to be sure, moved from the high cultural arena favoured by Berenson to the realms of photography and print culture, from the museum to the private collection. The material objects under scrutiny include green glasses and blue stones, and the pleasures and desires of looking and handling are explicitly gendered and sexualised; but a shared understanding of the materiality of visual experience enables this volume to offer a new articulation of 'corporealised vision' in the nineteenth century that pays proper attention to the neglected matter of touch.

Notes

1. René Descartes, *La Dioptrique*, Discours 1, quoted in Maurice Merleau-Ponty, 'Eye and Mind', *The Merleau-Ponty Aesthetics Reader: Philosophy and Painting*, ed. by Galen A. Johnson, trans. Michael B. Smith (Evanston, IL: Northwestern University Press, 1993), pp. 121–61: 131.
2. Jonathan Crary, *Techniques of the Observer: On Vision and Modernity in the Nineteenth Century* (Cambridge, MA and London: MIT Press, 1990), p. 19.
3. Merleau-Ponty, 'Eye and Mind', pp. 124–5.

4. Bernard Berenson, *Seeing and Knowing* (London: Evelyn, Adams & Mackay, 1968), pp. 23, 92.
5. Biblioteca Berenson, Villa I Tatti, Florence, B.B. to Field, 16 June 1893.
6. Kenneth Clark, *Another Part of the Wood: A Self-Portrait* (London: Harper & Row, 1974), p. 138.
7. Bernhard Berenson, *The Italian Painters of the Renaissance* (Oxford: Clarendon Press, 1930), pp. 63–4.
8. Biblioteca Berenson, B.B. to Michael, 24 October 1895.
9. Berenson, *The Italian Painters of the Renaissance*, pp. 62–3, hereafter in text.
10. Biblioteca Berenson, K.H. Bradley to Mrs Costelloe, 2 February 1892. The passage on Bonifazio may be found in Mary Logan, *Guide to the Italian Pictures at Hampton Court, with short studies of the artists*, The Kyrle Pamphlets, II (London: A. D. Innes & Co, 1894), p. 27.
11. Vernon Lee and Clementina Anstruther-Thomson, *Beauty and Ugliness and Other Studies in Psychological Aesthetics* (London: John Lane, The Bodley Head, 1912), pp. 25–6, hereafter in text.
12. Vineta Colby, *Vernon Lee: A Literary Biography* (Charlottesville: University Press of Virginia, 2003), pp. 158–65; René Wellek, 'Vernon Lee, Bernard Berenson and Aesthetics', in *Friendship's Garland: Essays Presented to Mario Praz*, ed. by Vittorio Gabrieli, 2 vols (Rome: Edizioni di Storia e Letteratura, 1966), II, 233–51.
13. Quoted in Colby, p. 167.
14. Biblioteca Berenson, B.B. to Michael, 22 February 1894.

Acknowledgements

This book brings together work on the materialities of reading and viewing in nineteenth-century culture. We are very grateful to our authors for their commitment to the project. At Palgrave Macmillan we would like to thank our editor Joseph Bristow for his intellectual support and Steven Hall for his efficiency in dealing with the material aspects of book production. We owe a lot to their patience and understanding during the long gestation of this book from conception to delivery as teaching commitments and more momentous life events enhanced and delayed the development of this book. The idea emerged at *The Verbal and the Visual in Nineteenth-Century Culture*, a conference which we organised on behalf of the Birkbeck Centre for Nineteenth-Century Studies in summer 2006 at the suggestion of Hilary Fraser. We would like to thank Hilary, our colleagues in the Centre, and our conference co-organisers Ella Dzelzainis and Sally Ledger. To the memory of Sally, our dear colleague and friend, we dedicate this volume.

An earlier version of Sophie Thomas's chapter appeared in her monograph *Romanticism and Visuality: Fragments, History, Spectacle* (Routledge, 2007). We are grateful to Routledge for permission to revise and reprint it.

Notes on the Contributors

The editors

Luisa Calè is lecturer in the Department of English and Humanities at Birkbeck, University of London. She is the author of *Fuseli's Milton Gallery: 'Turning Readers into Spectators'* (2006), and co-editor (with Antonella Braida) of *Dante on View: the Reception of Dante in the Visual and Performing Arts* (2007).

Patrizia Di Bello is lecturer in History and Theory of Photography in the Department of History of Art and Screen Media at Birkbeck, University of London. She is the author of *Women's Albums and Photography in Victorian England* (2007), and co-editor (with Gabriel Koureas) of *Art, History and the Senses* (2010).

The contributors

Stefano Evangelista is a tutorial fellow of Trinity College and university lecturer in English literature at the English Faculty, University of Oxford. He is the author of *British Aestheticism and Ancient Greece: Hellenism, Reception, Gods in Exile* (2009), and is currently editing a volume on the reception of Oscar Wilde in Europe.

Hilary Fraser is the Geoffrey Tillotson Professor in Nineteenth-Century Studies in the Department of English and Humanities at Birkbeck, University of London. She is the author of *Beauty and Belief: Aesthetics and Religion in Victorian Literature* (1986), *The Victorians and Renaissance Italy* (1992), *English Prose of the Nineteenth Century* (with Daniel Brown, 1997) and *Gender and the Victorian Periodical* (with Judith Johnston and Stephanie Green, 2003). She is currently working on an AHRC-funded project on *Gender, History, Visuality: Women Writing Art History in the Nineteenth Century*.

Michael Hatt is Professor of History of Art at the University of Warwick, having previously been Head of Research at the Yale Center for British Art. He is a specialist in the cultures of reading, viewing and collecting in the Victorian period and the fin de siècle, and has written widely on sculpture. He is the author (with Charlotte Klonk) of *Art History: a Critical Introduction to its Methods* (2006).

Lorraine Janzen Kooistra is Professor of English at Ryerson University in Toronto, Canada. She is the author of *Christina Rossetti and Illustration: a Publishing History* (2002), *The Artist as Critic: Bitextuality in Fin-de-Siècle Illustrated Books* (1995), and has published numerous chapters and articles on Victorian illustrated poetry. She is currently completing a monograph on the illustrated gift book and Victorian visual culture and co-editing an online scholarly edition of *The Yellow Book*.

Victoria Mills has both practical and academic experience in Museum studies. She worked for the Learning and Interpretation Department of the V&A, holds an MA in Museum Studies from Leicester University, where she is an Associate Tutor in the Department of Museum Studies, and is currently writing a Ph.D. on museum culture and writing at the fin de siècle at Birkbeck, University of London.

Graham Smith is Professor of Art History at the University of St Andrews and editor of the international quarterly *History of Photography*. He has published widely on Italian art and architecture of the sixteenth century and on photography in the nineteenth century. Among his publications are *The Casino of Pius IV*, *Sixteenth-Century Tuscan Drawings from the Uffizi*, *Disciples of Light: Photographs in the Brewster Album*, and *The Stone of Dante and Later Florentine Celebrations of the Poet*. His latest book, *Light that Dances in the Mind: Photographs and Memory in the Writings of E.M. Forster and his Contemporaries* (2007), reflects his current interests in the intersection of travel, literature and photography.

Lindsay Smith is Professor of English at the University of Sussex and Founding Director of the Sussex Centre for Visual Fields. She is the author of *The Politics of Focus: Women, Children, and Nineteenth-Century Photography* (1998), and of *Victorian Photography, Painting and Poetry: the Enigma of Visibility in Ruskin, Morris and the Pre-Raphaelites* (1995). She is currently writing a book on the photographs, letters and diaries of Lewis Carroll.

Sophie Thomas, Associate Professor of English at Ryerson University, Toronto, is the author of *Romanticism and Visuality: Fragments, History,*

Spectacle (2007). She has written essays on literature and visual culture in the Romantic period, and on fragments and ruins. She is currently writing a book on Romanticism and objects.

Heather Tilley has recently defended her Ph.D. thesis *Blindness and Writing: 1800–72* at Birkbeck College, University of London. She teaches English literature at Birkbeck and is currently project-managing the redevelopment of the e-journal *19: Interdisciplinary Studies in the Long Nineteenth Century*.

1
Introduction: Nineteenth-Century Objects and Beholders

Luisa Calè and Patrizia Di Bello

> I think and compare,
> See with an eye that can feel, feel with a hand that can see.
> (Goethe, *Erotica Romana*)

What happens to the objects that make up a 'literary and visual culture' when we try to imagine them not only through our minds, but also through our bodies and our senses? When we 're-member' their different materialities? In his *Italian Journey* Johann Wolfgang von Goethe remembers his experience of Rome through the story of Pygmalion and Galatea, 'the living woman' emerging from 'sculptured stone'. Encountering Rome 'in the flesh' gives a new life to the city which had so long been an object of the imagination, yet also felt already so familiar through etchings, drawings, paintings, or three-dimensional models in cork, woodcut, and plaster.[1] Through the physical pleasure implicit in the overlap between the experience of the city and the erotic discovery of the woman in the flesh, Goethe's Pygmalion stands for a multisensorial model of cultural encounter in which images are given a body and enlivened through touch.

Matthew Arnold argues that the critic's role is to 'see the object as it really is'.[2] Where he posits a detached free play of the mind, Walter Pater specifies that 'to see the object' one should 'know one's own impression as it really is'. For Pater what makes a critic is 'the power of being deeply moved by the presence of beautiful objects'.[3] Following Pater we go against the rise of a nineteenth-century history of objectivity; we look for the tangible qualities of media and for embodied modes of engagement with the practices of viewing, reading, collecting, and being with objects in the nineteenth century.

Questions about embodiment are particularly timely now that texts and images are likely to be mediated by digital as much as by older paper technologies. While the electronics industry is developing a pleasurable digital reading device to rival the paperback or the newspaper, objects such as books, magazines and all kinds of prints continue to play a strong part in our literary and visual cultures, which mix virtual pages with those bound into paper objects. This mixture and the sense that one day the digital might take over inform our need to look afresh at the history of looking and reading in their interaction with tangible objects such as books, illustrated magazines, letters, and photographs – objects whose present uses are still affected by their history as 'Victorian things'.[4]

The essays in this book are not part of a 'Great Exhibition' – a systematic and comprehensive account – but rather follow the logic of the chance encounter and the scrapbook. Faced with the impossible task of reconstructing what reading and looking might have felt like in the nineteenth century, we can but wander through the traces that might be embedded in the fragments that have survived. Like Asa Briggs in his study of *Victorian Things*, we are weary of 'imposing rules on disorderly "intelligible universes" rather than discovering them'.[5] In this volume, we bring together material aesthetic encounters from the beginning and the end of the century with no attempt at an even coverage. We follow, rather, Michel Serres' concept of history, which Lynda Nead describes as 'folded, pleated and kneaded [...] a dynamic volume rather than a linear sequence [...] continuously draw[ing] aspects of the past into its layers and folds'.[6] This description is also particularly suited to the experience of reading and looking, which the essays in this volume reveal as equally non-linear.[7] Our selection folds the early and the late nineteenth century onto each other, bringing to light 'unexpected networks' connecting 'apparently diverse or distant phenomena'.[8]

The essays collected here follow a meandering, spatial logic, which continually weaves in and out of the actual texts or images under consideration, getting caught into 'unpredictable proximities'.[9] For instance, Pygmalion's Galatea, Medusa, and Niobe offer tangible figures of petrification, mythological accounts of the work of media and their metamorphoses. A metamorphic Medusa works as a figure of movement across poetry, painting, and the phantasmagoria in Sophie Thomas's essay. Lindsay Smith thinks about sculpture and photography through the petrifications of Niobe. Yet the figure of Medusa also offers a mythological emblem of photography in its power to make tangible the opacity and anxieties of vision and blindness: in just one glance, one blink of the shutter, the camera petrifies a body, like Medusa metamorphosing it into a thing whose gaze and temporality are at once fixed in the moment and launched into the future. The mythical proximity between Medusa and photography did not escape the nineteenth-century imagination, at least not its margins: in a humorous poem from 1896, Fred Ghilett retells the story of Perseus's journey as a search for the 'The Camera Medusa':

> Now, the Camera-Medusa was no common button presser
> Confined to mere impressions and vignettes
> It left the carte-de-visite to the Kodaks which were lesser
> This camera took marble statuettes.[10]

Metamorphoses of stone into flesh, material memories and pleasures that recreate Romantic souvenirs in fleshly forms are more than just figures of speech or thought such as may be found in the pages of the 'art romances' analysed by Jonah Siegel.[11] Such literary forms should not be read in isolation. In their different ways, Stefano Evangelista, Lindsay Smith, Graham Smith, and Michael Hatt show the 'unexpected networks' of Italian travel, which can turn experiences of art into a vehicle of sexual freedom, or at least of a sexual desire at once carnal and fetishistically bound to objects. Photographs that reproduce or reference works of art, for instance, can fold into themselves memories, fantasies, and desires to be shared on site, by post, or through magazine circulation at home.

This edited collection considers material exchanges and relays between physical and mental objects. In Heather Tilley's essay on Wordsworth, the materiality of objects permeates the experience of blindness as an actual and poetic or metaphoric fear. Graham Smith demonstrates how visual representations work as 'material memories',[12] which are conjured up in the act of reading even when not reproduced as illustrations to the text. Evangelista explores how photographs circulate through commercial circuits and gifts between collectors, as tokens of exchange between cultural and sexual desires. The chapters by Lorraine Janzen Kooistra and Hatt analyse the multisensorial pleasures of reading, including the physical sensations evoked by textures and materials when handling magazines or books. As Henri Bergson argued, 'there is no perception that is not full of memories: with the immediate and present data of our senses, we mingle a thousand details out of our past experience.'[13]

The 'immediate and present data' of all of our senses also mingle in perception: the functions of the human eye are mediated by touch, affected by the bodies of writers and readers, makers and consumers, and by the social lives of both the bodies and the objects in question, from Percy Bysshe Shelley looking at a painting in the Uffizi in Florence, or re-constructing the experience while writing a poem (Thomas), to John Addington Symonds reading Plato in bed (Hatt). Jonathan Crary's influential work on 'vision, and its historical construction' posits viewers as 'observers' who 'comply with [...] rules, codes, regulations, and practices [...] within a prescribed set of possibilities', techniques, and visual apparatuses.[14] In this collection we privilege what may be termed 'beholders' for the coming together of the conceptual and the manual in an act of seeing that is also a grasping, or handling.

According to Crary, nineteenth-century optical toys reveal the embodied nature of vision and thus challenge an earlier, decorporealised, and dualist conception, in which the camera obscura articulated stable relations between outside reality and the autonomous rational inner vision of a free viewing subject (Crary 1990, pp. 25–66). The extent of this earlier concept of a decorporealised vision has been called into question, as has its demise in the nineteenth century.[15] What concerns us, however, is that the embodied observers that Crary posits for the nineteenth century are mostly reduced to a set of eyes and their neurological appurtenances.[16] Unlike Crary's observers, our beholders are as specific and contingent as possible, endowed with a full sensorium as well as a gender, a sexuality, and individual conditions such as poor sight and eye infections (Tilley), pulmonary disease (Evangelista), an inclination towards unusual jewels (Victoria Mills), or a propensity for reading in bed (Hatt). The protagonists of these essays have the financial and cultural capital enabling them to try out medical treatments, to dictate letters to female relations, and to travel to Italy to seek physically, artistically and sexually beneficial climates as well as a connection to its antiquities. They buy books and magazines; collect and exchange photographs; go to shows and art museums; and generally know about Romantic sites around Europe, gems and jewels, or classical culture.

Our essays discuss historically situated experiences that are as haptic as they are visual. Following the art historical endeavour initiated by Alois Riegl at the fin de siècle, we are keen to recuperate the haptic dimensions of seeing, but where he marked developments in style that went from a more haptic to a more disembodied optical perception,[17] we go against the grain and re-member the bodies and objects inherent in the optics of a material aesthetic. The experience of looking – whether reading texts or enjoying pictures – is never *just* visual, but it is also tactile, kinaesthetic, fully embodied, and affected by the material properties of the objects we do our looking and reading with. Meanings, memories and fantasies are engendered, transformed, inflected, given both cultural and emotional values. They are used to create individual and social identities, not only in the large brushstrokes of class, gender or race, but also in the more nuanced and subtle constructions of social sets, from respectable expat salons (Graham Smith) to classically-educated homosexual coteries (Evangelista, Mills, Hatt).[18] Unlike Crary, we do look at some of 'the marginal and local forms by which dominant practices of vision were resisted, deflected, or imperfectly constituted' (p. 7). As the essays in this volume suggest, practices of vision are rarely if ever perfectly constituted, because in the social life of objects and of the people experiencing them, such practices are always imbricated in a phenomenological, multi-sensorial world of desires and affects, which disturb, deflect, or indeed augment the experiences we have come to describe as *visual*.

In *Techniques of the Observer* Crary moves from science and philosophy, through optical toys and techniques of observation, to the wider realm of visual culture and the 'sociocultural field' (p. 118). This problematic sweep fails to explain how the 'separation of the senses' and the 'empirical isolation of vision' in nineteenth-century scientific and philosophical thought would affect actual visual experiences. It certainly did not stop people from touching books or photographs to look at them. Crary focuses on optical devices, such as the stereoscope, 'that operate directly on the body of the individual' (p. 7) as part of a 'process of modernization' (p. 9) that generates 'new needs, new production, and new consumption' (p. 10). But we should also consider how objects, old and new, might be used to navigate, cope with, or even resist the disjunctions and de-familiarisations of modernity. Objects and their tactile traces were crucial to nineteenth-century notions of comfort. As Walter Benjamin wrote, in the nineteenth century

> Coverings and antimacassars, boxes and casings, were devised in abundance, in which the traces of everyday objects were moulded. The resident's own traces were also moulded in the interior.[19]

To do so, the objects in the interior had to be preserved for the right touch. Servants, for example, should always hand letters to their employers on a tray, to disavow that they had in any way touched them. The touch of the woman of the house, on the other hand, working not for wages but for the love of her family, could cleanse a mass-produced object from the alienated and alienating touch of the worker, whose labour was mechanized and devalued into repetitive and deskilled manual operations. By contrast, a 'lady's touch' was endowed with the almost magic power to transform objects made and purchased through commercial transactions into gifts of love, which could bring comfort and harmony within the home.[20]

Many of the pleasures described as visual are immersed in a temporality that is more expansive and multisensorial than the visual temporality of afterimages. In this collection, Lindsay Smith discusses photography as a petrified moment let loose from its original temporal chain, free to travel through time and space, always at once of its own moment and immersed in the temporality of the actual photographic print as it is made, reproduced, bought, collected and looked at. Graham Smith calls attention to the temporal shifts of a short story by Henry James and how they chime with the actual experience of following the story as it was first serialised in a quarterly journal. Evangelista shows how afterimages are not only optical but also cultural and mnemonic: Greek sculptures come to life in the Sicilian youths captured in Von Gloeden's photographs and in the memory of those who looked at them.

For Crary, the nineteenth-century philosophical toy 'made unequivocally clear both the fabricated and hallucinatory nature of its image and the rupture between perception and its object'.[21] Yet a degree of rupture is inherent in any form of representation, verbal or visual. The here and now of listening to a story, looking at a painting or walking around a sculpture is imaginatively overlaid by the there and then of the story, the time reproduced or imagined, the myth. So the experience of the actual body here and now is dislocated by the imaginative body there and then, and at the same time the two are superimposed and fused into a single 'fabricated and hallucinatory' experience. Rather than new optical toys, this collection considers the apparently simpler, older technologies of the picture, the book, the letter, which were themselves modernised by new technologies – printing, mechanical production and reproduction, travel, postal systems, and the expanding capitalist economy used to fund their production and consumption. Yet these new temporalities of mechanised movement and production did not always impose faster rationalised rhythms onto the human body. Books, prints and magazines could be experienced through gestures that followed the individual rhythms of the human hand, not necessarily faster or standardised – and all the more precious because of it. As Lynda Nead has argued in her discussion of camera technologies at the end of the nineteenth century, modernity is a process of variable velocities.[22]

Rather than large narratives and bold philosophical sweeps, the essays in this collection pay attention to small details. Practising 'Keats's snail horn perception' (Hatt), we look for the objects, materials and conditions of aesthetic experience – the difference between Medusa painted on a shield or on canvas (Thomas); William Wordsworth's green glasses and what handwriting tells us about his corpus (Tilley); the degrees of transparency of glass and the refracting or reflecting possibilities of gems (Mills); the 'poetics of format' (Janzen Kooistra) shaping books and magazines: their paper quality, size, layout and margins; the borders and the interleaving tissues that 'stitch together' texts and images (Janzen Kooistra), and the effect they have on the experience of reading (Hatt).

Optics, objects, blinding visions

In the first section of this book Thomas and Tilley revisit works by Shelley and Wordsworth. From the mirror and the lamp to the camera obscura and the stereoscope, via the magic lantern and the phantasmagoria, optical devices have functioned as metaphors for the imagination, the textual condition, and a paradigmatic shift from a materialist Enlightenment to an idealist, or in any case inward, Romantic imagination.[23] The kinds of nineteenth-century optics we bring together in this book do not open ever-more transparent windows onto an objective world of separate objects; nor do they serve a 'blinding agenda', an idealist 'inward turn', as if the visible 'were secreting its own *medium*', as Derrida put it. Rather, our accent is on the material dimensions of viewing, which rearticulate what is opaque or blind as a 'punctum caecum', 'an analogical index of vision itself'.[24] In the vein of the late Merleau-Ponty, we look for the chiastic crossings of the visible and the tangible; we are interested in material visualities, an embodied optics of eyes and objects, bodies and pleasures.

Refractive rather than reflective, our media retain the material qualities of objects that call attention to the touch of sight. The interpenetration of the senses is indeed central to the history of optics in its hesitation between two paradigms that identify the source of vision in the object or in the eye. A materialist tradition conceives of visual phenomena in terms of the transmission of simulachra from the object to the eye of the viewer. Lucretius captured this tradition, which sees these simulachra, 'like films drawn from the outermost surface of things, flit about hither and thither through the air'.[25] The ghostly remnant of this visual paradigm haunts the spectacles of the phantasmagoria projected from a hidden magic lantern as they flit through the exhibition space, suggesting attenuated forms of embodiment. An intermediate, bidirectional and projectile model of vision, which touches the eye of the viewer, is captured in the mythical optics of Medusa, whose petrifying evil eye turns the viewer to stone. An attempt to sidestep this look of death articulates the optics and objects around her. As Thomas argues in her chapter, Medusa's presence is materialised in the 'fascinating slippage of object and image between the mirror, the shield, and the actual head, where reflection and representation *are* the thing itself'. This slippage in the object is reflected in the sidestepping, oblique, and indirect gazes, which 'glance off each other, like blows deflected by a shield (mirror)'. This strategy of indirection also characterises the media used to evoke Medusa, from Caravaggio's painting of Perseus's shield and the portrait of her dying, formerly attributed to Leonardo, to Shelley's poem, in which the gaze and the voice are turned away from the place of painter and viewer. Through the indirect and objectifying form of an utterance in the third person, Shelley deflects Medusa's gaze and projects it outwards.[26]

The other optical model posits the projection from the eye to the object. In this case, the process of vision is understood through the analogy of the blind man's staff, which needs to touch its objects in order to see them.[27] The blue stone and green glasses in Tilley's essay go beyond documenting the state of Wordsworth's eyes; these optical objects also suggest the aggressive agency of blinding visual rays and their impact on the retina. With their emphasis on colour as a dimension of vision, these objects protect the eye from both the blinding light coming from the outside and the blinding impulses of inspiration. Figures of optics articulate 'scenes in which our anxieties about images can express themselves in a variety of iconoclastic discourses', as W.J.T. Mitchell has argued.[28]

Beyond their metaphorical role as models for thinking, these optical props preserve traces that can help us flesh out what Merleau-Ponty termed 'conditioned thought',[29] the material conditions of aesthetic practice. Both Shelley and Wordsworth have been central in establishing an idealist turn, which would emancipate the powers of the imagination from a materialist enlightenment dependence on the body and thus open up an autonomous, ideally disembodied visionary Romanticism. Instead of serving such an idealist narrative, Tilley sees Wordsworth's blindness through the prism of his green glasses and blue stone. His vision is rooted in a physiology of the imagination that depends on its optical props instead of marking a 'disjunction', or 'rupture between perception and its object'.[30] For Crary, nineteenth-century physiology shows the 'adaptation of a human subject to productive tasks [...] The economic need for rapid coordination of eye and hand in performing repetitive actions required precise knowledge of human optical and sensory capacities'.[31] Tilley's work on the physiology of Wordsworth's vision unveils, rather, the uncoupling of eye, voice, and hand. Yet this uncoupling leads to rematerialising the conditions of Wordsworth's writing, and re-membering the 'productive tasks' and bodies of his work, from his ailing eyes to his faithful scribes, from the manuscript letter to the printed page.

Photographs, objects, pleasures

While Thomas's Medusa projects images of movement across painting, the phantasmagoria, and writing, for Lindsay Smith the petrifying qualities of photography make it more akin to sculpture than painting. As a kind of sculpture, photography participates in a moment in the nineteenth century when scaled-down reproductions of sculptures were much in demand. The implications of her analogy with sculpture chime with David Brewster's 1843 article on 'Photogenic Drawing', which compares photography to certain sculptural processes that substituted the human hand with machines. 'The art of multiplying statues by machinery' depended on carving machines endowed with two mechanical arms: one hand would touch the original to be copied, while the other would carve into a soft block a scaled down or scaled up version of the original. Like photography and casts, carving machines are indexical: their mode of reproduction is not mediated by the copying skills of human eyes and hands.

Photography or carving machines could not substitute the creative output of the artist, a noble occupation of the mind that was contrasted to mechanical copying as an occupation of the hand. As Steve Edwards has shown, this distinction was dependent on class differences. The irreplaceable nobility of creative work was opposed to mechanical, reproductive manual labour, which could be replaced by machines.[32] Once human copying could be substituted with reliable, scientifically mechanised copying, both photography and carving machines could preserve the original touch of the artist, no longer mediated by the inferior contaminating touch of the manual worker, prone to inconsistencies, imperfections, and to demanding better pay and conditions. Mechanised copies of works of art allow the beholder to disavow the human labour still involved in their making and to conceptualise the connection between original and reproduction as indexical – going directly from the object touched by the artist to the hands of the owner touching the reproduction. Touching mechanical reproductions enables an imaginative intimacy with their originals and their makers, even when they are dislocated by difference in size, materials, or between two and three dimensions. Like photography itself, this touch can bridge 'space and time' and become a way to assert 'domination'.[33] Carving machines literally touched the original while simultaneously making its reproduction. In photography, the tactile relationship works through the medium or agency of light, which was reflected off the body being photographed and brought into focus by the lens, until it finally touched the light-sensitive plate.[34]

Small and intimate objects, nineteenth-century photographs are easy to collect, store, transport, send through the post, or even use 'to paper a small room' (Evangelista). They exemplify the desire to 'get close', to handle and manipulate everything.[35] This focus on hands and touch helps us rethink indexicality:[36] handwriting and photography work as an indexical trace, which 'disturbs' vision with the desire for contact with the author, artist, or sitter (Tilley, Evangelista). Indexicality works as petrification rather than sign-making (Lindsay Smith); it is a continuous, rather than instantaneous process, which indexes what is in front of the camera as much as the desires of those who reach out to prints to look at them, buy them, collect them, send them around, and organise their publication (Evangelista). More than just visual processes of looking, these kinaesthetic and haptic journeys involve the bodies of both prints and collectors.

Our material rather than philosophical approach to the index participates in what might be called a 'sensual turn' in the humanities and social sciences, a movement from the textual and theoretical to the experiential and embodied.[37] As Elizabeth Edwards and Janice Hart remind us in one of the few systematic considerations of 'Photographs as Objects', 'a photograph is a three-dimensional thing, not only a two-dimensional image'; its functions as 'a socially salient object' depend on its practical and ritual uses.[38] Language-based semiotics turned the photograph into a carrier of meaning generated elsewhere. While the 'visual turn' emphasised the often disembodied gaze of the viewer / photographer, our multisensorial aesthetic restores the materiality of the visual to the body of the photograph and its various beholders (Evangelista, Hatt).

Illustrations and latent images

In this section both Graham Smith and Janzen Kooistra draw on Henry James's preface to *The Golden Bowl* to explore the relationship between texts and illustrations. James thought that illustration ought to 'stand off and on its own feet [...] as a separate and independent subject of publication, carrying its text in its spirit'.[39] For James 'to graft or "grow" [...] a picture by another hand on my own picture' (p. xlv) and thus turn a literary work into a 'picture-book' meant to renounce the peculiar qualities of writing. In a similar move, *The Yellow Book* chose to separate reading and looking, illustrations and letterpress (Janzen Kooistra). While seeking to avoid literature's being 'elbowed [...] by [...] a competitive process' (p. xlv), the rejection of commercial types of illustration did not entail a separation of literary from visual pleasures. To the contrary, following Aristotle, James argued that 'the essence of any representational work is of course to bristle with immediate images' (p. xlv). For all its literary power, James's 'vividness' is nonetheless fed by the kinds of visual material that he avoided as ornaments of his work.

Graham Smith has worked on the photographic repertoire of nineteenth-century tourism, showing how photography took over the tradition of the picturesque. If, as Marshall McLuhan argues, 'the "content" of any medium is always another medium',[40] the touristic photography studied by Graham Smith could be said to have as its 'content' the frames and material memories of the picturesque embedded in forms such as the album, the scrapbook, and the postcard. The question is whether the 'medium' acts as a transparent vehicle for these earlier forms and how its new mode of production transforms or metamorphoses them. In James's 'Daisy Miller' Graham Smith detects a series of commonplaces that could bring to the imagination of the reader a stock of familiar images. Reproductions of places such as the Rome of the Grand Tour were so well known that although they were not actually reproduced as illustrations of the story, they would act as 'latent pictures' imprinted on the mind of readers and developed like photographs by James's words. Graham Smith's analysis suggests that literary images depend on a material imagination, in which experiences and memories are structured by products and processes of mechanical reproduction. James's practice works against the ekphrastic relationship that might develop between text and illustration, yet still depends on the reader's awareness of the kinds of visual culture that might 'elbow' the writer into a predetermined corner of cultural production. His allusive strategy is similar to Shelley's, for the title of Shelley's poem – 'On the

Medusa of Leonardo da Vinci in the Florentine Gallery' – also alludes to a fashionable genre which it fails to deliver, the gallery poem which was a popular ingredient in ladies' albums and periodicals. Thus 'latent memory' resists, at the same time as it draws on, a culture of ekphrasis.

Ekphrasis wavers between the transparency of writing and the 'physical solidity' of the spatial arts. For Murray Krieger 'taking on Burckhardt's "corporeality", [language] tries to become an object with as much substance as the medium of the plastic arts'.[41] Whether or not aiming for the condition of other objects, as Pater would put it, the writing explored in this volume showcases painting, sculpture, and gems. Shelley's writing pierces through an invisible canvas to animate Medusa's gaze, while he and others experience or emulate the petrific qualities of sculpture at the Uffizi. The 'thing-like' qualities of language come through the fin-de-siècle aesthetic of J.K. Huysmans and Oscar Wilde, where the qualities of jewels are emulated in the choice of a 'lapidary language'. Yet this mimetic ability is far from a merely reproductive process. Through subtle 'transpositions', Mills argues, Huysmans and Wilde reorient the dynamics of subject, object and viewer, subverting any clear gendering of ornamentation. The power of ekphrasis is magnified in Shelley's display of the gigantic fragments of 'Ozymandias', which for James Heffernan articulate the monumental claims of ekphrasis, 'the poet's ambition to make his words outlast their ostensible subject, to displace visual representation with verbal representation'. In contrast to Krieger, Heffernan argues that ekphrasis 'foregrounds the *difference* between verbal and visual representation'.[42]

At the two extremes of ekphrasis we could place alternative figurations of the Medusa myth and different kinds of metamorphosis. Medusa dies of her own lethal optics when her gaze is reflected off her object of vision and comes back to strike her, fixing her in her own image, 'the same being that all of her victims have glimpsed at the moment of death'. This death by self reflection, which Louis Marin defines an 'automorphosis',[43] is a form of representation that fixes the medium in its specificity, in an intransitive reflection of itself, which keeps it separate from other media. At the other extreme is the 'ekphrastic fear' that the difference between writing and its object might be erased and that writing might become invisible, a 'self-consuming artifact' whose function is to give visibility to another medium.[44] In the petrification of Medusa's viewers metamorphosis exhibits the reversibility of subject and object, viewer and view. So too the more fluid relationships between media in the classical poses of Symonds's and Von Gloeden's nudes may suggest an alternative to Medusa's petrifications. Rather than a transfixing change, or a loss of identity, their homoerotic classicism has a potential for parodic difference in inhabiting another form, time, medium.

Precious objects

Objects – not only photographs, books, and magazines, but also letters, glasses, or jewels – are central to this collection, not just as 'stage settings for human actions and meanings, but integral to them'.[45] As Daniel Miller evocatively writes, relationships 'flow constantly between persons and things [...] the world of small things and intimate relationships [...] fill out our lives',[46] now as in the nineteenth century. These relationships are embodied in the personal objects and letters that materialised Wordsworth's blindness (Tilley), in the photographs exchanged by Symonds and his friends (Evangelista), in the real or imaginary collections put together by Huysmans and Wilde (Mills), or in the books handled and treasured by Fred Holland Day (Hatt). Such objects became 'evocative and therefore valuable to each specific person',[47] in ways that go beyond their primary function, meaning or subject matter, through being handled, exchanged, and used in close proximity to the body.

Nineteenth-century beholders used objects to blur the physical properties of bodies and their attributes. The essays in this section focus on the objects and agency of a homosexual imagination. For Proust a book can be a transformative optic instrument offered up to the reader: wandering inside the pages of Plato, John Addington Symmonds is conveyed to a utopian Greek setting where he can take part in a costume drama (Hatt). Gems and jewels helped Huysmans blur gender boundaries, but proximity to the body proved fatal in the attempt to merge organic with inorganic forms: the appeal of the inorganic went a step too far in Des Esseintes' decoration of a living tortoise: the gems took over the animal's substance and in the effort to 'live up' to its hybrid potential its precious 'still life' was metamorphosed into a dead thing (Mills).

Things have become 'objects' of study in materialist approaches from Marx to material culture, from phenomenology to thing theory. Marx considers objects are 'social hieroglyphics', because 'the definite relation between men themselves [...] assumes [...] the fantastic form of a relation between things'.[48] For Marx men distinguish themselves from animals by producing their means of existence: 'what they are [...] coincides with their production, both with *what* they produce and with *how* they produce'.[49] In an economy of alienated labour 'the object that labour produces – labour's product – confronts it as *something alien*, as a *power independent* of the producer'.[50] Even at its most dialectical, the relationship between subject and object is so imbricated as to take the form of 'material relations between persons and social relations between things',[51] a chiasmus in which people and things exchange properties. Recent approaches to material culture shift the focus from production to consumption in an attempt to 'transcend subject–object dualities'.[52] In *Capital* Marx indicated that people's 'movements within society' acquire 'the form of a movement made by things, and these things, far from being under their control, in fact control them'.[53] Modifying that formulation in *The Social Life of Things*, Arjun Appadurai argues that 'even though from a *theoretical* point of view human actors encode things with significance, from a *methodological* point of view it is the things-in-motion that illuminate their human and social context'.[54] Under the oxymoronic rubric of 'Thing Theory', Bill Brown invites us to rethink things for 'what exceeds their mere materialization as objects'. Amorphous remainders can help us think about 'how inanimate objects constitute human subjects, how they move them, how they threaten them, how they facilitate or threaten their relation to other subjects' to the point that 'the effort to rethink things becomes an effort to reinstitute society'.[55]

Poised between the precious and the ephemeral, the book as an object resists dualist notions which configure an ideal text as a disembodied, intangible spirit in the mind of the author or reader. William Morris talked about the book as a 'palpable work of art', which beholders handle, 'cosset and hug [...] as a material piece of goods': 'only the present age of superabundance of books makes some enthusiastic lovers of the spiritual part of books show their love for them by treating them as some men do their closest cronies and friends, speaking with familiar roughness to them'. Yet for Morris the reader who would 'take hold of his dearly beloved book-friend' in such a manner 'deserved to have his books read aloud to him henceforward, instead of being allowed to read them to himself'.[56] In formulating such a punishment, Morris discarded two Romantic experiences of the book – dismissed as a mere vessel of the word or invested with bibliomaniac pleasures and excesses of 'handling'.[57] Roughness in handling marked the textual condition at a time dominated by 'the utilitarian production of makeshifts', which Morris deplored (p. 1).

Throughout the nineteenth century, books became cheaper and the market more diversified into different levels of production values, from richly illustrated Gift Books published for the Christmas and New Year market to cheap Railway Books sold at train stations and almost intended to be discarded at the end of the journey. Illustrated materials of all kinds – from inexpensive illustrated magazines to free advertising leaflets – became widely available. Prints were no longer necessarily imbued with the connotations of an exclusive craft as they had been at the beginning of the century. Like many other previously exclusive commodities, by mid-century prints could be purchased in a variety of formats, from almost-art to almost-rubbish, blurring and complicating distinctions between the ephemeral and the precious. A precious production such as *The Yellow Book* was possible precisely because technological advancement had made printing both text and illustrations faster and cheaper, even if its 'distinctive format separating "pictures" from "letterpress"' (Janzen Kooistra) runs counter to the thrust of technological development aimed at finding ways to combine the production of the two in the interest of speed and economy.

At the beginning of the century, plates and letterpress belonged to different printing establishments, technical competences, and trade associations. Letterpress, printed from standardised raised ridges, was for books, newspaper, and general jobbing; images were printed from grooves cut into bespoke copper or other metal plate; they were slower, more expensive, and engravers enjoyed a higher status as artists or craftsmen.[58] As Michael Twyman emphasises, there was a 'fundamental difference of outlook between the two'.[59] In the production of early nineteenth-century illustrated Annuals, the copperplate illustrations came first – chronologically, economically and culturally; text was written on-demand to illustrate them.

By mid-century wood engraving had made it possible to print plates through a relief method which integrated them with lettering on the same printing block. Still produced by specialist firms, wood-engraved illustrations were now designed after the text had been letter-pressed and they were expected to follow its narratives accurately. John Everett Millais, for example, designed his illustrations for the instalments of Trollope's novels only after reading proofs of the text. He often left it to the last minute and had to draw the final version directly on the wood-block.[60] But this was expediency rather than a desire to return to the unified poetics of words and images of William Blake's illuminated books or of more 'autographic' printing techniques, in which the lines are the direct result of the action of the hand of the artist/engraver on the plate, as in the early nineteenth-century work of Thomas Bewick. In mid nineteenth-century wood engraving, the quality of an illustration's line was ultimately in the hand of 'woodpeckers', the labourers who hollowed out the wood around the drawn lines through repetitive 'pecks'.[61] Preparing the woodblock for relief printing was mechanical work rather than art or craft. For John Ruskin this type of wood-engraving epit-omised the vulgarity of 'the modern press – industry enslaved to the ghastly service of the [...] more bestial English mob, – railroad born and bred'.[62] He considered it a 'vile' printing method, because it imitated and debased the black line of metal engraving rather than using the white line characteristic of woodcut.[63] It was not a form of engraving, not a furrow in a plate, but a raised line like letterpress, although unlike letterpress it had to be cut away manually. Wood engraving might look like 'a sketch on wood', but it is only a 'most laborious and careful imi-tation of a sketch' (pp. 87–8). It is the work not of a 'noble hand' (p. 74) that moves 'under the direct influence of mental attention' (p. 75) and creates lines even if guided by an existing drawing, but of a 'base' hand performing 'some habitual dexterity of its own' (p. 75).

By the 1880s, 'process engraving' removed the need for the wood-pecker's repetitive mechanical labour. Illustrations could now be passed onto the block, and raised lines produced by photomechanical means. The image now relied on optical and chemical processes, rather than 'habitual dexterity'. This resulted in faster and cheaper illustrations. At the same time, process engraving ensured that the quirks and qualities of specific illustrators were less likely to be homogenised by the look asso-ciated with the engraving firm. For example, Aubrey Beardsley's 'black blots' and 'inscrutable faces' were not 'treated to a busy cosmetic of hatching and bracelet shading' or 'stock physiognomy appropriate to the subject'.[64] The mindless touch of the woodpecker was replaced by a hands-off process, which better preserved the more valued touch of the artist.

For Morris the touch of production had an impact on the aesthetic of the book. To the 'negative qualities' of 'makeshift' books Morris ascribed a 'crippling of the faculties' (pp. 1, 37). For the separation of reading and viewing, in his view, depended on the separate production of plates and letterpress, which meant that illustrations were 'in no respect a part of the tangible printed book' (p. 36). Those who were satisfied with read-ing the text and looking at pictures had a merely 'literary' interest in books. By contrast, Morris harked back to the organic aesthetic of illumi-nated manuscripts and noted that 'there is growing up a taste for books which are visible works of art' (p. 37).[65] The visual culture of precious books is richly represented in our collection, from Janzen Kooistra's work on *The Yellow Book* to the terse visual page of John Gray's *Silver-points*, which Hatt contrasts to the medievalising thickets encountered in Morris's Kelmscott edition of Chaucer.

Books, illustrated magazines and photographs might be mass or machine produced; they may lack the connection to a human hand that hand-written letters or original drawings would have, or the trace of a skilled artisan's hand. Nonetheless, as Daniel Miller shows us, they can be reinvested with human values by being actually or metaphorically touched – read, used, recommended, exchanged, passed around – by the hands of valorised others: 'meaningful relationships to things [and] with people [...] are much more akin and entwined than is commonly appreciated'.[66] The uses of objects are particularly relevant in homoerotic relationships, as if signifying the inhibition of men's desire to become objects of the care of other men. This desire is displaced onto the care of shared objects: 'Objects store and possess, take in and breathe out the emotions with which they have been associated' (p. 38). Objects, in particular small objects made to fit the scale of human bodies and hands, 'can embrace you as easily as you can embrace them' (p. 45).[67]

For us, reading takes place through the body as a whole multisensorial, rather than merely visual, experience. As an anthropologist, Miller can go and knock on people's doors and ask them about their things. We cannot do that when working with the past. What we can do, however, is to attend to the traces left by the social life of things: letters and diaries, fictions and essays, surviving collections, and domestic remains. Above all, we can sense the sense of things.

Notes

1. Johann Wolfgang von Goethe, *Italian Journey* (1786), trans. W.H. Auden and Elizabeth Mayer (London: Penguin, 1976), p. 129.
2. Matthew Arnold, 'The Function of Criticism at the Present Time', *The Complete Works of Matthew Arnold*, ed. by E.H. Super, 11 vols (Ann Arbor: University of Michigan Press, 1960–77), III, 258.
3. Walter Pater, 'Preface', *The Renaissance* (1873; London: Macmillan, 1910), pp. viii, x.
4. Asa Briggs, *Victorian Things* (1988; Thrupp, Glos: Sutton, 2003).
5. Briggs, *Victorian Things*, p. 17.
6. Lynda Nead, *The Haunted Gallery: Painting, Photography, Film c.1900* (New Haven and London: Yale University Press, 2007), p. 3, drawing on Michel Serres and Bruno Latour, *Conversations on Science, Culture and Time*, trans. Roxanne Lapidus (Ann Arbor: University of Michigan Press, 1995), pp. 57–60.
7. Recent books that have covered these themes without the multisensorial material aesthetic that informs this collection (and, in some cases, a more literary or mid nineteenth-century focus) include Julia Thomas, *Pictorial Victorians: The Inscription of Values in Word and Image* (Athens, Ohio: Ohio University Press, 2004); Gerard Curtis, *Visual Words: Art and the Material Book in Victorian England* (Aldershot: Ashgate, 2002); Kate Flint, *The Victorians and*

the Visual Imagination (Cambridge: Cambridge University Press, 2000); Carol T. Christ and John O. Jordan, eds, *Victorian Literature and the Victorian Visual Imagination* (Berkeley and London: University of California Press, 1995).

8. Nead, *Haunted Gallery*, p. 3.

9. Nead, p. 3.

10. Fred Ghilett, 'The Camera Medusa', *Cycling* (5 Dec 1896), 432; for a more recent example of a camera-medusa see Kobina Mercer, 'Reading Racial Fetishism: The Photographs of Robert Mapplethorpe', in Emily Apter and William Pietz, eds, *Fetishism as Cultural Discourse* (Ithaca and London: Cornell University Press, 1993), pp. 307–29: 312.

11. Jonah Siegel, *Haunted Museum: Longing, Travel, and the Art-Romance Tradition* (Princeton: Princeton University Press, 2005).

12. Marius Kwint, Christopher Breward and Jeremy Aynsley, eds, *Material Memories: Design and Evocation* (Oxford and New York: Berg, 1999).

13. Henri Bergson, *Matter and Memory*, trans. Nancy Margaret Paul and W. Scott Palmer (New York: Zone Books, 1988), p. 33.

14. Jonathan Crary, *Techniques of the Observer*, pp. 1–2, 5–6, hereafter in text.

15. Margaret Atherton, 'How to Write the History of Vision: Understanding the Relationship between Berkeley and Descartes', in David Michael Levin, ed., *Sites of Vision: The Discursive Construction of Sight in the History of Philosophy* (Cambridge, MA: MIT Press, 1996), pp. 139–66; John Plunkett, 'Touching Sight, Feeling Seeing: the Stereoscope and the History of the Senses 1830–1870', unpublished conference paper presented at the British Association for Victorian Studies, Leicester, 2008. We are grateful to Plunkett for letting us cite the manuscript.

16. See also Jonathan Crary, *Suspensions of Perception: Attention, Spectacle, and Modern Culture* (Cambridge, MA, and London: MIT Press, 2000), p. 3.

17. Alois Riegl, *Late Roman Art Industry*, trans. Rolf Winkes (Rome: Bretschneider, 1985), pp. 21–4.

18. For a social and historical geography of these coteries in London and some of its Europe-wide ramifications, see Matt Cook, *London and the Culture of Homosexuality 1885–1914* (Cambridge: Cambridge University Press, 2003).

19. Walter Benjamin, 'Paris – the Capital of the Nineteenth Century' (1935), *Charles Baudelaire: A Lyric Poet in the Era of High Capitalism*, trans. Harry Zohn (London: NLB, 1973), pp. 155–76: 169.

20. Patrizia Di Bello, *Women's Albums and Photography in Victorian England: Ladies, Mothers and Flirts* (Aldershot, Hampshire and Burlington, VT: Ashgate, 2007).

21. For instance, the Thaumatrope (literally, 'wonder-turner') was a simple card disc with, for example, a picture of a bird on one side and that of a cage on another, which, when turned quickly by twirling the strings at either side of it, appear unified in an image of a bird in a cage (Crary, *Techniques*, p. 106).

22. Nead, *Haunted Gallery*, p. 110.

23. M.H. Abrams, *The Mirror and the Lamp* (New York: Oxford University Press, 1953).

24. Jacques Derrida, *Memoirs of the Blind*, trans. Pascale-Anne Brault and Michael Naas (Chicago: University of Chicago Press, 1993), pp. 52–3 and Maurice Merleau-Ponty, *The Visible and the Invisible*, trans. Alphonso Lingis (Evanston: Northwestern University Press, 1968), p. 247.

25. Lucretius, *De Rerum Natura*, 4.24–35 and 88–9, trans. W.H.D. Rouse (Harvard University Press), pp. 279 and 281.
26. On the third person as the mode of the 'non person', see Émile Benveniste, *Problems in General Linguistics*, trans. Mary Elizabeth Meek (Coral Gables, FL: University of Miami Press, 1971), pp. 198, 200, 217, 221–2.
27. On the tradition of the blind man's staff, from Descartes' *Dioptrique* through Berkeley's *Theory of Vision*, see Atherton and also Alenca Zupančič, 'Philosophers' Blind Man's Buff', in Renata Salecl and Slavoj Žižek, eds, *Gaze and Voice as Love Objects* (Durham and London: Duke University Press, 1996), pp. 32–58.
28. W.J.T. Mitchell, *Iconology: Image, Text, Ideology* (Chicago: University of Chicago Press, 1986), p. 6.
29. Maurice Merleau-Ponty, 'Eye and Mind', pp. 121–49: 135–6, and Tilley's chapter in this volume.
30. Crary, *Techniques*, pp. 104, 106.
31. Crary, p. 85.
32. Steve Edwards, *The Making of English Photography: Allegories* (University Park, PA: Pennsylvania State University Press, 2006).
33. Constance Classen, 'Touch in the Museum', in Constance Classen, ed., *The Book of Touch* (London and New York: Berg, 2005), pp. 275–86: 278–9.
34. This argument is developed in Patrizia Di Bello, 'Photography and Sculpture: A "Light" Touch', in Patrizia Di Bello and Gabriel Koureas, eds, *Art, History and the Senses: 1830 to the Present* (Aldershot, Hampshire and Burlington, VT: Ashgate, 2010).
35. Walter Benjamin, 'The Work of Art in the Age of Mechanical Reproduction' (1936), *Illuminations*, trans. Harry Zohn (London: Fontana/Collins, 1973), pp. 219–53: 225.
36. Thus complicating ideas of indexicality that are still prevalent in theorising photography's relationship with its referent; see for example Helen Groth's *Victorian Photography and Literary Nostalgia* (Oxford and New York: Oxford University Press, 2004); Nancy Armstrong, *Fiction in the Age of Photography: the Legacy of British Realism* (Cambridge, MA and London: Harvard University Press, 1999). On photography's indexicality, see Rosalind Krauss, 'Notes on the Index: Part 1 and Part 2', in *The Originality of the Avant-Garde and Other Modernist Myths* (Cambridge, MA and London: MIT Press, 1986), pp. 196–219.
37. David Howes, 'Empires of the Senses', in David Howes, ed., *Empire of the Senses: The Sensual Culture Reader* (Oxford and New York: Berg, 2005), pp. 1–24; Howes, 'Charting the Sensorial Revolution', *Senses and Society*, 1 (2006), 113–28.
38. Elizabeth Edwards and Janice Hart, 'Photographs as Objects', in Edwards and Hart, eds, *Photographs, Objects, Histories* (London and New York: Routledge, 2004), pp. 1–15: 1–2; see also Geoffrey Batchen, *Forget Me Not: Photography and Remembrance* (New York: Princeton Architectural Press, 2004).
39. Henry James, 'Preface', *The Golden Bowl*, ed. by Virginia Llewellyn Smith (Oxford: Oxford University Press, 1999), p. xlvi, hereafter in text.
40. Marshall McLuhan, 'The Medium is the Message', *Understanding Media: the Extensions of Man* (London: Routledge, 1964, repr. 2002), p. 8.

41. Murray Krieger, 'Appendix: Ekphrasis and the Still Movement of Poetry; or *Laokoön* revisited (1967)', *Ekphrasis: The Illusion of the Natural Sign* (Baltimore: Johns Hopkins University Press, 1991), pp. 263–88: 285.

42. James Heffernan, *Museum of Words* (Chicago: The University of Chicago Press, 1993), pp. 191 and 118–19 for his discussion of Shelley's 'Ozymandias' and Medusa.

43. Louis Marin defines 'automorphosis' as the moment in which 'Medusa immobilizes herself at the acme of her violence, which differs considerably from a metamorphic transformation of one form into another, a process during which a prior identity is lost', see *To Destroy Painting*, trans. Mette Hjort (Chicago and London: The University of Chicago Press, 1995), p. 136.

44. On the difference between ekphrastic writing and its object, see W.J.T. Mitchell, *Picture Theory: Essays on Verbal and Visual Representation* (Chicago and London: University of Chicago Press, 1994), p. 154; on writing as a 'self-consuming artifact', see Stanley Fish, *Self-Consuming Artifacts: the Experience of Seventeenth-Century Literature* (Berkeley: University of California Press, 1972).

45. Edwards and Hart, *Photographs*, p. 4.

46. Daniel Miller, *The Comfort of Things* (Cambridge: Polity Press, 2008), pp. 6–7.

47. Miller, p. 30.

48. Karl Marx, *Capital Volume I*, trans. Ben Fowkes (London: Penguin, 1976), pp. 167, 165.

49. Karl Marx and Frederick Engels, *The German Ideology*, trans. C.J. Arthur (London: Lawrence, 1974), p. 42.

50. Karl Marx, *Economic and Philosophical Manuscripts of 1844*, trans. Martin Milligan (Amherst, NY: Prometheus Books, 1988), p. 71.

51. Marx, *Capital*, p. 166.

52. 'Editorial', *Journal of Material Culture*, 1 (1996), 5–14: 7.

53. Marx, *Capital*, pp. 167–8.

54. Arjun Appadurai, ed., *The Social Life of Things: Commodities in Cultural Perspective* (Cambridge: Cambridge University Press, 1986), p. 5.

55. Bill Brown, 'Thing Theory', *Critical Inquiry*, 28:1 (Autumn 2001), 1–22: 5, 7, 10.

56. William Morris, *The Ideal Book: Essays and Lectures on the Arts of the Book*, ed. by William S. Peterson (Berkeley: University of California Press, 1982), pp. 2, 1, hereafter in text.

57. On the Romantic pleasures of touch see Charles Lamb's 'Detached Thoughts on Books and Reading', *The London Magazine* VI: xxxi (July 1822) and the special issue of Romantic Circles on Romantic Bibliomania in *Romantic Libraries*, ed. Ina Ferris, http://www.rc.umd.edu/praxis/libraries/index.html, accessed 16 December 2008.

58. For a fuller and more carefully nuanced account, see Michael Twyman, *Printing 1770–1970: An Illustrated History of its Development and Uses in England* (1970; London: The British Library, 1998).

59. Twyman, p. 19.

60. Michael Mason, 'The Way We Look Now: Millais' Illustrations to Trollope', *Art History*,1:3 (1978), 309–40. See also Richard Maxwell, ed., *The Victorian Illustrated Book* (Charlottesville and London: University Press of Virginia, 2002).

61. Clive Ashwin, 'Graphic Imagery 1837–1901: A Victorian Revolution', *Art History*, 1:3 (1978), 360–70: 362.
62. John Ruskin, 'Appendix. Article I. Notes on the Present State of Engraving in England', *Ariadne Florentina: Six Lectures on Wood and Metal Engraving, with Appendix, Given before the University of Oxford in Michaelmas Term 1872* (London: George Allen, 1890), pp. 256–78: 267.
63. Ruskin, 'Lecture III: The Technics [*sic*] of Wood Engraving', *Ariadne Florentina*, pp. 74–107: 74; hereafter in text.
64. Ashwin, 'Graphic Imagery', p. 369. See also Trevor Fawcett, 'Graphic Versus Photographic in the Nineteenth-Century Reproduction', *Art History*, 9:2 (1986), 185–212.
65. For a Marxist take on Morris's practice, see Caroline Arscott, 'William Morris: Decoration and Materialism', in Andrew Hemingway, ed., *Marxism and the History of Art: from William Morris to the New Left* (London and Ann Arbor, MI: Pluto Press, 2006), pp. 9–27.
66. Miller, *Comfort*, p. 115; hereafter in text.
67. Objects can also embody, and at once reveal and keep, the secrets that are essential to the 'Epistemology of the Closet', see Eve Kosofsky Sedgwick, *Epistemology of the Closet* (Berkeley: University of California Press, 1990), in particular pp. 67–90.

Part I
Blinding Visions

2
Ekphrasis and Terror: Shelley, Medusa, and the Phantasmagoria

Sophie Thomas

As a central Romantic icon, the Medusa has been understood in terms of the ambivalence latent in the mythology surrounding her, in which she is identified with horror and beauty, with destruction and creativity, and as victim and tyrant. What tends to be overlooked, however, is what she might tell us about the act of looking itself, about the fear of sight, with all its generative anxieties and its relationship to Romantic discourses of visuality. This essay contrasts the use of the Medusa in Shelley's ekphrastic poem, 'On the Medusa of Leonardo da Vinci in the Florentine Gallery', with her appearance in contemporary visual spectacles such as the phantasmagoria, which was first developed in Paris in the 1790s. Shelley's poem, as a represented scene of seeing, brings a telling density to the act of looking figured by the Medusa. Ekphrasis itself, as the verbal representation of visual representation, presents a clear instance of dissonance between modes of representation, and of incongruity between the visible and the invisible: it appropriates the force of the visible in an attempt to make us 'see'.

At the phantasmagoria, meanwhile, the tension between the visible and the invisible was exploited as the basis for a popular form of 'ghost' show; projected apparitions loom out of darkness only to disappear again, playing fast and loose with the optics of materialisation. The image of the Medusa was a powerful one for the phantasmagoria, for while it raises the spectre of the contaminating (if not deadly) look, it also plays on a certain terror associated with the *mobile* image – the image awakening, 'actualising', so that the boundary between art and life is blurred or challenged. This is a function of illusion, the product of an increasingly sophisticated visual technology, but it speaks metaphorically for a kind of liberation, for an overturning of the usual (visual) order, associable with the revolutionary imagination. In both the content and the procedures of the phantasmagoria, the subversiveness of the image, and of the illusory, is precisely what is debated and displayed.

The figure of the Medusa functions as a link here between two interrelated discourses of visibility: the first related to public spectacles predicated upon the fear of the invisible and, secondly, the poet's more private struggles with the status of the imagination and its productions. As Shelley's poem suggests, the poet, seeking to master and convey the power of the visual, to embody it even, must radically reconfigure the petrifying potential of his subject. Phantasmagoric images were explicitly intended to 'astonish' the viewer – a word etymologically related to petrification (a-stony) and an effect potentially doubled, metaphorically at least, in the case of the Medusa head. On the one hand, the effects of illusion draw on the Medusa's ability to 'suspend the viewer's reflexive visual impulses', as Grant Scott has suggested.[1] On the other, the phantasmagoria might be said to undo or overturn the representational 'fix' of ekphrasis, by turning loose the Gorgon look – upon its audience, if not on the streets of revolutionary Paris.

Medusa and the petrific look

The myth of Medusa centres on a particularly frontal form of visual assault: she is the bearer of the petrific look that turns everything to stone. At the same time she is a handy figure for that upon which one must not and cannot look, actually and metaphorically; there is thus an ambiguity over whether it is looking at Medusa, or being looked at by her, that has petrific consequences. She is the horrifying (and horrified) figure whose head, severed by Perseus, is so effectively captured by Caravaggio – and from whom the viewer, in an echo of the serpentine movements of her locks, can only recoil (Plate 1). Yet from its inception, the story is beset by ambiguous details, directed by diversionary tactics. In some versions it is the Medusa's extraordinary beauty that stops all who behold her in their tracks; in others, however, it is her Gorgon monstrosity. Properly speaking it is both: her famed beauty was such that Neptune (Poseidon) forced himself upon her in the temple of Minerva (Athena), who in outrage turned Medusa into something hideous and fearsome; she exchanged her golden hair for writhing serpents and wished all who looked upon her turned to stone. Perseus, son of Zeus, was given the unenviable job of ridding the earth of this unbearably strange creature and the tyranny she unleashed. This he accomplished and gave the severed head of Medusa back to Minerva, who henceforth carried it on her shield, or on the breastplate of her armour.

As legend goes, Perseus succeeds in his task with the help of an array of objects, of certain aids, gifts from the gods: Mercury's wings for his feet, Pluto's invisibility helmet, and a shield from Pallas (not to mention the eye and the tooth 'borrowed' from the Graeae). When Perseus comes upon Medusa, she is, in fact, asleep: she is no threat, presumably, for her eyes are shut.[2] Not taking any chances, however, Perseus turns his back upon her, and uses her image mirrored in his shield to take his deadly aim. Her severed head was then, as Francis Bacon's recounting of the myth maintains, attached by Perseus to Pallas's shield, 'where it still retained its power of striking stiff, as if thunder or planet stricken, all who looked on it'.[3] Curiously though, at the moment of Perseus' attack, neither of them is actually looking. And yet the look is, and becomes, everything and everywhere. First, there is the fascinating slippage of object and image between the mirror, the shield, and the actual head, where reflection and representation *are* the thing itself (indeed, the terrifying head is itself already constituted as a representation). The head is borne like a shield before Perseus and as a shield thereafter, but where the actual head ends and the image of the head begins is noticeably unclear.

The unstable image of the Medusa thus begins to proliferate, and for this reason she has also been seen as a figure for doubleness: she bears the look that says thou shalt not look; she is simultaneously an invitation and prohibition. As Marjorie Garber and Nancy Vickers point out, she is 'at once monster and beauty, disease and cure, threat and protection, poison and remedy [...she] has come to stand for all that is obdurate and irresistible'.[4] Her head, moreover, is the ultimate apotropaic object, warding off terror with terror itself. In Freud's well-known reading of the myth, Medusa's head embodies the threat of castration: it suggests, or doubles for, the image of that other horrific site, the female genitalia, with its too visible lack.[5] At the same time though, in an apparent contradiction, the head is associable with the phallus in at least two ways: in the form of the serpents as replacement penises and in the very idea of petrification, of getting hard. While, by a transformation of affect, the spectator is reassured by being made 'stiff' with terror – for it affirms his possession of a penis – this only confirms, Freud claims, the 'technical rule according to which a multiplication of penis symbols signifies castration'.[6] There is clearly a paradoxical logic at work here, by which an appearance signals or is at the same time a disappearance; this corresponds to the paradox of the Medusa herself as both erection and castration, presence and absence, the look and its blinding consequence.

Medusa, the phantasmagoria, and the optics of materialisation

Medusa seems not to have been a popular subject for painters during the Romantic period, although she figures in fascinating if largely predictable ways in English political caricature, in connection with the French Revolution and its aftermath. However, there was one place where the terrifying sight of the Medusa could be had – repeatedly – and that is at the phantasmagoria shows in Paris and London. The phantasmagoria was effectively a modification of the magic lantern shows that had been popular throughout the eighteenth century. Magic lanterns were an early portable form of slide projector, which used an arrangement of a lamp and lenses to project images painted on glass slides.[7] The phantasmagoria incorporated two important changes: first, the image was projected from *behind* a screen, rather than in front, which made the operator invisible to the audience on the other side. It thus concealed the mechanism of illusion creation from view. Second, the earliest innovator of the spectacle, Paul de Philipsthal (under the pseudonym 'Philidor'), devised a set of rails upon which the projector could be made to move rapidly. Along with adjustable lenses, it was possible to create the appearance of movement (and un-nerving changes in size) in the projected image; the illusion of a figure's sudden advance or retreat enhanced the shows' purchase on the spectral and the supernatural.[8] The slides for use in the phantasmagoria lantern tended, in this vein, to depict frightening subjects: ghosts, skeletons, skulls, witches, devils, grave diggers and so on. The bleeding nun, from Lewis's *The Monk*, was a popular apparition, as were certain mythological themes, and portraits of infamous contemporaries, namely protagonists of the French Revolution such as Robespierre, Danton, Marat, and Bonaparte. Some slides included animated elements, such as skulls with wings, that could move in an uncanny manner; this was especially the case with the head of Medusa, whose eyes, and serpent hair, could be made to move (Plate 2), as well as to loom out frighteningly toward the audience.

The whole apparatus of the phantasmagoria – from eerie sound effects created with the glass harmonica, to images projected on clouds of smoke, to the total darkness surrounding the viewer (before the Diorama was developed in the 1820s, this was the first public, indoor entertainment to take place in the dark) – was contrived to induce fear. The subjects of the slides for ghost shows were set in opaque black, so that no superfluous light from the lantern could be perceived, with the result that the slide conjured up a ghost, a figure in complete darkness betraying no visible evidence that it was in fact an image on a screen.[9] Because the image was made to appear to float in the air, by being projected upon a semi-transparent screen and by appearing to move, the audience was unable to locate the image in space, and thus to see the illusion, so to speak. The ghost shows, moreover, were literally that: they claimed to raise the spirits of the dead, what Philipsthal called 'the phantoms of the absent' (he invited his patrons to request phantoms – with 'several days' notice' – of their own choosing).[10] A certain controversy surrounded Philipsthal's spectacle – perhaps related to the fact that the Terror was in full swing – and we next hear of him founding a phantasmagoria at the Lyceum in London in 1801 (the Lyceum was informally renamed the 'Phantoscopic Theatre'). A contemporary account, in David Brewster's *Letters on Natural Magic*, offers an evocative first-hand description of the show:

> The small theatre of exhibition was lighted only by one hanging lamp, the flame of which was drawn up into an opaque chimney or shade when the performance began. In this 'darkness visible' the curtain rose and displayed a cave with skeletons and other terrific figures in relief upon its walls. The flickering light was then drawn up beneath its shroud, and the spectators in total darkness found themselves in the middle of thunder and lightning. A thin transparent screen had, unknown to the spectators, been let down after the disappearance of the light, and upon it the flashes of lightning and all the subsequent appearances were represented. This screen being half-way between the spectators and the cave which was first shown, and being itself invisible, prevented the observers from having any idea of the real distance of the figures, and gave them the entire character of aerial pictures. The thunder and lightning were followed by the figures of ghosts, skeletons, and known individuals whose eyes and mouth were made to move by the shifting of combined sliders. After the first figure had been exhibited for a short time, it began to grow less and less, as if removed to a great distance, and at last vanished in a small cloud of light. Out of this same cloud the germ of another figure began to appear, and gradually grew larger and larger, and approached the spectators till it attained its perfect development. In this manner, the head of Dr. Franklin was transformed into a skull;

figures which retired with the freshness of life came back in the form of skeletons, and the retiring skeletons returned in the drapery of flesh and blood.[11]

Brewster's account further details the effects of apparitions advancing upon the audience, which left many with the impression that they could reach out and touch the looming figures. Indeed one of the definitive features of the phantasmagoria was its abandonment of the traditional procession of images projected by the magic lantern in favour of animated figures that loomed and disappeared with alarming suddenness, but which also traversed the screen from all directions and angles.

Meanwhile, in Paris, the phantasmagoria was being redeveloped by a Belgian showman, Etienne-Gaspard Robertson (an Anglicisation of 'Robert'), who mounted his spectacles at the Cour des Capucines from 1799. Robertson extended the repertoire of 'ghosts' at his disposal, and added to the spectacle in a number of other ways, such as by projecting three-dimensional, mechanically operated figures and tableaux and by using the principle of the camera obscura to project live actors into the scene. Other innovations contributed to a more frightening atmosphere: electric shocks, ventriloquism, life-size masked figures, the use of incense and smoke, and so on.[12] Nevertheless, illusionists such as Philipsthal and Robertson were careful to distance themselves from the charlatanism of magic or necromancy, and actually claimed to be scientists, rationalists – Robertson described himself with the words '*méchanicien, peintre, opticien*'.[13] Instead of playing on popular superstition, the spectacle was in fact positioned as instructive, a display of experiment and scientific theory; it claimed to pit revolutionary rationalism against the 'superstitious folk customs of the Catholic provinces'.[14] Paradoxically, this spectral display, which appeared to capitalise shamelessly on the widely held belief in the resurrection and apparition of the dead, was somehow also meant to display and thereby expose that very belief. In this way the phantasmagoria held up a mirror to its audience, and indeed in his memoirs Robertson explicitly used the term 'mirror' not just to describe the phantasmagoria, but also to designate the screen upon which 'shadows came and drew themselves, between the spectators and the *physicien*'.[15] The choice of the Capuchin convent, with its ruins and tombstones, was obviously perfect, but it is noteworthy that Robertson made use of several aspects of the site to mount a multi-faceted exhibition. The phantasmagoria was staged with great success in the cloister, but to get to it viewers had to pass through rooms containing a wide range of scientific and pseudo-scientific displays: in the first 'Salon de Physique', a range of optical devices (from prismatic mirrors to microscopes and peepshows); in another, a demonstration of Galvinism; in yet another, the spectacle of the invisible woman.[16]

One of the most innovative aspects of the phantasmagoria was, in addition to its moving rather than stationary illusions, its effective use of stark contrasts between light and darkness. There are obvious symbolic associations to which these extend, and which relate to the phantasmagoria's manipulation of the visual field by turning the visible into the invisible and vice versa. First, the century of the Enlightenment, as Jean Starobinski aptly noted in *The Invention of Liberty*, 'looked at things in the sharp clear light of the reasoning mind whose processes appear to have been closely akin to those of the seeing eye'.[17] What was visible, clearly, could at least be assessed for its truth value. Moreover, on the side of light or illumination, the valuation of light in the Christian tradition was supported by the Greek belief that 'all certainty was based on visibility'; central to Christianity's investment in the Second Coming is the idea that God himself, for so long hidden, will finally become visible.[18] Yet throughout much of the later eighteenth century, the Gothic investment in all things dark – Young's *Night Thoughts*, Novalis' *Hymns to the Night* – offers a parallel or counter-narrative to the (failed) promises of an enlightened age. Indeed, Martin Jay, in *Downcast Eyes*, points to a waning of trust in sight in the wake of the Enlightenment, and offers two reasons elaborated from Starobinski's analysis in *1789 – The Emblems of Reason*. The first corresponds to the revival of a (neo-Platonic) desire for the perception of an ideal beauty beyond 'the normal eyes of mundane observation'.[19] The second draws from a valorisation of darkness as 'the necessary complement, even the source of light',[20] in the way that the invisible functions as the secret counterpart of the visible.

As Starobinski argued, 'the solar myth of the Revolution delighted in the insubstantiality of darkness: Reason had only to appear, supported by will, and darkness disappeared [...but] the myth was an illusion'. France, in fact, 'experienced the intensest moments of its Revolution in a symbolism by which the light of principle merged with the opacity of the physical world and was lost'.[21] It follows from this argument that the failure of the Revolution (and the backlash of the Terror, which Norman Bryson has referred to as a period of 'generalized visual paranoia')[22] generated a new suspicion of the eye, which contributed to the Romantic emphasis on inner inspiration and unmediated vision,[23] but also perhaps signalled a return to darkness, and a denial, implicit in the entertaining spectacle of spectrality on display at the phantasmagoria, of what had previously been asserted in the name of reason. At the same time, as the fore-grounding of science and its mechanisms at the phantasmagoria suggest, dis-illusion was meant to be an important part of the exhibition. The projected image required darkness in order to be made visible, but staging the return to darkness under the aegis of its putative banishment was a curious, even uncanny, mixture of trap and release. Perhaps we can conclude from this that the drama of appearance and disappearance so effectively staged by the phantasmagoria offered a substitute revolution: a revolution this time of the senses, and of viewing in particular, in which that revolution – with its dependence on the simultaneous operation of belief and disbelief, the visible and the invisible, the petrified and the mobile – was itself the principal attraction.

Shelley's ekphrasis and the return of the Medusa

Shelley's ekphrastic poem on a Flemish-school painting of the Medusa addresses the subject of the Medusa directly and dramatises – textually – the struggle between seeing and imagining characteristic of the phantasmagoria. But to explore further this problem of 'represented sight' in connection with the Medusa I would like to turn back briefly to Caravaggio's *Head of Medusa*. Caravaggio's painting, which was executed upon a tournament shield dating from the sixteenth century, is remarkable for being a painting of the head alone, as though the painting *were* in fact the shield of Pallas/Perseus/Athena.[24] Caravaggio's image, as Louis Marin argues, represents the convergence of a number of looks, which are the subject of the painting: the Medusa's, Perseus', the painter's, the painting's, and the viewer's (p. 118). These gazes, however, glance off each other, like blows deflected by a shield (mirror), for the Medusa looks askance and not at the viewer, rendering the viewer transparent, or even absent, for what she looks at is offside, elsewhere. The look of the Medusa is of course unrepresentable – it cannot be seen – even while the image on the shield, or *as* a shield, is convex and round, indeed rather like an eye. Moreover, the event of the decapitation would appear to be equally unrepresentable, for the painting elides, Marin points out, two distinct moments: 'The fact that the moment of the blow itself cannot be presented is designated by the folding together of the moments just before and after the blow' (p. 139). First, the painting depicts the head of Medusa in the instant of her self-petrifaction, at the moment when she (purportedly) looks upon her image in Perseus' shield. Second, the head, as it has been painted, has already been severed and displayed upon the hero's shield. Marin suggests that the Medusa's automorphosis 'is also a *displacement* from one temporality to another, a passage from the moving, linear time of life and history to the time of representation with its immobility and permanence' (p. 136). For Marin, the example of Caravaggio's *Medusa* speaks to the 'ruse of pictorial representation' and to the operation by which painting 'destroys' itself. But such a displacement equally affects the transcription of this scene from image to text, or poem, where the inherent discontinuity between the visible and the invisible is reconfigured and, in a moment of imaginary ekphrasis, re-represented.

Caravaggio's *Medusa* has been in the collection of the Uffizi Gallery since at least 1631. Shelley would have seen it during his frequent visits to the gallery during his stay in Florence in 1819.[25] The painting he wrote about, however, was a 'Head of Medusa' ascribed at that time to Leonardo. It hung in a room devoted to Tuscan painters, close to the famous Tribuna, the octagonal room containing the most precious objects of the collection, including the sculptures of the Venus de' Medici, the Wrestlers, the Dancing Faun, as well as paintings by Michelangelo and Titian.[26] Many of these treasures are depicted in Johann Zoffany's 1780 painting of 'The Tribuna of the Uffizi', commissioned by Queen Charlotte and first displayed publicly at the inaugural Royal Academy exhibition held in the Great Room at Somerset House.[27] In contrast to the crowded scene of viewing depicted by Zoffany – crowded not only by the numbers of peering 'connoisseurs', but by the number of objects on display – evidence suggests that Shelley composed his poem from his memory of the painting. Moreover, far from reflecting what generic depictions of such scenes in the period tell us about the exhibition context as itself a form of social spectacle, the poem excludes any reference to the moment of viewing, and even to the status of the image *as a painting*, both common features of ekphrastic poems as a genre.[28] Here, the illusion created is of a private and *unmediated* scene of seeing.

The painting of the Medusa that inspired Shelley's poem, which was edited by Mary Shelley and first published in his *Posthumous Poems* of 1824, 'On the Medusa of Leonardo da Vinci in the Florentine Gallery', is strikingly different from Caravaggio's (Plate 3). The head of the Medusa is depicted on a horizontal plane, lying on the ground and looking upwards, which may remind the viewer of Géricault's paintings of severed heads (of 1818), where the horizontal arrangement and nestled sheeting has a disturbing erotic charge.[29] The prostrate position of the Medusa is established and emphasised in the first line of Shelley's opening stanza:

> It lieth, gazing on the midnight sky,
>   Upon the cloudy mountain-peak supine;
> Below, far lands are seen tremblingly;
>   Its horror and its beauty are divine.
> Upon its lips and eyelids seems to lie
>   Loveliness like a shadow, from which shine,
> Fiery and lurid, struggling underneath,
>   The agonies of anguish and of death.

While 'lieth' has an appropriate double meaning, alluding to the potential treachery of the look, of her look, its repetition in the fifth line suggests a lighter, transitory quality – something elusive (loveliness 'seems' to lie and it is shadow-like). In both poem and painting, the Medusa's gaze is again deflected: she looks upward, unthreateningly, so that air and sky become her mirror. But the trap has been laid: in the second stanza, the poem grapples with the mythic subject of the painting, displacing the conflict between Medusa and Perseus onto the tension between poet and subject, the speaker and the (gazing) object of his gaze:

> Yet it is less the horror than the grace
>   Which turns the gazer's spirit into stone
> Whereon the lineaments of that dead face
>   Are graven, till the characters be grown
> Into itself, and thought no more can trace;
>   'Tis the melodious hue of beauty thrown
> Athwart the darkness and the glare of pain,
>   Which humanize and harmonize the strain.

The Medusa's petrifying loveliness is emphasised by Shelley, who deflects attention away from the lurid, gothic potential inherent in the image, gestured toward in the first stanza, which was exploited by the phantasmagoria. The poet attends, however, to the transformation of the gazer at, or even in, the dying face – a different kind of automorphosis, perhaps – in which distinctive lineation becomes something uniform that resists the movement of thought.[30] While 'gazer' could as easily refer to the Medusa as the poet, it is also possible that the process of petrifaction is happening to both: the dying Medusa is not *looking* at the poet, but as 'thought no more can trace' passes without an object, the poet clearly feels the effects. The 'characters', evoking metaphorically the letters on the page that threaten to vanish and render it blank, become unreadable in a way that redirects the poet's thoughts toward more terrifying prospects, such as darkness and, by contrast, a pain that is said to glare like an intolerable light.

Subsequent stanzas attend to the snakes and the other creatures that, strikingly, occupy the foreground of the painting: these are fascinating appearances, hideous perhaps, but engaged in many cases in a complex play of light that the painting largely lacks evidence of. Many of the visual details in the poem are not in fact visible in the painting, which is dark, with elements of the background of the image now largely indistinct. It was precisely this shaded quality that suggested the hand of Leonardo, and for this reason many paintings were mistakenly attributed to him during this period. In Shelley's poem, meanwhile, the vipers 'curl and flow' in 'unending involutions' that convey their 'mailèd radiance'. A 'poisonous eft / Peeps idly into those Gorgonian eyes' while a bat, picking up the 'strain' or theme of light from the second stanza, is said to fly madly 'Out of the cave this hideous light had cleft'. It is all, the poet concludes paradoxically, 'the tempestuous loveliness of terror'. The poem concludes (provisionally) with the poet looking from a position of apparent neutrality upon its closing image: 'A woman's countenance, with serpent-locks, / Gazing in death on Heaven from those wet rocks'. The visible threat, still itself seeing, still seeing itself, has been stilled, as the poet steps outside the loop of looking.

Intriguingly, though, as Carol Jacobs has argued, there are at least two ways of looking at the severed head of Medusa in Shelley's poem. The first 'allows the spectator to regard it from a safe distance, as object'; the second 'draws the beholder into a conception of the Medusa as the performance of a radical figural transformation, of itself, of the beholder, of the language that attempts to represent it'.[31] Shelley's poem presents both possibilities, but they are suggestively implicit in the experience, the spectacle, of transformation at the phantasmagoria, where the objects of sight necessarily implicate the audience. In the poem, certainly, such transformations are very much in evidence. 'Fiery and lurid', the 'agonies of anguish and of death' are said to shine through the shadowy loveliness of the Medusa's 'lips and eyelids'; the gleaming serpents, emitting a kind of 'brazen glare', turn the 'thrilling' vaporous air into an 'ever-shifting mirror' of everything beneath, 'all the beauty and the terror there'. Meanwhile, the midnight sky 'flares a light more dread than obscurity'. Visually, all is contrast, opposition and change. Shelley's poem is intriguingly phantasmagoric in its images, which transform the dark canvas of the Uffizi painting into a screen across which all manner of terrifying lights and apparitions pass.

There is however an additional stanza associated with Shelley's poem, though not published with it until Neville Rogers included it in his article on the poem of 1961. It is not clear where this stanza could or should have fit – it is perhaps a kind of supplement to the poem, a fragment that (like other stanzas) contains its own blank spaces where words are missing, while drawing attention to the decapitated head of the Medusa as itself a fragment.[32] These are its final lines:

> It is a trunkless head, and on its feature
>   Death has met life, but there is life in death,
> The blood is frozen – but unconquered Nature
>   Seems struggling to the last – without a breath
> The fragment of an uncreated creature.

We look upon what is unambiguously the head of a corpse: dying, if not dead. Medusa's trunkless head, crudely put, suggests a curious kinship with Shelley's Ozymandias, whose 'vast and trunkless legs of stone / Stand in the desart'. His head, lying in the sand nearby, makes its own ironic statement about the effects of tyranny, and of the (im)permanence of art – about, that is, the possible outcomes of being turned to stone. Shelley's Medusa, however, is no cold relic: although 'it' is ostensibly drawing its last breath, it is a piece of something, finally, yet to be. This lack of 'fix', relates to the way in which the viewer in the poem moves beyond the apotropaic threat to an altered regard for the prostrate head, one that responds not to the prohibition against looking, but to the richer possibilities looking allows: leisurely looking, neither furtive nor fraught. Moreover, this 'unfixing' of the image of the Medusa, with its attendant suggestions of fragmentation and disembodiment, alludes directly to the dynamics of ekphrastic representation.

While a commonly held view of ekphrasis is that it has the effect of releasing, into verbal narrative, an otherwise static form, W.J.T. Mitchell's notion of ekphrastic fear addresses directly the possibility of the opposite: of artistic entrapment, should the ekphrastic conjuring act succeed too fully in recreating a static visual object.[33] This is only one of several stages or moments Mitchell claims as features of ekphrasis. In the first, the poet greets with 'indifference' what is perceived as the incommensurability of language on the one hand, and painting or sculpture on the other. This is followed by a moment of hope, that their differences might be overcome by the power of poetic language to stimulate or even simulate the visual imagination – but the very possibility of success threatens to freeze or petrify the dynamic temporal movement of language, to bring closer to death what otherwise bespeaks the vitality and independence of the mind. What this suggests is a transposition from painting and viewing to painting and language, or poetry, of what Mitchell refers to elsewhere as 'the Medusa effect', in which the image desires 'to change places with the beholder, to transfix or paralyze the beholder, turning him or her into an image for the gaze of the picture'.[34] The moment of succumbing, a 'Medusa-moment', is linked by Frederick Burwick to Thomas De Quincey's 'mighty antagonisms' with opium and with the fear of demoniacal intrusion that comes with it.[35] Mitchell addresses it however in terms of representation, emphasising an inherent otherness in the object that makes it a kind of 'resident alien' in the new textual artefact.

Ekphrastic texts represent representation; however, this repetition or redoubling of representation leads not to a more perfect or total representation, but rather to the recognition that representation and misrepresentation go hand in hand. Combining word and image sets up an internal conflict in which the inadequacies of each are exposed in the other. In Jacobs's reading of Shelley's poem, for example, 'intervals of non-coincidence', rather than meaning, are exposed in the endless mirroring by which 'the beholding subject, the producing subject, and the object produced can never coincide'.[36] Put differently, words displace the actual image-object, as Mitchell points out; they alienate and repress it in favour of the textual image, precisely to retain its visible power, to prevent it, in a manner of speaking, disappearing from view.[37] The actual image or object is thus a potent absence, an 'unapproachable and unpresentable "black hole" in the verbal structure, entirely absent from it, but shaping and affecting it in fundamental ways' (p. 158). The inherent dissonance between these two modes of representation can be mapped directly onto the tension between the visible and the invisible: the invisible (because inaccessible) image is brought before the reader's imagining eyes, but is exposed as lacking the supplement of textuality that accompanies the (ekphrastic) act of making visible.

In Shelley's poem, the Medusa, by being portrayed as gazing, 'exerts and reverses the power of the ekphrastic gaze': she is 'the image that turns the tables on the spectator and turns the spectator into an image'

(p. 172). This is a strikingly different 'image' to popular depictions of spectatorship, alluded to earlier, such as Thomas Rowlandson's marvellous prints of crowds at the Royal Academy summer exhibitions, with their eyes more on each other than on the walls. If for Shelley the moment of viewing, or of being viewed by, the Medusa is reconfigured without reference to the gallery context and never recorded *as such*, it is equally striking that features of his poem echo his detailed verbal accounts of the Uffizi's revered statues. In his 'Notices of the Sculpture in the Florence Gallery' Shelley devotes the most attention to the tension between irreversible grief and extreme beauty conveyed by two female figures, the Niobe and Minerva. The 'poetic harmony of marble' embodies, in the case of Niobe, 'the consummation of feminine majesty and loveliness, beyond which the imagination scarcely doubts that it can conceive anything'; and yet 'it seems as if despair and beauty had combined, and produced nothing but the sublimity of grief'.[38] There is 'no terror in the countenance, only grief – deep, remediless grief'. And again: 'It is difficult to speak of the beauty of the countenance, or to make intelligible in words, from what such astonishing loveliness results' (p. 404). The eloquent beauty of Minerva likewise pleads 'against some vast and inevitable wrong'; it encapsulates 'the joy and poetry of sorrow making grief beautiful, and giving it that nameless feeling which, from the imperfection of language, we call pain, but which is not all pain, though a feeling which makes not only its possessor, but the spectator of it, prefer it to what is called pleasure, in which all is not pleasure' (p. 405). Shelley's articulation of an unnameable feeling that is neither all pain nor all pleasure and yet both, and that infects the spectator as much as it does the possessor, informs his response-in-memory to the Medusa: performs, even, a displacement from stone, through 'imperfect language', to an image that (only) threatens petrification. Ekphrastic description in Shelley's essay is of a piece with his re-rendering of the Medusa.

Because Shelley's poem deconstructs the repressive force of ekphrasis, by not emphasising or referring explicitly to the act of textual framing (as conventionally, most ekphrastic poems do), it underscores the return of the repressed image in the form of the Medusa. This is a Medusa who does not tease us out of thought, in the manner of Keats' urn, but rather paralyses thought and renders it incapable of further 'tracing'. It is the inherently disturbing power wielded by the Medusa that stands behind Mitchell's claim that Shelley's poem on the Medusa is a, or rather *the*, primal scene of ekphrastic poetry and this disturbing power is synonymous with visual power. As a 'gazing' agent, the Medusa is a disturber of the order of representation; she can only be seen through the mediation of images, such as mirrors, paintings, and descriptions. Indeed, as Marin has pointed out, Perseus prevails against the Medusa by turning her threatening image into a representation: into something, like a shield, that can be held at a distance (and indeed pointed away). His victory is a function of *trompe l'oeil*, of optical deception, itself as much a feature of ekphrasis as it is of the phantasmagoria.

Shelley's treatment of the Medusa is more alert to what she can represent, or make visible, than to the conventions of ekphrastic poetry with which his poetry was, in any case, seldom engaged. Indeed, Shelley claimed for himself a habitual tendency to look for the manifestation 'beyond the present and tangible object'.[39] In the case of the Medusa, he accomplishes this by looking attentively *at* her, by penetrating almost without effort the clouds of myth and superstition that hang about her. Nevertheless, it is in relation to the dynamics of ekphrasis, which are caught up in the tension between the trap and release of aesthetic representation – a tension that is a generative feature of the Medusan play on visuality at the phantasmagoria – that the force of Shelley's repositioning of the Medusa becomes clear. In his poem, she is a potentially revolutionary figure, not because of her place in a narrative of violence and sexuality, and of wanton betrayal, but because she is the victim of the crushing power of others. In so far as her power of sight appears to persist in the face of death, Shelley's Medusa is a figure for resistance. The vaporous cloud emitting from her mouth, which suggests (last) breath and perhaps also alludes to the appearance of Pegasus, the symbol of inspiration and creative energy that legend holds sprang forth from her dying body, links her to the generation of new life. Even her ruined state, her 'monstrous mutilation', becomes, as Mitchell has argued, a pointed kind of revolutionary power. Shelley's treatment of the Medusa, then, works to demystify, to run counter to superstitious belief of the kind exposed at the phantasmagoria and exploited by political caricature. Enacting a radical humanisation as well as harmonisation of the 'strain', the poem returns to the image of a woman, lying prostrate, and we are not forbidden to look.

Notes

1. Grant F. Scott, 'Shelley, Medusa, and the Perils of Ekphrasis', in Frederick Burwick and Jürgen Klein, eds, *The Romantic Imagination: Literature and Art in England and Germany* (Amsterdam and Atlanta, GA: Rodopi, 1996), p. 329.

Scott's account ties the poem carefully to numerous aspects of the myth, and is especially revealing on the subject of male sexuality.

2. There is a significant ambiguity in the mirroring moment immediately before Medusa's death, as it is often held that she has petrified *herself* (hence the bulging eyes), by the sight of her own image in Perseus' shield, having woken up in that instant. This has had an impact on psychoanalytic readings of the myth, and on the susceptibility of the myth to both feminist and misogynist appropriations.

3. 'Perseus, or War', in *The Works of Francis Bacon*, 14 vols, ed. by James Spedding, Robert Leslie Ellis, and Douglas Denton Heath (London: Longman & Co., 1857–1874; repr. Stuttgart: Frommann, 1963), VI, 715.

4. Marjorie Garber and Nancy J. Vickers, eds, *The Medusa Reader* (New York and London: Routledge, 2003), p. 1.

5. Sigmund Freud, 'Medusa's Head', *The Standard Edition of the Complete Psychological Works of Sigmund Freud*, 24 vols, trans. and ed. by James Strachey (London: The Hogarth Press, 1953–1974), XVIII, 273–4.

6. Freud, 'Medusa's Head', p. 273.

7. Tradition holds that the magic lantern was invented by a Jesuit scientist, Athanasius Kircher, in the seventeenth century, though recently this credit has been more accurately assigned to the Dutch humanist Christiaan Huygens. See Laurent Mannoni's thorough account in *The Great Art of Light and Shadow: Archaeology of the Cinema*, trans. and ed. by Richard Crangle (Exeter, UK: University of Exeter Press, 2000). The lanternist was himself a popular visual and literary figure, often depicted travelling with his lamp and his images throughout the streets and squares of Europe.

8. See the excellent illustrations of the lantern in *Servants of Light: the Book of the Lantern*, ed. by Dennis Crompton et. al. (Ripon: The Magic Lantern Society, 1997).

9. *Encyclopaedia of the Magic Lantern*, ed. by David Robinson, Stephen Herbert, and Richard Crangle (London: Magic Lantern Society, 2001), p. 229.

10. Laurent Mannoni et al., eds, *Light and Movement: Incunabula of the Motion Picture 1420–1896* (Gemona: Giornate del Cinema Muto, 1995), p. 100. Philipsthal's resurrection of the dead extended to the raising of the devil himself, a 'spectre of fiery red, armed with claws, with horns and a satyr's tail'. The entry for 1792 further informs us that Philidor/Philipsthal's depiction of Jean-Paul Marat – the extremist revolutionary who was then still alive – 'conjured him under the form of a demon: he too appeared on the screen with claws and horns' (p. 100). The 'apparition' of Marat at the phantasmagoria took place in March of 1793, four months before he was assassinated. Philipsthal seems to have left Paris suddenly in April of that year. See also Mannoni's deft account of the phantasmagoria in *The Great Art of Light and Shadow* (chapter six), which notes that Marat was himself an amateur of projected images.

11. Richard Altick, *The Shows of London* (Cambridge, MA and London: Belknap/Harvard University Press, 1978), pp. 217–18, quoting from David Brewster, *Letters on Natural Magic* (London, 1832), pp. 80–1.

12. *Encyclopaedia of the Magic Lantern*, pp. 227–8. Further descriptions of Robertson's spectacle, including its export to the United States in the early 1800s, are to be found in Theodore Barber, 'Phantasmagorical Wonders: the Magic

Lantern Ghost Show in Nineteenth-Century America', *Film History*, 3 (1989), 73–86.
13. E.-G. Robertson, *Mémoires récréatifs, scientifiques, et anecdotiques d'un physicien-aéronaute*, 2 vols (Paris, 1830–34), I, 178. Robertson was initially ordained as a priest, which puts a slightly different slant on his denunciation of the false claims of charlatans. Philipsthal made comparable assertions: 'I am neither priest nor magician; I do not wish to deceive you; but I will astonish you', see Mannoni, *The Great Art of Light and Shadow*, p. 144. Robertson was also an avid balloonist – or *aéronaute* – and took his balloon (itself quite a spectacle) over wondrous sights, such as the Kremlin in flames, the site of the battle of Moscow, and so on, as his memoirs relate.
14. Roberston, *Mémoires*, I, 149–50. What this suggests of course is that the effect of the phantasmagoria was closely connected to the persistence of primitive beliefs that Freud thought might be central to the experience of the uncanny.
15. '…on appelle *miroir* le rideau de percale sur lequel viennent se dessiner les ombres entre les spectateurs et le physicien.' Robertson, *Mémoires*, I, vj (*avant propos*).
16. For full details of Robertson's displays, see the *Programme Instructif* reproduced in Mannoni et al., eds, *Light and Movement*, pp. 118–19.
17. Jean Starobinski, *The Invention of Liberty, 1700–1789*, trans. Bernard C. Swift (Geneva: Skira, 1964), p. 210.
18. Hans Blumenberg, 'Light as a Metaphor for Truth: at the Preliminary Stage of Philosophical Concept Formation', in David Michael Levin, ed., *Modernity and the Hegemony of Vision* (Berkeley: University of California Press, 1993), pp. 46–7. This is noted in contrast to the Hebrew tradition, where 'the impossibility of beholding God is absolute and not merely temporary', and where hearing tends, as a result, to surpass or predetermine sight.
19. Martin Jay, *Downcast Eyes: the Denigration of Vision in Twentieth-Century French Thought* (Berkeley, Los Angeles and London: University of California Press, 1993), p. 106; Jean Starobinski, *1789 – The Emblems of Reason*, trans. Barbara Bray (Cambridge, MA and London: MIT Press, 1988), p. 40f.
20. Jay, *Downcast Eyes*, p. 107.
21. Jay, *Downcast Eyes*, p. 107; Starobinski, *1789*, p. 196.
22. *Tradition and Desire* (Cambridge: Cambridge University Press, 1984), p. 96.
23. Jay, *Downcast Eyes*, p. 107.
24. See Marin, *To Destroy Painting*, pp. 112–13, hereafter in text. Such shields were common enough in the sixteenth and seventeenth centuries; referred to as 'parade' shields, they were either round or oblong, and displayed upon them was a representation (either painted or in relief) of a Medusa head. In these cases, the head played its traditional apotropaic role, to ward off the enemy, to announce the triumph of the bearer.
25. Mary Shelley's journals inform us of a first visit to the gallery on 11 September; there are notes of P.B. Shelley returning thereafter. *The Journals of Mary Shelley 1814–1844*, ed. by Paula R. Feldman and Diana Scott-Kilvert (Baltimore and London: Johns Hopkins University Press, 1995), pp. 298–9. Shelley comments in a letter to Hogg of April 1820 that they had spent the 'severe' winter at Florence, and that he 'dedicated every sunny day to the study of the gallery there', see *The Letters of Percy Bysshe Shelley*, 3 vols, ed. by Frederick

L. Jones (Oxford: Clarendon Press, 1964), II, 186. Mary dates Shelley's poem to 1819; no further details, and no holograph of the poem, have survived.

26. Although the painting would seem to approximate one of Leonardo's, described in detail by Vasari, its attribution to Leonardo was mistaken – the painter of the Florentine Medusa is unknown, and the painting is now attributed to the Flemish School. It hangs in a corridor containing sixteenth century works (in room 33 of the Uffizi Gallery). An 1822 Uffizi catalogue lists it under 'École Toscane', immediately after the entry on 'La Tribune', see *Galerie Impériale et Royale de Florence. Nouvelle edition ornée des planches de la Vénus des Médécis, de celle de Canova, et de l'Apollon. Avec des changements faits en 1821* (Florence, 1822), pp. 165–6. Neville Rogers, in 'Shelley and the Visual Arts', in the *Keats–Shelley Memorial Bulletin*, 12 (1961), was the first to connect Shelley's poem with this painting, and offers a close analysis of the relation between the two. He suggests that Shelley was working from memory, but argues for his skill as a 'translator' between media as between languages.

27. See David H. Solkin's introductory essay in *Art on the Line: the Royal Academy Exhibitions at Somerset House 1780–1836* (New Haven and London: Yale University Press, 2001).

28. Zoffany was, no doubt, taking liberties by filling the Uffizi so blatantly with a flock of English tourists as well as by rearranging elements of the museum's displays, as Judith Pascoe notes in *The Hummingbird Cabinet: a Rare and Curious History of Romantic Collectors* (Ithaca and London: Cornell University Press, 2006), pp. 65–6.

29. See Linda Nochlin's discussion of these paintings in *The Body in Pieces: the Fragment as a Metaphor of Modernity* (London: Thames and Hudson, 1994), pp. 19–22.

30. Who exactly the gazer is, in this line, is the subject of some controversy. As Carol Jacobs notes, there are several possibilities: Perseus, his predecessors, the painter, the poet, the reader, see Carol Jacobs, 'On Looking at Shelley's Medusa', *Yale French Studies*, 69 (1985), 163–79. Jacobs and other commentators tend to assume that the gazer is the spectator. Clearly, 'gazer' in this line can indicate any one of these viewing positions and has, to my mind, a suggestively inclusive sense. James Heffernan, however, troubled by how in every other instance in the poem 'gazing' is attributed to Medusa, reads this instance of 'gazer' accordingly, such that 'the poem becomes a study in the petrifaction of beauty, in what happens when the petrifying impact of Medusa's gaze is turned inward on her own spirit'. This seems to me to limit unnecessarily the interpretive possibilities of the poem. See Heffernan, *Museum of Words*, p. 122.

31. Jacobs, 'On Looking at Shelley's Medusa', p. 172.

32. Jay Clayton argues that Mary Shelley may have omitted this stanza in her edition of her husband's *Posthumous Poems* (1824) because of the implicit bearing of this 'uncreated creature' on the relationship between monstrosity and vision articulated in *Frankenstein*, see Jay Clayton, 'Concealed Circuits: Frankenstein's Monster, the Medusa, and the Cyborg', *Raritan*, 15 (Spring 1996), 62–3.

33. The view of ekphrasis as capable of releasing, from graphic art, an 'embryonically narrative impulse', is articulated by Heffernan in 'Ekphrasis and

Representation', *NLH*, 22 (1991), 301–2. W.J.T. Mitchell examines the anxiety inherent in ekphrastic representations in his chapter on ekphrasis in *Picture Theory*.

34. W.J.T. Mitchell, *What Do Pictures Want? The Lives and Loves of Images* (Chicago and London: Chicago University Press, 2005), p. 36.

35. The importance of the 'Medusa-moment' in relation to a sense of personal crisis that manifests itself in dreams (related in turn to opium use), can be extended to Coleridge, see Frederick Burwick, *Mimesis and its Romantic Reflections* (University Park, PA: Pennsylvania State University Press, 2001), p. 111.

36. Jacobs, 'On Looking at Shelley's Medusa', p. 179.

37. Mitchell, *Picture Theory*, p. 157 n. 19, hereafter in text.

38. *Shelley's Prose Works*, 2 vols, ed. by R.H. Shepherd (London: Chatto & Windus, 1906), I, 402, hereafter in text.

39. As Shelley wrote to Thomas Love Peacock, 'You know I always seek in what I see the manifestation of something beyond the present & tangible object', 6 November 1818, *Letters*, II, 47.

3
Wordsworth's Glasses:
the Materiality of Blindness
in the Romantic Vision

Heather Tilley

Among the memorabilia on display at Dove Cottage, Grasmere, are the green eyeshades that Wordsworth wore to alleviate the symptoms of the eye disorders that accompanied his writing career, and a blue stone thought to be the one used to relieve his eye inflammations. Several unpublished letters in the Wordsworth Trust collection discuss and document the nature and impact of Wordsworth's eye disorders. From 1805 until his death, throughout the period in which he redrafted major sections of *The Prelude*, Wordsworth experienced sustained attacks of chronic trachoma. These attacks often confined him to darkened rooms for days at a time and prevented his travelling. The fear of permanent blindness also hastened the publication of his poetry. The trachoma left Wordsworth sensitive to light and reliant upon wearing these green eyeshades to relieve his photophobia. Through these objects and letters, I will offer a new materialist perspective on Wordsworth's blindness and explore the intimate relationship between the materiality of blindness and of writing in the poet's imagination. This materialist approach questions the use of blindness in the construction of the Romantic literary canon, in which Wordsworth's interest in blindness is often taken to uphold an idealist model of the mind and imagination, which privileges the sovereignty of the mind above the senses.

Figures of blindness haunt Wordsworth's writing, from blind Herbert in *The Borderers* to 'Lines Written a Few Miles Above Tintern Abbey', 'The Blind Highland Boy', the blind man of *The Excursion,* and the blind beggar of *The Prelude.* However, little critical attention has been paid to the poet's experience of visual disorders. Meyer H. Abrams, Geoffrey Hartman and Harold Bloom have traditionally focused on the visionary nature of romantic poetry and philosophy, in which blindness produces a space where the distinction between inner and outer vision can be upheld. Although the topic of blindness continues to be addressed in more recent critical studies, Wordsworth's physical experience of eye disorders remains neglected. Jeffrey Baker, for example, offers a Bloomian reading of the figures of the deaf and blind in Wordsworth's writings interpreted as signs of his fear of his poetic father John Milton.[1] More recently, Edward Larrissy has comprehensively documented the episodes of blindness in Wordsworth's writing as border states, in which the terms of blindness and insight signal the limits between self and other. He also notes that Wordsworth's thought is characteristically 'modelled on the idea of compensatory enhancement of aural sensitivity in the blind'.[2] However, Larrissy's study overlooks the impact of personal experience on these texts, which are marked by complex revision processes and protracted publication histories.

Wordsworth's glasses and the blue stone suggest the poet's fragile and distressing experience of physical sight. In its precariousness, Wordsworth's vision exemplifies what Merleau-Ponty defines as 'conditioned thought', occasioned 'by what happens in the body'.[3] The objects and traces of Wordsworth's eye disorders indicate that blindness and writing occupy a shared terrain in the poet's textual imagination, pointing to the supplementary nature of vision and, by extension, the text. Wordsworth's anxious experience of blindness also raises questions about the act of writing itself. Restoring Wordsworth's vision to a more phenomenological model, the green glasses and blue stone challenge the dominant critical paradigms concerning the visionary nature of Romantic poetry. These objects counter Bloom's heavily rhetoricised claims that Wordsworth pays little attention to the materiality and spatiality of sight and attempts to 'defeat the eye'.[4] By contrast, these objects suggest the poet's fear of the loss of his physical vision and indicate his care for the eye at a sensual, epistemological and ontological level. 'Eye', 'vision', and 'material' are complex terms, which slip in and out of fixed categories of meaning in the Romantic imagination.

Romantic ophthalmia

Wordsworth seems to have first experienced symptoms of the trachoma in 1804, shortly after his sister Dorothy noted she had caught an eye infection.[5] Endemic at the time, trachoma caused the formation of pustules along the eyelashes and eyelid margins and could lead to permanent loss of vision if it spread to the eyeball. This chronic inflammation is likely to have been a case of Egyptian ophthalmia, brought over by soldiers returning from the Napoleonic wars.[6] As ophthalmic historian Julius Hirschberg argues, this Egyptian strain was crucial to the development of the treatment of eye disease in Britain at the start of the nineteenth century. Hirschberg argues that ophthalmology was shaped by the political and social issues of the day, particularly the French Revolution. Interest in ophthalmology waned at the end of the eighteenth century, as the war against France drained resources. However, the war instigated the need for new investment in ophthalmology at the start of the nineteenth century, as soldiers returning from the campaign in Egypt (1798–1801), carried eye disease back to Britain, where it rapidly spread from the naval and military forces to the civilian population. Hirschberg notes that 'the conjunctivitis and especially its sequelae, the papillary occlusion, must have presented a tremendous challenge to English surgeons'.[7] By the early nineteenth century, along with smallpox, ophthalmia was one of the most common causes of blindness.[8] John Stevenson, one of the early leading ophthalmologists in Britain, attributes part of the rapid growth of the field to the effect of the Egyptian ophthalmia:

> Of late years [...] a dreadful Ophthalmia, before unknown amongst us, has been introduced into the country from Egypt, and has not only added greatly to the frequency of their occurrence, but also at the same time not a little increased the malignancy of their character.[9]

He goes on to suggest that the seriousness of the disease attracted the attention of 'regular practitioners' of medicine to the site of the eye. Ophthalmology advanced rapidly in the period. By the 1830s, Hirschberg argues, new hospitals were being built and specialisation led to the development of new surgical techniques.

The professionalisation of ophthalmology is also marked by its growth as a textual discipline at the time. The development of print culture shaped the field and helped construct a rational discourse around the diseased eye as textbooks and specialist journals disseminated ideas and discoveries across the country. One of the earliest British ophthalmic texts, James Wardrop's *Essays on the Morbid Anatomy of the Eye* (1808), claimed that despite the publication of 'several excellent practical treatises and detached essays', and as 'no attempt has yet been made in this country to treat of the pathology of the human eye, little apology seems necessary for the present undertaking'.[10] The construction of the eye as a figure of linguistic discourse in these texts invites a return to Michel Foucault's reflections on the relationship between vision, knowledge and the emergence of the rational discourse of the clinic. Foucault argues that modern medicine 'succeeded in striking a balance between *seeing* and *knowing* (*le voir et le savoir*) that protected it from error', as the clinic evolved into a disciplinary space in which the doctor learns to 'see what he saw' when examining the human body – that is, give name to the new layers of the visible body emerging in medical investigation.[11] In Foucault's argument, philosophy is traditionally figured as a discourse proceeding from blindness, with language awaiting in the dark 'for us to attain awareness before emerging into the light of day and speaking' (p. xvi). If we must look to the region where 'things' and 'words' have not yet been separated, where seeing and saying are still one, in order to determine the mutations in discourse that mark the birth of the clinic, then further ruptures emerge when the object of that language is blindness itself (p. xi).

Janis Caldwell usefully terms 'Romantic materialism' the 'double vision' of leading doctors and writers in this period, who shared a concern with consciousness and self-expression and an investment in what natural philosophy revealed about the material world. For Caldwell Romantic materialism involves a dialectical hermeneutic, an interpretive method which tacked 'back and forth between physical evidence and inner, imaginative understanding', moving between and accepting disjunctions between 'the book of Nature and the Book of Scripture'. This dialectical hermeneutic opens up the shared space between medical diagnostics and literary representations. Medical lectures, textbooks, and journal articles were shaped by imaginative literature, and participated in a textual economy which reshaped the imaginative and epistemological claims of literature in texts addressed to the medical body published between 1800 and 1859.[12]

Medical discourses at the time abound in literary examples of blindness. Such an interest demonstrates the desire to construct an authentic, authoritative voice in such texts. Quotations from Milton were frequently excerpted in early ophthalmologic texts. His poetry was recognised as inextricably bound up with the experience of his physical and material body and was read autobiographically for evidence of his blindness.[13] Milton's presence in these texts demonstrates the reciprocity between material and imaginative states of blindness in early ophthalmologic discourse. Building on Caldwell's 'Romantic materialism', this study sets the objects that mark Wordsworth's blindness alongside the medical diagnoses alluded to in various letters and thus restores materiality to the poet's fragile eye.

The materiality of Wordsworth's blindness: objects and spaces

Private letters record that Wordsworth experienced several bouts of trachoma throughout the 1810s–40s. Family and friends frequently commented on the inflammation of his eyes. The trachoma left him sensitive to light and reliant upon wearing green eyeshades when out walking in bright sunlight. The medical advice he sought to alleviate symptoms of the inflammation initially focused on altering his diet, whilst using a few restoratives.[14] Sara Hutchinson, Wordsworth's sister-in-law, describes some of the remedies in a letter to John Monkhouse, which provides us with an account of Wordsworth as a patient, as well as suggesting how common trachoma was:

> You give no particulars of the state of your eyes at present – therefore 'I guess' they are not materially worse or better – William has been sadly teezed lately with inflammation on the Lids, & consequent heat & irritation of the eyeballs – Tillbrook had the same when he was here – and since his return to College he has been to Town consulting Alexander whose prescriptions would, we are sure, be of use to William – but he is a most refractory Patient – Alexander recommends nothing more than bathing in water (morning and Evg) as hot as the eye can bear till the water becomes nearly cool – to accustom the eye to the light, & variety of colours – not to stick to green – else nothing else in time would be endured – to eat & drink moderately no 'condiments' to use Wms favourite word & [...] and abstinence in Tea.[15]

Wordsworth started to wear green eyeshades in 1820.[16] Green glass had been used in eyeshades to treat photophobia since at least the seventeenth century. In 1666 Samuel Pepys recorded that he bought a pair of green spectacles to help alleviate the pain he was experiencing in his eyes.[17] In Oliver Goldsmith's sentimental novel *The Vicar of Wakefield: a Tale Supposed to be Written by Himself* (1766) the vicar's son Moses exchanges the family's horse for 'a gross of green spectacles with silver rims and shagreen cases'.[18] However, by the time Wordsworth began wearing green glasses, their function in managing ocular dysfunctions was coming under ophthalmologic scrutiny. For instance, Stevenson argued that:

> By using *green* spectacles, especially those of a *deep tint*, the eye is subjected to frequent, and not inconsiderable variations in respect to

the degree of light; and every such sudden and violent change, must of necessity be detrimental to the organ of vision.[19]

In a populist ophthalmic treatise, *The Art of Preserving the Sight Unimpaired to an Extreme Old Age; and of Re-establishing and Strengthening it When it is Become Weak* (1813), Georg Beer notes that although most people of weak sight use spectacles to improve their vision, others go further and imagine 'that since green silk has such beneficial effects upon the eyes, so green glasses cannot fail to have the same influence'.[20] As Beer implies, the fabric as well as the colour is recognised to impact upon the eyes. Yet the effect is challenged in a later guidebook to spectacles and glasses: 'green, or any coloured glasses' veil objects 'with a gloomy obscurity' and therefore should not be recommended. Nor does it approve of 'other ridiculous refinements', such as 'thin *Green-Gauze* or *Crape*, instead of Green Glass', recommended 'under the pretence, that while it moderates the Light [...] it still admits the Air, and is, therefore, cooler to the Eyes'.[21] Wordsworth's physician must have been aware of the ophthalmologic concern over the effects of green light, because he advised him to use a 'variety of colours – not to stick to green'. According to Beer, this concern is due to their representing 'objects different from what they are in reality, giving them a dark and obscure outline, by which the weakness of the eyes may absolutely be increased, instead of being diminished'.[22]

Green eyeshades are frequently mentioned in literature of the period, associated with distorted vision and figuring the gap between reality and perception of the external world. Heinrich von Kleist used green glasses as a metaphor to articulate the Kantian realignment of the phenomenal and noumenal world. In 1801 he anxiously wrote to his fiancée that if everyone saw the world through them 'they would be forced to judge that everything they saw *was* green, and could never be sure whether their eyes saw things as they really are, or did not add something of their own to what they saw'.[23] In an early journalistic paper published in *Bentley's Miscellany* (1838), Charles Dickens plays with the idea of coloured spectacles when Mr Tickle proudly displays his 'new-invented spectacles', at the 'Second Meeting of the Mudfog Association for the Advancement of Everything'. In a satirical swipe at scientific and philosophic societies, the narrator argues that the glasses 'enabled the wearer to discern, in very bright colours, objects at a great distance, and rendered him wholly blind to those immediately before him. It was, he said, a most valuable and useful invention, based strictly upon the principle of the human eye'.[24]

In 1825 Wordsworth began experimenting with other palliatives, notably copper sulphate, also known as the blue stone. The properties of copper sulphate had long been used to treat eye conditions; the ancient Egyptians, for example, are believed to have used it to treat trachoma.[25] Sara Hutchinson reported that Frederic Reynolds, editor of the *Keepsake*, prescribed touching the eyes with the blue stone in 1826. She noted that it 'acted like magic' upon Wordsworth eyes: 'I never saw him look so well & *bonny* as he did yesterday, upon his return from Keswick, for many years'.[26] A few months later, following a few applications of the blue stone, his sister Dorothy reports that Wordsworth's eyes 'are become useful again'. She notes: 'he holds the pen himself, and even reads aloud to us by candlelight. This happy change, through God's blessing, has been brought about by touching the eyelids with blue stone.'[27] Despite this experiment, however, symptoms flared up again in 1829; Sara Coleridge writes that 'Mr Wordsworth is suffering from an attack in his eyes – his left eye is very much affected; this is most vexatious as we all hoped the enemy was put to flight forever'.[28] These experiments with blue stone and green eyeshades demonstrate the use of supplements to manage the body and to bring it back to normal functioning.

The material conditions of reading and writing (not least the scarcity of light) were understood to put great strain upon the eyes.[29] The ophthalmologist Stevenson noted that many instances of 'weakness of sight' and eye diseases were brought on by 'inordinate indulgence in literary pursuits protracted frequently to late hours'.[30] Wordsworth's blindness opens up the link between writing and the material space of the interior, which structures and shapes the mind, mirroring the space of human interiority. The interior of Dove Cottage exemplifies the material factors that might have impacted upon his eye condition: many of the rooms had dark wood panelling and the small-sized windows admitted limited light. The domestic space, including the writer's study, depended upon artificial light sources, which in the early nineteenth century were mainly candles.[31] Although there were major advancements in the use of artificial light over the course of the century, the expense of candles limited their use in bourgeois households. The material evolution of the lamp during this period makes it a doubly apt metaphor for the romantic imagination.[32] The domestic interior in the early nineteenth century thus oscillates between being a space of blindness and one of illumination.[33]

The retreat into the dark room is like a retreat into a blind cavern, a psychological retreat into a space of the imagination. From blindness emerge not only writing, but subjectivity itself – the self in both nature and culture (the 'works of man' and 'face of human life'):

> This faculty [imagination] has been the moving soul
> Of our long labour: we have traced the stream
> From darkness and the very place of birth
> In its blind cavern, whence is faintly heard
> The sound of waters; followed it to light
> And open day, accompanied its course
> Among the ways of nature, afterwards
> Lost sight of it bewildered and engulfed,
> Then given it greeting as it rose once more
> With strength, reflecting in its solemn breast
> The works of man and face of human life [...][34]

Wordsworth's Platonic invocation of the 'blind cavern' towards the conclusion of *The Prelude* is also a remedy for his ailing sight. Withdrawing from light seems to have been a regular way of dealing with the attacks. As Wordsworth's daughter Dora notes in 1837, her father had been compelled to sit in darkened rooms for ten days, after a 'most severe' attack.[35] Imagination does not only proceed from blindness; it causes blindness.

Dora suggests that the attacks of blindness disrupted not only the mechanical act of reading and writing, but also the metaphysics of writing, the mental activities of thinking and composing poetry. In an important letter of 1829, she records:

> My greatest anxiety now is for my dear Father's eye, which I am grieved to say is almost worse this morning than it has ever been. The inflammation seems to have moved from the lid to the eye itself – though not being able to read or write is bad enough but this is the least disturbing consequence to him – he cannot amuse himself by any mental occupations – if he attempts to think or to compose the eye instantly suffers.[36]

The eye is materially threatened by the activity of the mind, which strangely resonates with Wordsworth's desire to thwart the 'tyranny' of the eye. In a letter from 1834, William's nephew Chris notes: 'My uncle's eyes are [...] much better, indeed they would be quite well, if he did not write verses: but this he will do; and therefore it is extremely difficult to prevent him from ruining his eyesight'.[37] The notion that mental disturbance aggravates the eyes is borne out in a letter of 1833, in which

Dora writes, again to her cousin Christopher, that her father has been 'a prisoner in a dark room' because of a recurrence of the inflammation:

> for my father is still a blind man – but thank god the inflammation has entirely subsided. Tonics were applied to his eyes and he has now permission to go into the garden; for the last ten days he has been a prisoner to a dark room & so very very patient but not very good; for compose sonnets he will in spite of all the dreadful threats of his medical attendant, nor will the recollection of blisters on blisters or leaches on leaches keep him quiet. Within the last few weeks he has composed upwards of 40 sonnets, I believe principally on subjects connected with his late tour [...] now that the inflammations in the eyes have taken so alarming a form we are all extremely anxious that he should consult Alexander or some oculist of note and we hope by & bye to persuade him to go to London for the purpose.[38]

Thus blindness is not only brought on by reading and writing, but by the act of thinking itself. The relationship between vision and writing is emphasised still further by the detail that the sonnets he composes are 'on subjects connected with his late tour', suggesting that he wants to record the visual experience of the tour in case he should become permanently blind. This instance records the reciprocal nature of composition and vision – composing poetry requires the perception of an original, real object (the tour) to stimulate mental activity, yet that activity is recognised as potentially destroying vision.

The image of Wordsworth enclosed in a dark room, withdrawn from the light and the sun that he loves, suggests the supplementary nature of writing. As Derrida writes:

> Blindness thus produces that which is born at the same time as society: the languages, the regulated substitution of signs for things, the order of the supplement. One goes *from blindness to the supplement*. But the blind person cannot see, in its origin, the very thing he produces to supplement his sight. *Blindness to the supplement* is the law.[39]

Sight and language are intimately connected in Derrida's thinking. Standing for the double absence of vision, the figure of the blind engenders language and writing (which stand for things beyond direct perception). The physical experience of Wordsworth's blindness demonstrates that writing takes place through supplements – the materials and technologies of writing, including the hands that record Wordsworth's voice when he cannot see to write. As a material act, writing is here a feminine supplement of a masculine composition which otherwise remains unheard. The biographical evidence of Wordsworth's blindness impacts on the production of his poetry in a way that thickens the visual implications of his writing and allows other histories to come forward and speak, voices which are silent, yet present in the text: the women who nursed Wordsworth in his blindness, communicated his blindness to their own friends, and acted as his amanuenses when he was unable to write. The material existence of these letters signals the collective and gendered nature of writing.

Wordsworth's amanuenses

When he became blind, Wordsworth relied upon dictation and transcription. Most of the letters that relate to Wordsworth's blindness are written by other, predominantly female, hands. Dorothy writes of an occasion when his eyes were so bad that 'he was utterly unable to use a pen himself; and for many days suffered so much from inflammation in his eyes that it was injurious to him even to dictate to another person'.[40] As Wordsworth's sight disappears, so too does his voice. As a result, he is doubly absent from us as readers. When Wordsworth is blind, we literally lose the trace of his writing; another hand stands in for his writing. Wordsworth's letters are often transcribed by unknown hands, which write 'I hold the pen for Mr W., whose eyes, I grieve to say, do not serve him for this & scarcely any other purpose at present'.[41]

Handling these letters today we readers are in touch with the body of a text's author, with our desire for the presence of the author. Reading the trace of a hand transcribing another's voice produces a double loss: of the presence of the voice speaking and of the voice of the hand transcribing. The experience of reading the hand that writes plays on the same desires at stake in looking at a photograph of a person, because handwriting too makes a claim to the immediacy of presence: they both promise that the person must have been there, in the space captured in the writing or in the image, which bears the trace of an original presence. This immediacy is central to Roland Barthes' reflections on photography, in which he claims that a photograph 'always carries its referent with itself'; there is no photograph 'without *something* or *someone*'. Yet blindness and invisibility also haunt the photograph, as 'whatever it grants to vision and whatever its manner, a photograph is always invisible; it is not it that we see'.[42] Like the photograph, the letters detailing Wordsworth's blindness are forms of writing conditioned by light, acts dependent upon illumination. These letters also signal the mechanics of the text, mediated through the eyes, hands and bodies of others, as much as the implements of writing. They demonstrate that writing is supplementary, for as Derrida articulates the supplement 'will always be the moving of the tongue or acting through the hands of others'.[43]

This supplementary nature of writing is poignant in Dora's letters from the 1830s, in which she describes her father as a prisoner and as a blind man, read alongside Wordsworth's 1816 poem 'A little onward lend thy guiding hands'. Whilst enjoying the idea of walking with Dora in the English countryside, Wordsworth's mind is disturbed by Milton's voice. The opening of his poem quotes the opening lines of Milton's *Samson Agonistes* and thus also echoes the opening of Sophocles' *Oedipus at Colonus*, in which the blind Oedipus is guided by his daughter Antigone. The disturbance exercised by these voices emphasises his anxiety: instead of a father leading his child into the Lake District, and perhaps the Alps, the poem depicts a blind man led by his daughter.[44] Anticipating, and indeed engendering, his own future blindness, the speaker foresees that 'Time' will enrol him 'among those who lean / Upon a living staff, with borrowed sight'. In anticipating Wordsworth's dependence upon his daughter – 'O my own Dora, my beloved child! / Should that day come' – the poem presents the traumatic tension between the activity of the mind and the experience of the body. The topography of the Lake District over which the father, as his daughter's 'happy guide', envisages travelling across also doubles as a more disturbing metaphor for the limits of the mind as a physical object. The speaker registers the limits of their geographical excursion; he imagines them gaining the top of 'some smooth ridge, whose brink precipitous / Kindles intense desire for powers withheld / From this corporeal frame'. The preceding vision of his future as blind man imbues this image with a foreboding anxiety that an absence of vision signals an absence of the sights from which writing springs.

Read alongside Hartman's analysis, Dora's letters and Wordsworth's poem reveal the fuller, more fluid relationship between gender, vision, blindness, generation, and writing.[45] In this essay, Hartman assesses the relationship between Wordsworth's eye troubles, the emotions he felt when he could visit his illegitimate daughter Caroline in France for the first time since 1803 (the Continent had opened up again to English travellers after Napoleon's fall), and Dora's approaching puberty.

Although Hartman offers an insightful and provoking reading of this poem, which draws on psychoanalytic theory to focus on the similarity of the quotation to an inner voice, the poem also acknowledges and plays out a traumatic response to the physical experience of blindness. Reciprocally, the activity of composing the poem itself invokes further anxieties about perpetuating the state of blindness. The speaker's physical blindness is anticipated and constructed through the dialogue with his literary predecessors and along masculine hierarchal lines; yet the feelings expressed towards his daughter indicate a fear of the blindness that is the unknown, and yet not unrealistic. Situated between his literary forebears and his young daughter, stripped of vision and dependent upon both, the speaker anticipates and fears not only this future blindness, but also his absence.[46]

Blindness and auto/biography: the blind beggar's written paper

The material condition and experience of Wordsworth's blindness invites a critique of the relationship between biographical material and the poetics of autobiography. Paul de Man sees the blind beggars of *The Prelude* and *The Excursion* as figures of Wordsworth's own 'poetic self'.[47] My investigation of Wordsworth's blindness contradicts de Man's claim that the question of whether the writer is himself blind is 'somewhat irrelevant'.[48] By contrast, Wordsworth's anxiety that his language may indeed be 'blind to its own statement' is inherently connected to his actual experience of blindness, as are the gaps and absences that punctuate the material production of the text. Wordsworth's experience of the trachoma alerts us to the sensitivity and preoccupation with the material conditions of writing in the poet's imagination, especially in his later poetic project. While Larrissy acknowledges that there is 'sometimes an autobiographical element at play' in Wordsworth's references to blindness after 1805 and notes the impact of the trachoma, he fails to analyse the material experience of his blindness, partly because the poet's interest in blindness predates his condition.[49] However, Larrissy's claim reveals an inherent blindness in his own critical approach, for he overlooks the publication history of Wordsworth's writings. For example, *The Borderers* was first drafted in 1797–99, but it was only published (with extensive revisions) in 1842; yet Larrissy focuses on the version of the first draft exclusively. Taking account of the later date adds a material autobiographical layer that connects Wordsworth's play with the poetic fragment discussed by Hartman. In fact, the description of blind Herbert, repeatedly referred to as 'old, feeble, meek and blind', imbues the revision and publication of this text with clear autobiographical resonances, in which the literary allusions to Lear and Milton overlap with the poet's own sense of his ageing material body.

Commenting on Wordsworth's lack of smell (but not his eye disorders), Alan Richardson speculates:

> In the present critical climate, however, with unprecedented attention given to the centrality of sensation, of 'organic sensibility', perception, and the body within Romantic writing, Wordsworth's limitation to four of the five external senses seems at least worth noting. If, as an influential critic has declared, Wordsworth's poetic project is 'grounded in a regimen of the senses', does the ground shift when one considers Wordsworth's alienated relation to at least one of those senses?[50]

As I have suggested in this essay, Wordsworth's 'alienated relation' to vision opens up a range of questions and implications for our understanding of blindness in both his own writing and the writing of the Romantic period more generally. Indeed, to reflect on the movement between the two periods of speculation on and experience of blindness in Wordsworth's writing (before and after the trachoma) is to encompass the border between 'self and other' in his own poetic identity.[51] Wordsworth's different selves emerge and coalesce; the young Romantic poet's idealising of blindness coalesces with the mature writer suffering from prolonged and protracted pain in his eyes, while conterminously revising his great autobiographical project. The complex textual history and existence of *The Prelude* perpetuates a system of blindness and deferral, for to try to hold in focus Wordsworth's autobiography in its parallel texts of 1805 and 1850 requires turning (away) from one to the other.

Wordsworth's description of the blind beggar in *The Prelude*, composed around the time of Wordsworth's first experience of blindness, turns on the relationship between blindness and writing. The speaker encounters a blind beggar wearing a placard in the context of an anxiety about the limits of reading and interpreting the bewildering visual spectacles of the newly unfolding city spaces. The details we are given about the beggar, and the label he wears, connect blindness with a more explicit anxiety about the limits to self-knowledge, which undercuts the very premise of *The Prelude* itself. The speaker is abruptly smitten 'with the view' of the blind beggar, whom we are told:

> [...] with upright face
> Stood propped against a wall, upon his chest
> Wearing a written paper to explain
> The story of the man and who he was.
> My mind did at this spectacle turn round
> As with the might of waters,
> And it seemed
> To me that in this label was a type
> Or emblem of the utmost that we know
> Both of ourselves and of the universe;
> And, on the shape of this unmoving man,
> His fixed face and sightless eyes, I looked
> As if admonished from another world.[52]
>
> (*Prelude*, 1805, 286)

In a double denial of the blind man's subjective agency, communication between the blind man and the sighted is reduced to a system of visible signs (writing). As such, the blind man cannot have access to his own history. Yet, ironically, this impasse marks the moment when the speaker's own self is brought into being by the poem, his existence figured through language. The passivity with which the speaker records the event – being 'smitten with the view' – signals the blind man's function as an object which disturbs the speaker's subjectivity, revealing the limits of vision and the arbitrary association of knowledge and sight. This preoccupation with the relationship between blindness and knowledge is reflected in the original manuscript version, which had argued that 'the whole of what is written to our view, / Is but a label on a blind man's chest'.[53]

The man's history is a visible, material object that comes into existence through the eyes of others, as the speaker reads the words of the beggar's story and re-verbalises it within his own personal history. However, insofar as the blind man cannot read his own written narrative, he stands for the limits of self-knowledge. This is the metaphoric blindness that structures Coleridge's *Biographia Literaria*. As David M. Baulsch points out, Coleridge's invocation of the Kantian I of transcendental apperception introduces into his autobiography a figure for the impossibility of self-perception.[54] Moreover, in *The Prelude*, as the blind man echoes Wordsworth's poetic self, so his 'written paper' stands as an uncanny reminder that Wordsworth's life, itself materialised in the text, has no real transcendental existence. Rather, the self is haunted by a blindness, materially-wrought, at both the subjective and objective edges of its existence; it can neither see nor read itself; as a result, the boundaries between self and others begin to blur. Disappearing from the visual field, the text loses its semblance of autonomy and authority and is revealed to be an object threaded through different eyes, voices, hands, and experiences, constructed in and through impermanent and shifting material conditions.

Conclusion

By outlining the tension between the idealist and material construction of blindness in Wordsworth's writings, witnessed through objects and letters, I hope to have begun to suggest a new way of thinking about the experience of vision in his poetry. In opening up the materiality of Wordsworth's blindness via a reading of these objects and accounts, we also open up a reading of Wordsworth's writing which returns it to the thickness of the material field. Thus, to interrogate Wordsworth's physiological experience of visual disorders and blindness is not to limit, but to extend our reading of the text. This critical practice goes someway to fulfil Merleau-Ponty's dream of reversal in the experience of reading, 'no longer [...] a matter of speaking about space and light, but of making space and light, which are *there*, speak to us'.[55]

Notes

1. Jeffrey Baker, 'The Deaf Man and the Blind Man', *Critical Survey*, 8:3 (1996), 259–69.
2. Edward Larrissy, 'Wordsworth's Transitions', in *The Blind and Blindness in Literature of the Romantic Period* (Edinburgh: Edinburgh University Press, 2007), pp. 102–40: 103.
3. Maurice Merleau-Ponty, 'Eye and Mind', pp. 135–6.
4. Bloom argues that Wordsworth would have found the space of the cinema theatre 'merely irrelevant to the inward eye of his solitude, which is the eye of his song', see Harold Bloom, 'Visionary Cinema of Romantic Poetry', in *The Ringers in the Towers: Studies in Romantic Tradition* (Chicago and London: University of Chicago Press, 1971), pp. 37–52: 45.
5. On 24 August 1804, she wrote to Lady Beaumont, 'I have got a disorder in my eyes, I do not know whether it is occasioned by being disturbed in my

rest of late, or if it be the same disease I am told has of late been common all over England', in *The Letters of William and Dorothy Wordsworth: The Early Years: 1787–1805*, ed. by E.D. Selincourt, revsd by Chester L. Shaver, 2nd edn (Oxford: Clarendon Press, 1967), I, 496.

6. J.N.G. Lloyd notes that the trachoma was also known as the Egyptian ophthalmia, ' "The Dear Faculty": Some Observations on the Sight of William Wordsworth', *The Optician* (1 March 1968), 214–15.

7. Julius Hirschberg, *The History of Ophthalmology*, trans. Frederick C. Blodi Hirschberg, 11 vols (Bonn, 1987), VIII, 8.

8. Hirschberg, *History of Ophthalmology*, p. 25.

9. John Stevenson, *On the Morbid Sensibility of the Eye, Commonly Called Weakness of Sight* (London: Samuel Highley, 1810), pp. 1–2.

10. James Wardrop, *Essays on the Morbid Anatomy of the Eye* (Edinburgh: George Ramsay, 1808), pp. vi–vii.

11. Michel Foucault, *The Birth of the Clinic: an Archaeology of Medical Perception*, trans. A.M. Sheridan Smith (London: Tavistock, 1973; repr. 1975), p. 55, hereafter in text.

12. Gillian Beer and George Levine used the term 'materialism' in reference to Charles Darwin, but for Caldwell 'Romantic materialism' is also 'particularly apt for pre-Darwinian science and literature', *Literature and Medicine in Nineteenth-Century Britain: From Mary Shelley to George Eliot* (Cambridge: Cambridge University Press, 2004), pp. 1–2.

13. John Stevenson quotes passages from *Paradise Lost* on the frontispieces and as framing devices in throughout his treatises, which were published between 1810 and 1834.

14. Dorothy Wordsworth to Charles Lloyd, 30 May 1820, unpublished letter, Wordsworth Trust, sig. 2003.48.151.

15. Sara Hutchinson to John Monkhouse, 12 December 1825, unpublished letter, Wordsworth Trust, sig. WLMS Hutchinson/1/6/6.

16. Stephen Gill, *William Wordsworth* (Oxford: Oxford University Press, 1990), p. 287 and footnote.

17. 24 December 1666, quoted in Cecil S. Flick, *A Gross of Green Spectacles* (London: Hatton Press, 1951), p. 15.

18. Oliver Goldsmith, *The Vicar of Wakefield: a Tale Supposed to be Written by Himself*, ed. by Arthur Friedman (London: Oxford University Press, 1974), p. 61.

19. Stevenson, *On the Morbid Sensibility of the Eye*, p. 103.

20. Georg Joseph Beer, *The Art of Preserving the Sight Unimpaired to an Extreme Old Age; and of Re-establishing and Strengthening it When it is Become Weak* (London: Henry Colburn, 1813), pp. 178–9.

21. William Kitchener, *The Economy of the Eyes: Precepts for the Improvement and Preservation of the Sight* (London: Hurst, Robinson, & Co., 1824), pp. 91–2.

22. Beer, *The Art of Preserving the Sight*, pp. 178–9. Although rarely used today, green spectacles may have been beneficial to those with eye disorders in their impact upon intraocular pressure – fluid pressure in the eye which can be affected by factors such as inflammation: see R.B. Zaretskaya, 'Some Experiments with Green Spectacles Prescribed to Glaucomatous Patients', *American Journal of Ophthalmology*, 31 (1948), 985–9: 989, 988.

23. Quoted in Seán Allan, *The Stories of Heinrich Von Kleist: Fictions of Security* (New York: Camden House, 2001), p. 19.

24. First published in *Bentley's Miscellany*, 4 (September 1838), 209–27; see *Sketches by Boz and Other Early Papers, 1833–39*, ed. by Michael Slater (London: J.M. Dent, 1994), p. 546.

25. The first effective therapeutic use of copper sulphate sticks was described by early Egyptians, see Khalid F. Tabbara, 'Blinding Trachoma: the Forgotten Problem', *British Journal of Ophthalmology*, 85 (2001), 1397–9: 1398.

26. Sara Hutchinson to Edward Quillinan, *The Letters of Sara Hutchinson, from 1800 to 1835*, ed. by Kathleen Coburn (London: Routledge, 1954), p. 329.

27. Letter to Miss Laing, 23 January 1827, Wordsworth Trust, sig. DWLMS 15/15.

28. Sara Coleridge to Elizabeth Wardell, 13 April 1829, Wordsworth Trust, sig. WLMS A/Coleridge, Sara/23.

29. On the impact of the cost of domestic lighting on reading practices in the first half of the nineteenth century, see Simon Eliot, ' "Never Mind the Value, What about the Price?"; Or, How Much did "Marmion" Cost St. John Rivers?', *Nineteenth-Century Literature*, 56:2 (2001), 160–97: 170–8.

30. Stevenson, *On the Morbid Sensibility of the Eye*, p. 32.

31. William T. O'Dea, *The Social History of Lighting* (London: Routledge, 1958), p. 53.

32. For an analysis of the impact of technology upon the material and spatial experience of light during the nineteenth century, see Wolfgang Schivelbusch, *Disenchanted Night: the Industrialisation of Light in the Nineteenth Century*, trans. Angela Davies (Berkeley: University of California Press, 1995), in particular chapter 1, 'The Lamp', pp. 1–78.

33. For an analysis of how writers inhabit domestic space and how domestic space inhabits writing, see Diana Fuss, *The Sense of an Interior: Four Writers and the Rooms that Shaped Them* (New York: Routledge, 2004).

34. William Wordsworth, *The Prelude: The Four Texts (1798, 1799, 1805, 1850)*, ed. by Jonathan Wordsworth (Harmondsworth: Penguin, 1995), Book XIII, lines 171–81, p. 520. All references from 1805 version unless otherwise stated.

35. Letter to her cousins, 5 October, 1837, Wordsworth Trust, sig. WLL/Wordsworth, Dora/1/67.

36. Letter to Christopher Wordsworth, cousin, 12 April 1829, Wordsworth Trust, sig. WLL/Wordsworth, Dora/1/19.

37. Quoted in Juliet Barker, *Wordsworth: A Life* (Harmondsworth: Penguin, 2000), p. 434.

38. 5 May 1833, Wordsworth Trust, sig. WLL/Wordsworth, Dora/1/53.

39. Jacques Derrida, *Of Grammatology*, trans. Gayatri Chakravorty Spivak, 3rd edn (Baltimore: Johns Hopkins University Press, 1974, repr. 1997), p. 149.

40. Dorothy Wordsworth to Frances Merewether, 13 September 1831, *The Letters of William and Dorothy Wordsworth*, 8 vols, ed. by Ernest de Selincourt, revsd by Alan G. Hill, 2nd edn (Oxford: Oxford University Press, 1979), V, 430.

41. Sara Hutchinson, letter for William Wordsworth to Edward Quillinan, 10 July 1832, *Letters of William and Dorothy Wordsworth*, V, 540.

42. Roland Barthes, *Camera Lucida: Reflections on Photography* trans. Richard Howard (1981; London: Vintage, 2000), pp. 5–6.
43. Derrida, *Of Grammatology*, p. 147.
44. Geoffrey H. Hartman, 'Diction and Defense', in *The Unremarkable Wordsworth* (London: Methuen, 1987), p. 120.
45. Hartman, 'Diction and Defense', pp. 120–8. See Appendix 1.
46. Movingly, the image of Dora as guide to Wordsworth in his blindness is realised in later years, when she literally acted as his guide and driver during a visit to Sir Walter Scott in August 1831.
47. Paul de Man, 'Autobiography as De-Facement', *The Rhetoric of Romanticism* (New York: Columbia University Press, 1984), pp. 67–82.
48. Paul de Man, 'The Rhetoric of Blindness: Jacques Derrida's Reading of Rousseau', *Blindness and Insight: Essays in the Rhetoric of Contemporary Criticism*, 2nd edn (London: Routledge, 1983, repr. 2005), p. 137.
49. Larrissy, *The Blind and Blindness*, p. 103.
50. Alan Richardson, *British Romanticism and the Science of the Mind* (Cambridge: Cambridge University Press, 2001), p. xiii. Richardson does not note Wordsworth's prolonged experiences of blindness between 1805 and his death in 1850.
51. Larrissy, *The Blind and Blindness*, p. 106.
52. Wordsworth, *The Prelude*, Book VII, lines 610–22, p. 286.
53. Wordsworth, *The Prelude*, p. 607, footnote.
54. David M. Baulsch, 'The "Perpetual Exercise of an Interminable Quest": *The Biographia Literaria* and the Kantian Revolution', *Studies in Romanticism*, 43 (2004), 557–81: 560.
55. Merleau-Ponty, 'Eye and Mind', p. 138.

Part II
Photographs and their Pleasures

4
The Wont of Photography, or the Pleasure of Mimesis

Lindsay Smith

It remains common to assume that the invention of photography in the nineteenth century represented the epitome of imitation, a perfect culmination of the age-old debate on mimesis. By enabling the faithful reproduction of an original, a photograph held the capacity to establish as its own wont or habit that ancient aesthetic category. The extreme verisimilitude of photography, the miraculous closeness to an original of an aptly termed photographic 'likeness', had widespread implications for the representational status of painting as one of the fine arts chiefly determined by its mimetic qualities. A photograph's causal connection to a referent, its physical proximity to an object through the chemical fixity of light, signalled in one sense a trumping of the painter's art. For it made possible an impression of grapes or of a faithfully rendered curtain that in classical accounts of mimesis no Zeuxis or Parrhasius could have imagined. Indeed, photography seemed to close the gap between appearance and reality, an achievement which would have profound ramifications. On a practical level a great many painters, especially portraitists and miniaturists, would find their livelihood threatened while on a conceptual one the pleasure of *trompe l'oeil*, the process of tricking the eye of the beholder, would no longer be dependent simply upon the virtuosity of a painter.

Yet, as the work of Jacques Lacan suggests, we should not necessarily assume that the birds pecked at Zeuxis's fruit because it appeared illusionistically plausible to a human, but rather because to a bird's eye the representation bore 'something more reduced', something akin to the sign.[1] That founding story of mimesis makes a different phenomenological proposition, which by extension checks the possibility of a clear-cut relationship between photography and illusionism. Since it resembles John Ruskin's earlier attempts to imagine appearance from the perspective of the 'rattlesnake retina' or from the 'eye of an eagle in flight',[2] Lacan's questioning of the predilection of those fabled birds tests the limits of illusionism and thereby reconfigures the classical story. In turn, his speculation prompts us to question once more the nature and extent to which the reproduction of the visible world newly pictured in photographs transforms that aesthetic category of mimesis and its relationship to the art of pleasing. As Ruskin's art criticism bears witness, the implications for visual perception of a new monochromatic technology for reproducing the visible world extend far beyond the realm of photography itself. Indeed, the very inability of early photography to reproduce colour embodies in some ways, as if for the first time, that larger and fundamental gap between representation and reality. A photograph newly begs the question of the extent to which it is neither the object itself nor simply a 'reflection' or mimetic version of the object.

Lacan ousts *trompe l'oeil* as a key to successful illusionism in the classical tale by replacing it with something at odds with accepted visual and cognitive hierarchies. 'The point is', Lacan writes, 'not that painting gives an illusory equivalence to the object, even if Plato seems to be saying this', but rather that 'the *trompe l'oeil* of painting pretends to be something other than what it is'.[3] In attributing to the success of Zeuxis's representation a proximity to 'the sign', Lacan reconfigures the extent to which the appearance of reality as given by the photographic medium might hold not only a special relationship to the concept of mimesis but also dramatise the peculiar determinants, or limits, of that concept. In such a context the question of how to interpret the deception of Zeuxis's birds becomes newly resonant. Stephen Bann in *The True Vine* (p. 20) has shown us that we need not insist upon reading 'as a founding myth' the Zeuxis Parrhasius story. There are indeed ways of interpreting the narrative without imagining the pictorial image as historically enslaved to the natural world.[4] But while Bann is concerned with ekphrasis and the genre of Pliny's writing in interpretations of the ancient story, I am primarily interested in the intervention of nineteenth-century photography in both a tradition of mimesis and the means by which it might, retrospectively, allow for such a different story of the origins, in painting, of imitation. I want to claim that in producing, somewhat perversely, its own 'enslavement' to 'things', its dependence upon the visible realm, the medium of photography inaugurates a particular break in the aesthetic of mimesis. I do not mean here to identify a historical moment at which realism gives way to abstraction, a post-photographic world in which painters are liberated from depicting the visible. Instead, I want to explore a fundamentally ontological turn in which photography's singular testing of the limits of mimesis retrospectively changes the story.

We will find that photography intervenes powerfully in narratives of mimesis in large part owing to its unique relationship to temporality, especially its peculiar attachment to the future tense (anterior future). As a vital part of this intervention photography's seemingly perfect and easy production of a mimetic relationship to the object calls up a proximity to the medium of sculpture, a medium with which we might consider it bears less direct association than painting. Perceived as arrested life or petrified form, with all the classical implications of potential shape-shifting and metamorphosis, sculpture more emphatically shares qualities with photography in its potential to petrify animate form. Indeed 'petrification' is a more helpful metaphor than 'freezing' to describe such a process since it harbours the potential for physical transformation in a more potent form and alludes in particular ways to futurity. At the same time, photography uniquely produces resemblance as a process of referring to an original in a movement that is distinct from an imitative one; far, that is, from the playful function of *trompe l'oeil*. That particular version of photographic resemblance to an object is at a fundamental level produced by its causal connection to a referent, its chemical and physical origins in light as harnessed by sensitised salts. But that quality of resemblance is also bound up with the medium's relationship to temporality. Unlike the well-rehearsed sense of a frozen moment, a petrified moment in which 'stone' substitutes for 'ice' encapsulates the anterior future tense of that which will be yet has reciprocally already been. Moreover, a photograph approximates the petrification of sculpture by that quality of perpetually having 'almost all [its] life still before [it]', as Maurice Merleau-Ponty might say, or by its capacity to allude to the future almost in spite of itself.[5]

To be sure, resemblance to an original is that condition that most of all crystallises an understanding of mimesis as imitation; it is that quality of which photography, like classical sculpture, appears to provide a surfeit. Yet, reciprocally and somewhat paradoxically, photographic resemblance might also elude mimesis in the form of imitation. Indeed, rather than providing a key to the mimetic function, photographic 'resemblance' points up a potential break in the story of mimesis. It does so, not by offering up a more perfect representation than any hand could achieve, but by re-defining the relationship of imitation to resemblance as a temporal prospect. What appears to be an unprecedented formal predisposition of a photograph to mimetic possibility precisely generates a conceptual departure from it. The close resemblance to photography of an original invites us to re-think the very concept of 'resemblance' as inherent to a process of mimesis. Both Plato and, much more recently, Emmanuel Lévinas uniquely focus such a fundamental concept of 'resemblance'.

Resemblance and the relationship between appearance and reality are central to the concept of mimesis in Book X of *The Republic*, Plato's well-known dialogue that ends with the banishment of mimic poetry aimed at pleasure from the model city. To Socrates' question whether the art of painting is designed to be an appearance of things 'as they are' or 'as they appear', the answer is 'as they appear'.[6] In the famous example of the three types of bed, the painter's bed, as opposed to the carpenter's physically constructed bed, is a likeness of an actual bed distinct from the thing itself (596b–598c, pp. 319–20). The painter in turn is designated the imitator at a 'third remove from King and truth'. However, as Christopher Janaway has remarked in *Images of Excellence*, 'if something is a mere appearance and not a reality, it does not follow that it is an appearance taken for a reality'.[7] Janaway refutes a crude *trompe l'oeil* definition of mimesis based upon the ability to fool or trick those whom Plato refers to as 'children or simple persons' (p. 122). In setting aside a notion of the confusion of appearance and reality, Janaway reminds us that Plato considers representation in terms of resemblance, justifying 'the traditional translation of mimesis as "imitation" ' (p. 118). The definition that answers Socrates' question about mimesis is that 'mimetic art is far removed from the truth, and that is why [...] it can make everything, because it touches only a small part of each thing' (598b6–8). As Janaway explains, the image (*eidolon*) produced by mimetic art is 'an example of what we would call a representation and the activity we would call representing' (p. 118).

In an acute manner photography poses the conceptual slippage inherent in such a distinction between an appearance of reality and an appearance taken for reality, the distinction between a representation and an imitation. For in being the thing itself a photograph complicates that relationship of an object to its representation. In a literal sense, of course, a photographic image is unable to erase a distinction between object and image because it is a two-dimensional reduction of three dimensions. However, as a reprographic medium photography holds a different relationship from painting to an original. On a primary level, that distinctiveness inheres in the extent to which a photograph might be called imitative, or rather the extent to which in fact the photographic process may connote imitation when the art of imitating is taken out of the artist's hand to become mechanical, when pigments aren't undergoing the alchemy of becoming imitated 'things'. A photograph of a bed is neither Plato's original bed nor the painter's secondary bed. Yet might it not be newly equivalent to the carpenter's bed or indeed constitute a fourth type in Plato's hierarchy? Furthermore, if illusionism is central to an understanding of the mimetic process, in the relationship of photography to those objects it 'perfectly' represents what happens to the pleasure generated by the power of an illusion?

The erasure of the material distinctiveness of a work of art in discussions of mimesis in the visual arts is well rehearsed, a condition that Janaway, following Arthur Danto, has termed 'the logical invisibility of the medium' (p. 118). Such 'invisibility' operates for some theoreticians 'as a feature of imitative theory' in the sense that the nature of the medium does not determine the imitation of the object produced by a painter. In coming to his conclusions upon visual mimesis, Plato does not discuss the artist's technique, the use of line or colouring or a particular 'set of marks in a physical medium on a physical surface' (p. 118). For him the physical process by which the representation is created is not important: 'the product of the painter's activity [for Plato] is just something secondary to other objects' (p. 118). In an understanding of mimesis as 'imitation' such a concept of a logical invisibility of the medium might serve in several ways as a description of photographic representation. But, as I hope to demonstrate, although photography appears to provide such a seamless relation to an original, the potential of medium invisibility inherent in an unprecedented resemblance to an original is forever undermined by a photograph's acute inscription of temporality. More particularly, such seamlessness is undermined by the ways in which a photograph reconfigures temporality through a quality of resemblance itself.

In 'Reality and its Shadow', published in 1948 in *Les Temps Modernes*, Lévinas uses the concept of resemblance to focus the complication of transparency in the phenomenology of images.[8] I want to take up Lévinas's term 'resemblance' together with his concept of the 'petrification of an instant' (p. 134) in order to explore the way in which the assault on time performed by a photograph compromises a simple imitative relationship to the object. Both concepts manifest what it is about photographic representation that checks the legacy of mimesis, stops it dead, so to speak, rather than epitomising it. As we shall find, both 'resemblance' and 'petrification' newly realise the singular interrelationship of photography and sculpture. In 'Reality and its Shadow', Lévinas notes that 'the intention of one who contemplates an image is said to go directly through the image, as through a window, into the world it represents'. 'Yet', he remarks, 'nothing is more mysterious than the term "world it represents" since representation expresses just that function of an image that remains to be determined' (p. 135). Implicit in Lévinas's allusion to a future state here is a sense of that which is yet to be, that remains to be conjured as residing in the passage between an image and that which it represents. In defining the peculiarity of the visual image, its difference from a symbol or a sign or a word, he settles upon 'the very way in which it refers to its object: resemblance' (p. 135). 'But', he writes,

> that [resemblance] supposes that thought stops in the image itself; it consequently supposes a certain opacity of the image. A sign, for its part, is pure transparency, nowise counting for itself. Must we then come back to taking the image as an independent reality which resembles the original? No, but on condition that we take resemblance not as the result of a comparison between an image and the original, but as the very movement that engenders the image.
>
> (p. 135)

Lévinas is thus proposing a distinctive concept of 'resemblance'. Rather than that condition produced by the comparison of an image with an original, resemblance inheres in 'the very movement' that produces the image, from which it springs. His use of the verb 'engender' denotes a sense of giving existence to an image as offspring. By extension, as a visual medium of irrefutable resemblance photography 'refers' to an object, in Lévinas's sense of the term, rather than 'replicates' it. Through a seemingly perfect congruence with the thing it represents – together with those negative/positive and shadow/light dichotomies that mark a temporal dimension to its presence as burnt into the emulsion – a photograph is belatedly always the thing itself. Moreover, it is always the thing itself through the metamorphosis of age.

In a related context, Lévinas has written about Marcel Proust, distinguishing the artist from the philosopher: 'the theory put forward by a poet [...] is concerned not to express but to create the object'.[9] For Lévinas 'the real interiorisation of the Proustian world [...] stems not from a subjective vision of reality, nor even from interior coordinates that exclude objective references [...] but from the very structure of appearances which are both what they are and the infinity of what they exclude' (p. 162). It is the case that in *A La Recherche* Proust is fascinated by the visual and imaginative complexity to be found in the simplicity of an originally familiar object changed by aging into something else.

Such a process of transmutation constitutes the method by which an object is created. For example, lime flowers before their infusion as tea in which to dip a now mythic Madeleine approximate 'the most disparate things, the transparent wing of a fly, the blank side of a label, the petal of a rose, which had all been piled together, pounded or interwoven like the materials for a nest'.[10] Owing to 'their metamorphosis from something earlier' (and metamorphosis is central here), Proust's petals mark 'as the glow upon an old wall still marks the place of a vanished fresco, the difference between those parts of the tree which had and those which had not been "in colour"' (p. 60). The analogy of petals with 'the glow' that marks the place of a vanished fresco suggests a magical resurrection of that which was considered lost. At the same time, lime flowers are 'like a book in which one reads with astonished delight the name of a person one knows, the pleasure of finding that these were sprigs of real lime-trees, [...] altered indeed, precisely because they were not imitations but themselves, and because they had aged' (p. 60). For Proust this is a vital distinction, for lime flowers are not imitations, representations or copies of an original, but those very originals changed by time. Proust's flowers, like photographs, imprint themselves without being made, prompting us to ponder the tantalising proposition that the medium of photography may engender such transformations implicit in a concept of resemblance. Susan Sontag goes so far as to say that photographs, unlike other art forms, become more attractive with age, their vulnerable and flimsy nature being a type of their ontological status.[11] As ephemeral objects subject to time photographs eventually fade. Thus in a manner not unrelated to sculpture, a photograph deteriorates and gains a certain authority both by way of its age and also by the aging it represents, the inherent transmutation of those things depicted. At the same time, the additionally complex condition of a photograph, in its independence from the hand of a maker, denotes a material existence distinct from that of painting or sculpture. It is somewhat paradoxical, then, to identify a profound sense in which the photographer comes closest to the sculptor's art through a quality of petrification, through that very turning to stone which is not final but contains yet metamorphic potential. Just as in Ovid, stones may be animated (most famously in the case of Pygmalion) while flesh may be turned to stone, the kinship between photograph and sculpture resides in the fact that both breathe life into inanimate form. What is more, they simultaneously petrify and vitalise through a temporal inscription in which, by a kind of metaphysical method, past, present and future come to dwell simultaneously within. In truth, that paper thin object, the photograph, that seems far removed from the firm physical bulk of a sculpture, turns out to be its obscure but most recent relative.

The encapsulation of 'resemblance' as played out in Proust is, at first glance, far from the second of Lévinas's concepts that I wish to take up, that of petrification, but it relates directly to a photograph's assault on temporality as a kind of metamorphosis. Towards the end of 'Reality and its Shadow' Lévinas introduces the term 'petrification' in his discussion of temporality: 'since Bergson it has been customary to take the continuity of time to be the very essence of duration' (p. 140). The result, he states, has been a disregard for discontinuity of duration in favour of an acceptance 'as a truism' of 'a photographic metaphor of a snapshot of movement' (p. 140). Lévinas is referring here to the type of photographic image produced in chronophotography where serial movement is captured, in which duration is evidenced by a flow of movement traceable in the sequential quality of a static image. His point is that in such a type of visual representation paradoxically something of a quality of duration is lost. As a consequence, he writes,

> [w]e on the contrary have been sensitive to the paradox that an instant can stop. The fact that humanity could have provided itself with art reveals in time the uncertainty of time's continuation and something like a death doubling impulse of life. The petrification of the instant in the heart of duration – Niobe's punishment – the insecurity of a being which has a presentiment of fate, is the great obsession of the artist's world, the pagan world.

> (p. 140)

Lévinas identifies 'the petrification of the instant' (a type of grammatical future tense) not to describe the photographic process but more generally to identify a notion of 'a presentiment of fate' at the centre of a concept of duration in art. Yet in alluding to the mythological figure of Niobe, who must endure the archetypal fate of being turned to stone, we have both that sense in which the photographic medium marks each of its images with death and the meaning of a semblance of a direct perception of something about to happen. The temporal formulation evident in the term 'presentiment' mixes both impression and perception. And, by extension, Lévinas's reading of 'the great obsession of the artist's world' invites us to re-conceptualise photographic simultaneity, that disarmingly simple yet irrefutable quality of the medium of photography that enables a subject looking at a photograph to occupy at the same time more than one temporal reality: to experience, in effect, a quality of the already having been of that which is yet to come. Such is the presentiment of fate in photography, the immobility or imprisonment in the image whose paradoxical subjection to duration has the power to 'sear' the subject, to borrow Walter Benjamin's term.[12]

In his seminal 'Small History of Photography', Benjamin reads something like Lévinas's 'instant' (at the heart of duration) as a quality unique to those photographs produced up until the 1840s, prior to the rapid commercialisation of the medium. The technical restrictions of early lenses, that meant long exposure times during which subjects had to pose motionless, lent for Benjamin an air of permanence to these early photographs. 'The procedure itself', he writes, 'caused the subject to focus his life in the moment rather than hurrying on past it'; it enabled a subject to grow into the image (p. 245). Such a quality of 'duration' links further to the sculptor's art of breathing life into a block of marble, of animating the dead. But, for Benjamin, the material difference of portrait photographs of this early period from later ones of the 1860s is distinguished by an 'absence of contact between actuality and photography', which is at the same time the reason why early photographs produce for him a more lasting impression than later ones. We might further read Benjamin's notion of a lack of contact as a kind of anti-imitative tendency and one that is captured in his suggestive statement that theoreticians of the medium 'undertook nothing less than to legitimize the photographer before the very tribunal he was in the process of overturning' (p. 241).

The somewhat perverse anti-mimetic character of photography, or that quality of the medium that prompts a re-telling of the tale of mimesis (those birds and grapes) along the lines that Lacan proposes, means that, following the invention of the medium, it becomes 'less and less plausible to reflect upon an experience according to [a Platonic] distinction between images and things, copies and originals'.[13] Such a quality is especially evidenced by those photographs in which there occurs a presentiment of fate in the assault on temporality that the medium performs. Yet the ability of early photography to question its own seamless replication of the world is inherent in qualities additional to those to which Benjamin refers, such as the reduction in size of an original, in combination printing, and the absence of colour, all of which I've discussed elsewhere.[14] It is profoundly persistent in the temporal dislocation or, as Bann has called it, the 'gradual convergence of the otherness of *space* [...] into an otherness of *time*, which is guaranteed by the indexical nature – the "close contact" – of the photographic process'.[15] For Barthes such a quality is that telling of death in the future as exemplified by Alexander Gardner's photographs of Lewis Payne, who had attempted to assassinate W.H. Seward, American Secretary. In these photographs the youth is petrified photographically as a prisoner in his cell prior to execution, an image of which it is true to say both that 'he is dead and he is going to die'.[16] This temporality of the medium is also captured in Benjamin's poignant and seemingly random reference to a photograph of Karl Dauthendey, 'from the time of his engagement to that woman whom he then found one day, shortly after the birth of her sixth child, lying in the bedroom of his Moscow house with her arteries severed'. Dauthendey becomes a figure for whom we may say a tragic future is writ large in the prophecy of the photographic portrait. Benjamin's spark of contingency, which marks his well-known theory of the optical unconscious, is a type of Lévinas's 'presentiment of fate': 'immerse yourself in such a picture long enough' writes Benjamin 'and you will recognize how alive the contradictions are [...] the most precise technology can give its products a magical value, such as a painted picture can never again have for us'.[17] Rather than simply prefiguring the fate of his wife, Dauthendey's photograph registers the temporal disjunction of the image and provides the perfect type of that 'presentiment of fate'.

In related terms, but in an earlier daguerreotype image that evacuates such human drama, Daguerre's 'Parisien Boulevard' of 1838 petrifies the instant to produce a quality of duration that feels like the presentiment of fate. The busy street is emptied of human presence by the long exposure time. Yet one human figure remains posed at its centre, a person who has lingered at the water pump long enough for his image to be inscribed on the plate. The sense of arrested movement here differs vastly from that captured in later sequential chronophotographs by Etienne-Jules Marey or Edweard Muybridge that show the gait of a galloping horse or the wings of a bird in flight. For in Daguerre's photograph there is something closer to petrification in an image bearing the endurance of time. Moreover, we encounter here a quality of petrification as much in the sense of metamorphosis of what no longer remains, what has been transformed, as much as in what endures, in the image. Such a quality is differently resonant in the negative/positive process of William Henry Fox Talbot's 'The Milliner's Window' (1842), in which we find neatly displayed rows of women's bonnets that appear fossilised. Here, inanimate objects, photographed hats have become very unlike those objects they represent – silenced, stilled as it were, leant a curious stasis by the medium. Whether by emptying or fossilising the scene, the daguerreotype and the Talbotype show how the early forms of the photographic medium embody a process of petrification intrinsic to those larger temporal issues under discussion. What is more, the medium is again here somewhat oddly akin to that of sculpture. Throughout the 'Small History' Benjamin insists upon a distinction between painting and photograph that resides in photography's temporal status. This temporality of photography, alongside a general focus upon a process of petrification, recalls Lévinas's allusion to metamorphosis in his reference to the mythological figure of Niobe. Lévinas, we recall, refers to the tragic Niobe, whose many children were murdered by the gods in return for her sin of pride, precisely to dramatise the concept of petrification as the stopping of time. But his reference to an instant at the heart of duration in art is equally applicable to photographs and to sculptures and it allows us to develop further the relationship of photography to mimesis via its kinship with the three-dimensional art of sculpture rather than the two-dimensional one of painting.

Within classical writing Niobe appears as the daughter of Tantalus who boasts about her fertility and about motherhood (she has variously 12 or 14 children) and claims her superiority over the Goddess Leto who has only twins. Leto's offence at the insult results in her sending her children Artemis and Apollo to murder all of Niobe's offspring. In her extreme grief, but resisting suicide, Niobe is finally transformed into a stone that is blown by the wind to Mount Sipylus. In Ovid, the rock, which bears some vague resemblance to the human form, sheds tears. Several other classical writers refer to Niobe as one of many figures turned to stone. Apollodorus focuses upon the slaying of her children,[18] while Homer introduces her in *The Iliad* as part of a past tale recounted in a dialogue between Achilles and Priam. She is cited in Homer's epic as the most extreme example of grief and as a reassuring anchor for the endurance of the base instinct of survival: 'We are told / that even Niobe in her extremity / took thought for bread – though all her brood had perished, / her young girls and six tall sons'.[19]

However, in Ovid's account, by comparison, we are reminded that Niobe's fate of metamorphosis follows directly that of Arachne transformed into a spider for the related sin of hubris or pride. But not only does Arachne's punishment operate as a presentiment of the subsequent fate of Niobe (Tieresias' daughter Manto warned the women of Thebes of foreboding), but her triumph in the visual art of imitation is the cause of tragic events. For Ovid, Niobe should have heeded the warning inherent in the example of Arachne who 'in her web did portray to the full / How Europe was by royall Jove beguiled in shape of Bull'. These images, 'a swimming Bull, a swelling Sea, so lively had she wrought / That Bull and Sea in very deede ye might them wee have thought'.[20] Thereby, the example of a visual mimesis as imitative over-reaching signals Arachne's downfall. Niobe, by comparison, through her metamorphosis into stone,[21] represents a kind of anti-mimesis that for Lévinas emblematises the artist's obsession with petrifying the instant.

There exist surprisingly few painted representations of Niobe's meta-morphosis in the fine arts but sculptural ones have had significant influence.[22] Indeed, as we shall find, the impact of a particular ancient statue of the Niobe has generated two fascinating modern photographic versions of the goddess. It may be somewhat ironic that one of the most enduring representations of the figure of Niobe takes the mimetic form of the Roman sculpture displayed in the Uffizi Gallery in Florence.[23] The statue of Niobe in the Uffizi became a hugely meaningful monu-ment for several nineteenth-century artists and writers, perhaps most famously Percy Shelley, who writes of the sculpture both in his 'Criti-cal Notices of the Sculpture in the Florence Gallery' and in a letter to his friend Thomas Jefferson Hogg on 20 April 1820.[24] The latter records an encounter with the statue that, as Clifton Spargo has pointed out, came almost 'directly a year before the composition of Adonais',[25] his pastoral elegy on the death of John Keats, a missive in which Shelley referred to the famous statues in the gallery including 'the famous Venus, the Minerva, the Apollino – and more than all, the Niobe and her children'.[26] Shelley went on to claim that 'no production of sculp-ture, not even the Apollo, ever produced on me so strong an effect as this Niobe' (p. 186). In his comment to Hogg, Shelley provides a digest of what he clearly felt had been a major effect upon him of the Niobe when he had first seen it on his earlier visit to the Uffizi with Mary Shelley in 1819. She and Shelley had lost their first two children (Clara in 1818, William in 1819), and Mary was pregnant when they first saw the Niobe in 1819. As a consequence of such actual human loss and of Mary Shelley's reference to Niobe's 'maternal, remediless grief that sheds a solemn sadness around',[27] critics tend to quote only those parts of Percy Shelley's 'note' on the sculpture that dwell on the perfect representation of the mother's grief. While clearly mater-nal anguish is key to the effect of the statue upon both Mary and Percy Shelley, there are also in Percy Shelley's account curious ways in which the Niobe statue focuses larger issues of mimesis and tem-porality with which we are concerned. I thereby quote substantially from the 'note' in order to demonstrate those ways in which mater-nal fear and grief become, for Shelley, part of a larger philosophical meditation upon the remarkable presence of metamorphosis within the sculptural form:

> This figure of Niobe is probably the most consummate personification of loveliness, with regard to its countenance, as that of the Apollo of the Vatican is with regard to its entire form, that remains to us of Greek antiquity. It is a colossal figure; the size of a work of art rather adds to its beauty, because it allows to the spectator the choice of a greater number of points of view, and affords him a more analytical one, in which to catch a greater number of the infinite modes of expression, of which any form approaching ideal beauty is necessarily composed. It is the figure of *a mother in the act of sheltering, from some divine and inevitable peril, the last, we will imagine, of her surviving children.*
>
> The child, terrified, we may conceive, at the strange destruction of all its kindred, has fled to its mother, and hiding its head in the folds of her robe, and casting back one arm, as in a passionate appeal for defence, where it never before could have been sought in vain, *seems in the marble to have scarcely suspended the motion of her terror; as though conceived to be yet in the act of arrival.* […] Niobe is enveloped in profuse drapery, a portion of which the left hand has gathered up, and is in the act of extending it over the child in the instinct of defending her from what reason knows to be inevitable. The right – as the restorer of it has justly comprehended, – is gathering up her child to her, and with a like instinctive gesture is encouraging by its gentle pressure the child to believe that it can give security. The countenance, which is the consummation of feminine majesty and loveliness, beyond which the imagination scarcely doubts that it can conceive anything, that masterpiece of the poetic harmony of marble, expresses other feelings. *There is embodied a sense of the inevitable and rapid destiny which is consummating around her, as if it were already over.* It seems as if despair and beauty had combined, and produced nothing but the sublime loveliness of grief. As the motions of the form expresses the instinctive sense of the possibility of protecting the child, and the accustomed and affectionate assurance that she would find an protection in her arms, so reason and imagination speak in the countenance the certainty that no mortal defence is of avail.
>
> There is no terror in the countenance – only grief, deep, remediless grief. There is no anger – of what avail is indignation against what is known to be omnipotent? There is no selfish shrinking from personal

pain; there is no panic at supernatural agency; there is no advertising to herself as herself; the calamity is mightier than to leave scope for such emotions.

Everything is swallowed up in sorrow. Her countenance, in assured expectation of the arrow piercing its last victim in her embrace, is fixed on her omnipotent enemy. *The pathetic beauty of the expression of her tender, and serene despair, which is yet so profound and so incapable of being ever worn away, is beyond the effect of sculpture. As soon as the arrow shall have pierced her last child, the fable that she was dissolved into a fountain of tears, will be but a feeble emblem of the sadness of despair, in which the years of her remaining life, we feel, must flow away.*[28] [my italics]

In his extended 'Note', Shelley reacts on many levels to the statue. He begins by referring to a general effect upon the spectator of its 'colossal' proportions as 'adding to its beauty because it allows the spectator a multitude of positions from which to view it and 'catch a greater number of the infinite modes of expression [...] of a mother in the act of sheltering from some divine and inevitable peril the last, we may imagine, of her children'. The poet's syntax defers the anguish of the mother to which invariably it is leading. The qualification 'we may imagine' encapsulates a peculiar temporal function of the sculpture in an aesthetic of metamorphosis. For Shelley chooses to 'imagine' the daughter portrayed in the sculpture as the 'last' surviving Niobid. While clearly to do so is to heighten the dramatic plight of the mother and the overall effect of the work of art, the use of the word 'may' here simultaneously suggests a choice, albeit a kind of inevitable one. For Shelley the truth is that the viewer cannot but 'imagine' in the future, and thus reciprocally in the past, that the child here petrified in marble will be, and reciprocally will always have been, the last of Niobe's children. But, more emphatically, the child will serve the perpetual function of being the last in a narrative that records ultimate loss and subsequent metamorphosis.

For Shelley and other commentators, the Niobe sculpture is unique. Unlike Bernini's famous marble 'Apollo and Daphne' (1622–1625), in which Daphne is shown metamorphosing into a laurel tree,[29] whereby the filigree working of the stone confounds the viewer's sense of the limits of the material, the Niobe impresses a shift within the organic matter of marble itself to a new creation of animate form. In his 'Note' Shelley strengthens his initial interest in the facility of multiple viewpoints when he refers to the child's attempts to hide 'its head in the folds of [Niobe's] robes', who, he notes, 'seems in the marble to have scarcely suspended the motion of her terror; as though conceived to be yet in the act of arrival'. And most notable in this comment is the poet's sense of movement, or metamorphosis within the sculpted form, as both arrested and yet to come – that which is simultaneously (or will be post 1839) the future tense of photography. Later in the extract, Shelley remarks again upon a temporal disruption in which Niobe's fate exists as if already having taken place: 'there is embodied a sense of the inevitable and rapid destiny which is consummating around her as if it were already over'. On the one hand, Shelley refers to the way in which the sculptural form of the artefact is a correlate of Niobe's ultimate fate of stone, while on the other he alludes to incipient transformation as a destiny 'already over', and manifestly yet to come.

Shelley's seemingly distinctive method of reading the Niobe in the Uffizi owes much, of course, to the aesthetic tradition of Winckelmann and Lessing. For Winckelmann, in *The History of the Art of Antiquity* (1764), the Niobe and the Laocoön are 'two of the most beautiful works of antiquity'. The Niobe is 'a representation of the fear of death', the Laocoön of 'extreme suffering and pain'.[30] It is striking to compare Winckelmann's reading of 1764 with Shelley's response, for it is evident from Shelley's sustained account that he had read Winckelmann, since he responds to the statue with some similar sentiment. Both writers are fascinated by the type of physical paralysis, of petrification, that provides the embodiment of a state 'in which sensation and reflection cease and which resembles apathy, does not disturb a limb or a feature' (p. 125). Winckelmann directly compares the Niobe with the Laocoön in his well-known discussion of how, in representing heroes, 'the artist is allowed less licence than the poet because the artist's having to select the most beautiful parts of the most beautiful forms' means he must not express the passions 'to a degree which will not conflict with the physical beauty of the figure which he models' (p. 124). The governing aesthetic principle is that the expression in the figure must not upset the components of ideal beauty from which it has been created. As Alex Potts has pointed out, in Winckelmann's reading of the Niobe:

> the figure in the high mode becomes the visual embodiment of the irresistible power of a high idea only by way of a deadly paradox, by being stilled and purified simplified to the point where it no longer exists as a living being. The figure of Niobe is 'pure spirit' and 'divine soul' in a state of extreme 'fear of death' when total impassivity takes over.[31]

Interestingly, Winckelmann plays down the maternal significance of the figure with which Shelley is subsequently concerned in order to stress the sculptor's portrayal of that 'state of mind, where feeling and thought cease'. For Lessing, writing in response to Winckelmann's reading and disagreeing with certain of its premises, there is nonetheless a related emphasis upon reconciling 'with the demands of beauty' in classical sculpture the depiction of pain 'in all its disfiguring violence'.[32] Therefore, in the Laocoön, Lessing claims 'the scream had to be softened to a sigh, not because screaming betrays an ignoble soul, but because it distorts the features in a disgusting manner'. Distress, such as that in the Niobe, is 'transformed, through beauty, into the tender feeling of pity' (p. 17). However, it is specifically through Shelley's later emphasis upon the temporal components of the Niobe that we may return again to Lévinas, this time to his comments upon sculpture to pursue further those larger arguments of metamorphosis and mimesis as raised by the coming together of statue and photograph.

Lévinas, following Winckelmann and Lessing, refers to the Laocoön and to the Mona Lisa as works of art realising 'the paradox of an instant that endures without a future'. He claims that the duration of a statue 'is not really an instant. It does not give itself out here as an infinitesimal element of duration [...] it has in its own way a quasi-eternal duration'.[33] Rather,

> Within the life, or rather the death, of a statue, an instant endures infinitely: eternally Laocoön will be caught in the grip of serpents; the Mona Lisa will smile eternally. Eternally the future announced in the strained muscles of Laocoön will be unable to become present [...] An eternally suspended future floats around the congealed position of a statue like a future forever to come. The immanence of the future lost before an instant stripped of the essential characteristics of the present; its evanescence.
>
> (p. 138)

Such a relationship of the statue to duration as theorised by Lévinas is newly inflected when we come to consider nineteenth-century photographic images of the Niobe room at the Uffizi in which we encounter a complex interweave of the two media, sculpture and photography. In photographs by the Fratelli Alinari we are reminded on the one hand of the uses of early photography to document artefacts, especially ancient sculpture as for example evidenced by those photographs of the 1850s by Roger Fenton of statues in the British Museum.[34] But something profound occurs when we consider the Alinari photographs of 'Gallery of

Niobe in the Uffizi' (1856–7) (Plate 4). The Alinari photograph makes manifest the sense that a photograph of a sculpture constitutes a double form of petrification. In this photograph we find pictured the neoclassical gallery lit by strong sunlight in which the main figure of Niobe and her 'youngest' daughter casts a decisive shadow. The extreme height of the figures displayed on decorative pedestals is exacerbated by the low viewpoint of the camera which focuses those pedestals at the eye-level of the viewer. Yet at the same time the sculptures are somewhat dwarfed by the vast walls. Such formal qualities of the nineteenth-century photograph are thrown into relief by comparison with the more recent twentieth-century photograph by E. George Talge from the 1990s. This later image not only shows changes to the display of the paintings, the addition of a vase not present in the earlier one, but also the change in the camera angle that lengthens the viewpoint and in which the immensity of the Niobe fails to register. However, at the same time, the presence of two framed paintings displayed on easels on either side of the Niobe impresses, as belonging to the sculpture, an absolute difference of form. But with regard to mimesis and the larger relationship of photography to sculpture the presence of polychrome in the modern photograph serves to point up the perfect congruency between the monochromatic photographic medium and the sculptural medium. For the presence of colour impresses the centrality of monochrome to the unique relationship that statue and photograph each bear to concepts of petrification and metamorphosis.

Photography works like sculpture of the human form to petrify an instant. Whether or not they capture an actual gesture or movement, both photograph and sculpture arrest a quality of duration. What is particularly notable about the Niobe is that medium and subject, form and content, are congruent in a rare, almost unprecedented way. For the mythological figure whose *future* fate will be to be turned to stone is here, as it were, already turned, her fate consummately anticipated by the sculptor's art. Such congruence is part of the great attraction of the Uffizi statue, which combines petrification as a fearful, negative state exemplified by the Medusa with petrification as harbouring metamorphosis, the breathing of life into stone, implicit movement and temporal disturbance as states of change.

The transformational fate of the Niobe emerges quite distinctively in the early twentieth century where we find two curious photographic versions of the myth that dwell upon the figure of Niobe herself. The first is the surrealist Man Ray's 'Glass Tears' of 1930 in which Niobe's tears have become petrified like herself, turned to glass beads on her cheek.

Madame Yevonde, the London portraitist celebrated for her introduction of the vivex colour process, translates Man Ray's 'Glass Tears' into her 'Niobe' as part of her *Goddess Series* of 1935. In these twentieth-century photographs there is a focus upon the physiognomy of Niobe, of her grief as taking the form of glass tears or mascara induced ones. Both photographers, Man Ray and Yevonde, choose to realise a close up of the face of the weeping figure. The body has gone, so too has any evidence of those lost children that in ancient art she was caught in the act of shielding, and in the eternal act of weeping for. It is as if in these two twentieth-century realisations of the mythic woman, photography as a process is particularly at home. This is the case not because in these modern photographs there occurs, as with the ancient sculpture, a perfect balancing between medium and object, but rather because, in terms of an aesthetic of imitation, something curious with regard to duration is present in the attempt by both Man Ray and Yevonde to represent the implausibility of the dual states of Niobe's petrification and tears.

For, in re-inscribing 'Glass Tears' as 'Niobe', in giving the mythological name to the anonymous subject of 'Glass Tears', Yevonde above all finds metamorphosis in Man Ray's image, which in itself is rather spare. But where in the image does she find it evidenced? Yevonde's own version of the figure of Niobe is more orthodox than Man Ray's; the tears wet the goddess's cheek and a larger proportion of the face is visible in the cropping. The glass or stone tears of Niobe here metamorphose back to human tears in a passage entailed by the temporal slippage of the photographic medium. However, in both photographs that focus so emphatically on the face of the goddess we have a metonymy of the Niobe sculpture. There are no Niobids present, just the face of a female figure and a focus upon her visible grief.

What, then, might it mean in larger terms to realise photographically this mythological figure? But also what might it mean to photograph sculptures of the figure of Niobe, as do the Alinari, with all that is implied by the doubling back of the photograph of sculpture? The improbability of a stone that weeps is, I believe, what makes the analogy of Niobe so powerful for Lévinas, and for Shelley, Man Ray and Yevonde before him. It encapsulates its suggestiveness for an understanding of the radical temporal qualities of photography and in turn renders the metaphor of petrification a type of the anti-mimetic quality of photography. For, in a very obvious regard the turning to stone of Niobe in the myth makes her into an artefact or imitation. Indeed, the ancient statue in the Uffizi apparently bore the following epigram: 'To stone the gods have changed her, but in vain, The sculptor's art has made her breathe again'. Here we find the paradox of the perfect equivalent of the art of sculpture with the petrified figure. The sculptor's art, itself a form of petrification, animates the figure of Niobe. Yet for the mythic stone of Mount Sipylus to weep is absolutely to break the imitative correspondence in the same way that the invisible temporal dislocation inherent to photography (in the form of duration) fractures the smooth surface of the image – the way in which a captured moment in the present can never remain simply present to us.

In the story of Niobe – Lévinas' petrification of the instant – there remains something anti-imitative about the event of metamorphosis. It is because as a process that frustrates organic development metamorphosis likewise frustrates a simple relationship between object and image, original and copy. What is more, metamorphosis can work both ways: it describes this type of frustration of duality upon which Platonic accounts of mimesis rely. Indeed, metamorphosis articulates that which eludes the seeming imitative sovereignty of photographic representation, and thereby defines Lévinas's term 'resemblance', 'not as the result of a comparison between an image and the original, but as the very movement that engenders the image'.[35] Furthermore, in what Lévinas refers to as 'the instant of a statue, in its eternally suspended future', we find that 'the tragic simultaneity of necessity and liberty, can come to pass: the power of freedom congeals into impotence' (pp. 138–9). In the figure of Niobe who weeps through her petrification we have, long before its actual possibility as a medium, the indwellingness of the photographic, a conceptual movement that differentiates the place of the photograph in stories of imitation and illusionism. In the manner of ancient sculpture photography provides a check to mimesis precisely by newly espousing the object; by couching in its apparent mirroring relation to the world the secret of metamorphosis as temporal dislocation.

Notes

1. Jacques Lacan, *The Four Fundamental Concepts of Psychoanalysis*, trans. Alan Sheridan (London: Penguin, 1977), pp. 111–12.
2. John Ruskin, Lecture VI: 'Relation to Art of Science of Light', *The Eagle's Nest* (1872), *The Complete Works of John Ruskin* (Library edn), ed. by E.T. Cook and A. Wedderburn, 39 vols (London: George Allen, 1903–12), XXII, 200–1.
3. Lacan, *Four Fundamental Concepts*, p. 112.

4. Stephen Bann, *The True Vine: on Visual Representation and the Western Tradition* (Cambridge: Cambridge University Press, 1989), p. 20.

5. Maurice Merleau-Ponty, *The Primacy of Perception and Other Essays on Phenomenological Psychology, the Philosophy of Art, History and Politics*, ed. by James M. Edie (Chicago: North Western University Press, 1964), p. 190.

6. *The Republic of Plato*, trans. with an introduction and notes by Francis Macdonald Cornford (Oxford: Clarendon Press), Book X, 598b, p. 318, hereafter in text.

7. Christopher Janaway, *Images of Excellence: Plato's Critique of the Arts* (Oxford: Oxford University Press, 1998), p. 122; hereafter in text.

8. Emmanuel Lévinas, 'Reality and its Shadow', trans. Alphonso Lingis, *The Levinas Reader*, ed. by Seán Hand (Oxford: Basil Blackwell, 1989), pp. 129–43; hereafter in text.

9. Emmanuel Lévinas, 'The Other in Proust', trans. Seán Hand, *The Levinas Reader*, p. 161; hereafter in text.

10. Marcel Proust, *In Search of Lost Time: Swann's Way*, trans. C.K. Scott Moncrieff and Terence Kilmartin, revised D.J. Enwright (London: Vintage, 1996) pp. 59–60; hereafter in text.

11. Susan Sontag, *On Photography* (1973; Harmondsworth, Middlesex: Penguin, 1979), p. 79.

12. Walter Benjamin, 'A Small History of Photography', *One Way Street and Other Writings*, trans. Edmund Jephcott and Kingsley Shorter (London: Verso, 1985), pp. 240–57: 243; hereafter in text.

13. Sontag, *On Photography*, p. 179.

14. See in particular Lindsay Smith, *The Politics of Focus: Women, Children and Nineteenth Century Photography* (Manchester: Manchester University Press, 1998); ' "Thinking blues": the memory of colour in nineteenth-century photography', in Roger Luckhurst and Josephine McDonagh, eds, *Transactions and Encounters: Science and Culture in the Nineteenth Century* (Manchester: Manchester University Press, 2002), pp. 55–74.

15. Stephen Bann, *The Clothing of Clio: a Study of the Representation of History in Nineteenth-Century Britain and France* (Cambridge and New York: Cambridge University Press, 1984), p. 134.

16. Roland Barthes, *Camera Lucida: Reflections on Photography*, trans. Richard Howard (New York: Hill and Wang, 1981), p. 95.

17. Benjamin, 'A Small History', p. 243.

18. Apollodorus, *The Library*, trans. Sir James George Fraser, 2 vols (London: William Heineman, 1963), I, 341–3.

19. Homer, *The Iliad*, trans. Robert Fitzgerald (Oxford: Oxford University Press, 1987), Book XXIV, Lines 607–12:

> Apollo,
> Making his silver long bow whip and sing,
> Shot the lads down, and Artemis with raining
> Arrows killed the daughters – all this after
> Niobe had compared herself with Leto,
> The smooth-cheeked goddess.

20. Ovid's *Metamorphoses*, The Arthur Golding Translation 1567, ed. and intr. by Frederick Nims (New York: Macmillan, 1965), Book 6, lines 184–8:

> Before hir marriage Niobe had knowen [Arachne] verie well,
> When yet a Maide in Meonie and Sipyle she did dwell.
> And yet Arachnes punishment at home before hir eyes,
> To use discreter kinde of talke it could hir not advise,
> Nor (as behoveth) to the Gods to yeelde in humble wise.

21. Ibid., lines: 390–5:

> Hir pulses ceased for to beate, hir necke did cease to bow,
> Hir armes to stir, hir feete to go, all powre forwent as now.
> And into stone hir verie wombe and bowels also bind.
> But yet she wept: and being hoyst by force of whirling wind
> Was carried into Phrygie. There upon a mountaines top
> She weepeth still in stone. From stone the drerie teares do drop.

22. See for example the following paintings: Abraham Bloemaert, *The Death of Niobe's Children*, 1591 (Statens Museum for Kunst, Copenhagen); Jacques-Louis David, *Apollo and Diana Attacking the Children of Niobe*, 1772 (Dallas Museum of Art); Anicet-Charles-Gabriel Lemonnier, *Apollo and Diana Attacking Niobe and her Children*, 1772 (Musee des Beaux Arts, Rouen); Pierre Jombert, *The Children of Niobe Killed by Apollo and Diana*, 1772, (École Nationale Supérieure des Beaux-Arts, Paris); Richard Wilson, *The Destruction of Niobe's Children*, 1760 (Yale Center for British Art).
23. The Niobe room at the Uffizi Gallery, Florence, was built by the Grand Duke Pietro Leopoldo for the reception of the statues of Niobe and her Niobids, part of a celebrated group of antiquity brought from the Villa Medici, Rome, in 1775. The centrepiece, the figure of Niobe herself shielding her daughter, was originally found near the Porta S. Paolo, Rome, in 1683. Many sources date the sculpture of Niobe to *c*.300 BC, while others date the work to the second or first century BC. Pliny believed the Niobe group to be by Praxiteles or Skopas active in the fourth century BC, but most dispute this view.
24. Percy Bysshe Shelley, letter to Thomas Jefferson Hogg, Pisa 20 April 1820, *The Letters of Percy Bysshe Shelley*, II, 185–7.
25. Clifton Spargo, *The Ethics of Mourning: Grief and Responsibility in Elegaic Literature* (Baltimore and London: Johns Hopkins University Press, 2004), p. 153.
26. Percy Bysshe Shelley, letter to Hogg, Pisa 20 April 1820, *Letters*, II, 186; hereafter in text.
27. Following the grief that marked her first visit in 1819, Mary Shelley records her reluctance to revisit the gallery in the 1840s:

> With slow steps my feet almost unwillingly first moved to the collection in the Reali Uffizi. As I entered the Tribune, I felt a crowd of associations rise up around me, gifted with painful vitality. I was long lost in tears.

However, her subsequent visits to the gallery during the 1840s appear to have been cathartic for she notes that: 'these saddest ghosts were laid; and the affliction calmed'. [Quoted in Helen M. Buss, David Lorne MacDonald and Anne McWhir, *Mary Wollstonecraft and Mary Shelley: Writing Lives* (Windsor, Ontario: Wilfred Laurier University Press, 2001) p. 208]. Later nineteenth-century travellers, such as Sophia Peabody Hawthorne, did not identify so exclusively with the anguish of the Niobe. Instead, Hawthorne focuses upon the way in which the de-contextualisation of the antique sculptures, the severing of the interconnections between them, radically alters the viewing experience:

> To-day is distinguished by my first seeing Niobe and her children, arranged round a vast hall – the very original marbles [...] The dying son is very beautiful, as well as the daughter, who is looking down upon him – or who *was* – for they are separated now. The light in the hall is not good for sculpture, and these noble forms are at great disadvantage. [*Notes on Italy 1853–1860* (London: Sampson Low, 1869), pp. 374–5]

28. Percy Bysshe Shelley, 'Critical Notices of the Sculpture in the Florence Gallery' (1819), *Shelley's Prose Works*, I, 402–5.
29. Gian Lorenzo Bernini, *Apollo and Daphne* (1622–1625) marble, height 243 cm (Galleria Borghese, Rome).
30. Johann Joachim Winckelmann, *History of Ancient Art among the Greeks*, trans. G.H. Lodge (Boston, MA: J.R. Osgod & Co.,1880), p. 125; hereafter in text.
31. Alex Potts, *Flesh and the Ideal: Winckelmann and the Origins of Art History* (New Haven and London: Yale University Press, 1994), p. 111.
32. Gotthold Ephraim Lessing, *Laocoon: an Essay on the Limits of Painting and Poetry*, trans. Edward Allen McCormick (Baltimore and London: Johns Hopkins University Press, 1984), p. 17; hereafter in text.
33. Lévinas, 'Reality and its Shadow', p. 138; hereafter in text.
34. From 1852 Roger Fenton was employed to photograph drawings, prints and sculptures at the British Museum, and the art dealers Colnaghi sold prints of the photographed objects. Particularly striking are Fenton's photographs of Greek and Roman sculpture and in *Students Day, The Graeco-Roman Saloon*, 1857 (stereoscopic albumen print), for example, the antique statues on either side of the gallery are pictured in such a way that their apparent interaction defies a sense of complete stasis. Interestingly, in a review in the *New York Observer* (21 Aug. 2005) of the exhibition 'All the Mighty World: the Photographs of Roger Fenton 1852–1860' at the Metropolitan Museum of Art, New York, Mario Naves, in making the point that 'people were quite peripheral to [Fenton's] aesthetic', identifies a 'photograph of an antique sculpture – a hermaphrodite feeding a bird, from the British Museum's collection', as exhibiting 'more animism than Fenton's pictures of flesh-and-blood subjects do'. Both examples further raise the fascinating question of what is precisely being reproduced when early cameras are turned to ancient sculpture.
35. Lévinas, 'Reality and its Shadow' p. 135; hereafter in text.

5
Aesthetic Encounters: the Erotic Visions of John Addington Symonds and Wilhelm Von Gloeden

Stefano Evangelista

In 1877, after an unpleasant episode of homosexual blackmailing, the classical scholar and critic John Addington Symonds permanently set up home abroad. Symonds and his family moved to the fashionable small town of Davos in the Swiss Alps, and from there Symonds frequently left for Italy on his own, leaving his wife and daughters behind. The dry climate made Italy an ideal place for those who, like Symonds, had been diagnosed with lung disease. But Italy was also an attractive destination for wealthy homosexual men from Britain and other Northern European countries, who used the Italian journey to combine healing, learning, and the sexual pleasure available through well-established networks of locals and expatriates that catered for sexual tastes that had to be hidden for fear of scandal and of the repressive legislation back home.

Symonds's impressions of Italy are recorded in a number of travel essays, most of which originally appeared separately in periodicals and were later collected in book form. In 1874, when he was still living in England, he published *Sketches in Italy and Greece* – a mixture of travel descriptions and essays on literature, history, and the visual arts. This was followed by *Sketches and Studies in Italy* (1879) and *Italian Byways* (1883), both of which retained the eclectic nature of the first collection. Symonds's essays are full of evocative descriptions written in striking aesthetic prose, which emphasise the *genius loci* and local or folkloric elements of various Italian locations. The essays contain several detailed descriptions of buildings, frescos, and paintings, but Symonds often digresses in order to recount legends (such as the miracles of a local saint), to provide fully researched literary and historical references, or to offer general reflections on aesthetics or religion. He also gives many travel tips, directing British tourists to unusual and lesser known sights and monuments, advising them on wine and food to enjoy in specific locations. In fact, the sketches are clearly meant as a supplement to standard tourist guides that cultured British travellers could carry with them on their Italian journey. Like Ruskin in *The Stones of Venice* (1851–53), Symonds exploited the ever increasing demand in England for more imaginative and challenging texts to be taken on holiday or to be read or reread in Britain for the virtual travel or to recall the sensations of past trips. These successful books went through several editions during Symonds's lifetime and were soon translated into German. After Symonds's death, his literary executor Horatio Brown collected all Symonds's sketches into a single three-volume edition in 1898, *Sketches and Studies in Italy and Greece*, which he rearranged geographically 'for the convenience of travellers', as an imaginary journey through Italy from North to South, starting in the Alps and ending, through Capri and Sicily, in Athens.

The persona adopted by Symonds is that of the eighteenth-century sentimental traveller, perfected in the Italian works of German authors like Goethe (who is often quoted in the sketches) and Heinrich Heine. These Romantic writers are the most representative figures of what, by the end of the nineteenth century, was a well-established tradition of Northern Europeans using the experience of the Italian journey to contribute to the debate on the arts back home. Part of the pleasure offered by these texts was to invite the leisured readers in Northern Europe to recognise the cultural allusions, mainly from classical antiquity and the Renaissance, with which the Italian cities and landscapes are scattered. But there was also the more risqué pleasure, inseparable from the 'sentimental' appeal of the genre, of following the writer through a journey of erotic, as well as intellectual, discovery. Italy was projected both as a land of culture and of sexual liberation or even libertinism, attributable, among other factors, to freer social customs, good weather, and the ready availability of prostitutes. The sexual encounter became a generic trope of travel narrative just as it functioned as an important *rite de passage* in the sentimental autobiography of the author. The fact that these encounters would often be with Italians of lower social status also bears the mark of a slightly old-fashioned eighteenth-century sensibility that conflates sexual and social freedom, and that has an almost revolutionary or utopian taste. So in *Reisebilder* (1826–31) Heine recounts his adventures in a brothel; and Goethe's *Roman Elegies* and *Venetian Epigrams* offer a detailed exploration of the mood of erotic anticipation that pervades the *Italian Journey* (1816–17).

Reading Symonds's travel essays, one is similarly struck by the sexual tension with which they are charged. The sketches are interwoven with the erotic autobiography of a homosexual man who scans the back-streets of Italian cities for chances of talking to young soldiers, who befriends peasants on country roads and stops to observe the bodies of workmen in the sun. In the first essay in *Italian Byways*, 'Autumn Wanderings', Symonds describes the arrival in Italy from Switzerland over a mountain pass. His first sight of Italy is in the form of:

> a dozen Italian workmen, arm linked in arm in two rows, tramping in rhythmic stride, and singing as they went. Two of them were such nobly-built young men, that for a moment the beauty of the land-scape faded from my sight, and I was saddened. They moved to their singing, like some of Mason or Fredrick Walker's figures, with the free grace of living statues, and laughed as we drove by.[1]

A few pages on, in 'Monte Oliveto', he points out 'two young con-tadini in one field, whom Frederick Walker might have painted with the dignity of Pheidian form', remarking that Tuscan peasants 'have an eminently noble carriage, and are fashioned on the lines of antique statues'.[2] Sometimes Symonds describes talking to these men. He con-stantly asks his readers to stop to admire the handsome faces of male youths or their muscular bodies, their physical beauty, their powerful masculinity, redolent of an idealised classicism and of a modern demo-cratic ideal borrowed from Walt Whitman. Symonds's encounters with young men often serve as epiphanies in the writings, disclosing a cer-tain *genius loci* to the author: the Italian working-class men momentarily embody, unbeknownst to themselves, the mark of the great tradition of the Italian past, which is suddenly made visible to the English tourist.

Symonds's published writings operate under the prevalent nineteenth-century conventions of euphemism and restraint. In order to make full sense of the encounters narrated in the sketches, it is necessary to turn to the franker evidence contained in Symonds's diaries and let-ters from these years. In his posthumously-published *Memoirs* (1984) he looks back to the early Italian travels that provided the basis for *Sketches and Studies in Italy*, describing the erotic imagination that forms the subtext of the travel essays in terms of 'uneasiness' and obsession:

> [a]ll kinds of young men – peasants on the Riviera, Corsican drivers, Florentine lads upon the Lungarno in the evenings, *facchini* at Venice, and especially a handsome Bernese guide who attended to the strong horse I rode – used to pluck at the sleeve of my heart, inviting me to fraternize, drawing out of me the sympathy I felt for male beauty and vigour. The sustained resistance to these appeals, the prolonged reversion to mere study as an anodyne for these desires, worried my nerves; and sometimes I broke out rebelliously into poems of passionate longing.[3]

The poem referred to, 'Phallus Impudicus', which is actually transcribed at this point in the *Memoirs*, includes an extended voyeuristic fantasy of spying on a naked Italian boy asleep in an inn room. Verse-writing, which sublimates homoerotic fulfilment in the form of textuality, is presented as a type of sexual neurosis and referred to as 'mental masturbation' by Symonds himself.[4] The private, pornographic text complements the public texts of the travel essays, giving a voice to the neurotic sexual energies that have been imperfectly purged from them.

While, as a young man, Symonds experienced an uneasy tension between desire and morality, in later years he would come to believe that sexual activity with men was beneficial to his mental health. From the 1880s Venice became Symonds's second home: he made annual trips there from his new home in Davos and eventually rented the mezzanine flat in his friend Horatio Brown's house on the Zattere, which he used as a base for his jaunts into other regions of the country. Symonds frequently complained that it was difficult to break the class barrier that separated him from ordinary Italians, but he believed that in Venice social boundaries were more fluid than in most other places. Here it was relatively easy to approach porters, soldiers, gondoliers, and other types of working-class men. Symonds also frequented brothels in Venice (which, it is worth noticing, was a relatively chaste spot on the map of the grand tour) and got to know male prostitutes in several Italian cities. He was convinced that these erotic or erotically-tinged encounters with working-class men provided him with a privileged experience of Italy that was deeper and more authentic than what was available to the average heterosexual traveller.

Symonds corresponded with a number of male friends in England who were either homosexual or sympathetic to homosexuality, including Edmond Gosse, Horatio Brown, Charles Philip Kains-Jackson, and Henry Graham Dakyns. Writing to Gosse from Venice in 1890, he lists, among the cultural attractions of the city, the view from his window:

> I am just above a bridge [...] up & down wh[ich] go divine beings: sailors of the marine, soldiers, blue vested & trousered fishermen, swaggering gondoliers. I can almost see their faces as they top the bridge. By rising from the chair a little I do so at once and get some smiles from passing strangers.[5]

In a similar vein, while confined to his flat by ill health, he fantasises to Kains-Jackson about St Mark's square, which he imagines 'ringing with a military band, while bright-eyed, sleek-necked sailors shot ceaseless invitations as they passed'.[6] Sometimes Symonds focuses on particular men: again in a letter to Gosse, he describes a 'soldier friend' as being 'like the Hermes of Praxiteles with the coloring of a Giorgione St. Sebastian, just over six foot high, & 20 years of age'.[7] In this way Symonds effectively draws his correspondents into erotic triangulations in which the desire for the young male body is shared across languages and nations. Italy, and Venice in particular, functioned for Symonds as an erotic theatre, in which the healthy male body was displayed and available everywhere for erotic contemplation and sometimes for sexual consumption. In this scenario the opportunities for sexual pleasure were multiplied and, what is more important, experienced as legitimate. In Italy the tension between desire and moral conventions, which is central to the problem of homosexuality in nineteenth-century Britain, was more easily reconciled. While in England homosexuality was associated with secrecy, repression, trauma, and abuse, in Italy homoerotic desire was connected to nature (of which the working-class men described by Symonds clearly are an emanation), health, and visibility.[8] This contrast is best illustrated by the diametrically opposite trends in the legislations of the two countries: in England the repressive laws already in existence were toughened by the Labouchere Amendment of 1885; in Italy the punishment for homosexual crimes was completely abolished in 1889.

In the letters, as in the published essays, homosexual *eros* is persistently fused with discourses of art and artistic appreciation. The body of the working-class male is idealised, 'understood', and translated through reference to the high cultural traditions of the classics and the Renaissance. This practice has several ramifications. It elevates the working-class man through the democratising energy of the homoerotic gaze, which, in this idealised conception, breaks down social and linguistic barriers. By comparing workmen and porters to figures from

Praxiteles, Giorgione, and Fredrick Walker, though, Symonds also constructs a high-cultural framework that legitimises his own interest in these young men as, effectively, a type of study. In this act the more carnal side of desire is somewhat tempered and detached from its specific object through the displacing action of intertextuality. A few years earlier, in a fundamental essay in the history of aestheticism, Symonds's Oxford colleague Walter Pater had claimed that the German art historian Johann Winckelmann had perfected his study of ancient sculpture through his erotic friendships with young men in Rome, which functioned as a practical education in the aesthetics of masculine form.[9] Symonds projects a similar image of himself as at once student of art and lover of men in Italy. He creates a universe in which erotic and aesthetic desires and values are somewhat interchangeable or complementary, and in which, as a consequence, homoerotic desires and practices must also be understood as somehow aiding the study of art and aesthetics.

Photography and networks of desire

In 1889 Symonds bought a Kodak. The revolutionary roll-film camera that made photography accessible to middle-class amateurs had only been launched the previous year.[10] Amateur photography appealed to Symonds as an inveterate traveller who often spent the best part of each year exploring new areas of Italy or revisiting familiar places. Like leisured travellers today, Symonds used photography as a way of keeping memories of places and sharing them with his friends. Symonds also frequently asked his close friends and correspondents to send him portraits of themselves and seemed especially keen to collect photographs of other homosexual men, as if he sought to build, through the photographic medium, a virtual gallery of like-minded men.[11] But photography also provided him with the technology to record his erotic encounters and to share them with friends, reproducing, in this exchange, the mixture of anthropological interest and erotic frisson that characterised his Italian journeys.

From the late 1880s till his death in 1893, Symonds regularly sent photographs of Swiss and Italian men whom he knew to correspondents in Britain, including Gosse, Kains-Jackson, Henry Dakyns, and Mary Robinson. Symonds was keen to turn these young men into actual art objects, having them photographed clothed or semi-nude by professional photographers.[12] He made, for instance, several photographic studies of his own gondolier and lover Angelo Fusato, which he distributed amongst some of his closer friends. In a letter to Dakyns he describes one of these studies, in which Fusato is 'nude to the waste', as being 'worthy of a place beside the finest chalk drawings of a realistic master';[13] writing to Kains-Jackson about another of these photographs, he notices that the 'strange thing about Angelo is that he has the shoulders, thorax, belly & thighs of a Bacchus, in spite of that delicate neurotic face. Nude, he is really very remarkable'.[14] The gaze of the art connoisseur, familiar with the canon of classical sculpture, and the erotic gaze of the modern lover of boys become one as Symonds expertly surveys Angelo's body, as a study, but also as the object of pornography. The 'perverse' homosexual pleasure aroused by the living body is conveyed as the acceptable aesthetic pleasure of the art object. Photography, for Symonds, opens up a new space for the convergence of aesthetic and erotic interests present in the travel writings. The perfect *mimesis* of the photographic image turns its subject into an art object even more effectively than the intertextual technique analysed above. The represented naked male body can be enjoyed more openly than the flesh-and-blood one: it is telling that the passage quoted above, in which Symonds compares his lover to a Bacchus, is ostensibly the description of a photograph, not of the real thing (to which he, presumably, would have had equal access). Through the photographic medium, in other words, the contemplation of the naked body of a young gondolier gains equal status to the pleasure of contemplating the male nude as it is displayed in museums or art galleries. But at the same time the photograph preserves the perfect memory of a private desire, which can be endlessly reproduced and circulated, in the form of erotica, among a community of homosexual men, for whom it provides a material referent to cement a shared sexual identity. The photograph also helps to develop a language about male homosexuality that is based on desire and eroticism rather than medicine ('inversion') or the ancient world ('paederasty').[15]

Symonds was an avid collector of photographs of the male nude and homoerotic pornography more generally. He became interested in the German bodybuilder Eugen Sandow (1867–1925), whose nude studies he used as reference material for his work on aesthetics and later had displayed in a gymnasium in Davos.[16] He was in contact with photographic studios that specialised in the male nude in Italy and other European countries, purchasing hundreds of photographs from them and circulating them among his friends in England, where the National Vigilance Association had been effective in curtailing the production of home-grown pornographic material.[17] In 1890 he started sending Gosse and Kains-Jackson examples of 'Sicilian Studies' by the German artist Wilhelm Von Gloeden, who had set up a photographic studio in the small Sicilian town of Taormina. Here Von Gloeden took pictures of young men and boys, often in classical attitudes or classical settings, which he reconstructed through the use of stage props or quotations such as garlands, vine wreaths, Pan-pipes, vases, leopard skins and so on. Like Symonds, Von Gloeden had moved South to look after his health, after having been diagnosed with a lung condition; and, like Symonds, he found in Italy an antidote against the sexually-repressive climate of his native North.

Von Gloeden's art is pervaded by a strong homoeroticism evoked by the eroticised male nude or played out by groups of boys and adolescents portrayed in intimate or affectionate attitudes. Not all of his photographs, however, are sexually explicit. In many of the pictures homoerotic desire is masked by an appeal to ethnographic interests and references to the socially acceptable tradition of classical sculpture, from which Von Gloeden copied models' poses and attitudes. This is why he became a successful photographer whose public was not limited to homoerotically inclined men. His fame helped to develop the tourist industry of the little-known Taormina, where his studio became, like the Alinari shop in Florence, a favourite place to purchase Italian 'studies' as souvenirs for friends or for travel albums. The treatment of the homoerotic theme made Von Gloeden's photographs attractive to the nascent homosexual press in Germany, where they were regularly published in pioneering magazines such as *Die Schönheit*, *Der Eigene*, and *Die Freundschaft*. His studies of the naked male body in the open air (his most characteristic setting) became popular *academies* – figure studies for the use of amateur and professional painters. At the same time the more risqué material was circulated on the pornographic market: explicit photographs and, later, picture postcards could be obtained through the post, directly from his studio, or via distributors in Germany and elsewhere.

In the early 1890s Symonds corresponded with Von Gloeden and the other homophile German photographer Wilhelm Plüschow (1852–1930), who was based in Rome, and whose subjects, style, and technique had been the inspiration for Von Gloeden's own. Collecting nudes by Von Gloeden and Plüschow became an obsession for Symonds. In May 1890 he could boast to Gosse: 'Nudes pour in on me from Sicily & Naples. I have a vast collection now – enough to paper a little room I think'.[18] Symonds was in fact directly responsible for introducing the work of Von Gloeden and Plüschow to Britain via his friend Charles Kains-Jackson, who was, between 1888 and 1894, the editor of the homoerotically-oriented periodical *The Artist and Journal of Home*

Culture. Through this circle some of Von Gloeden's photographs came to be published in one of the first issues of *The Studio*, an illustrated magazine of fine and applied art edited by the decadent Gleeson White (1851–1898). Like *The Artist*, *The Studio* specialised in skirting the fringes of the acceptable in the matters of homoeroticism. In the years preceding the conservative backlash of the Wilde trials, both periodicals helped to focus a community of homosexual men that was making itself increasingly visible through daring homoerotic discourse in the press.[19]

In June 1893, *The Studio* brought out an issue which was almost entirely devoted to the question of how to read artistic photography and how to place it in relation to the other visual arts. An anonymous article, probably written by White, entitled 'The Nude in Photography, with Seven Studies from Life', features several unmistakably homoerotic photographs by Von Gloeden and Baron Corvo (Frederick William Rolfe). The latter include a portrait of the young Cecil Castle, Charles Kains-Jackson's lover.[20] The article examines the new genre of nude open-air pictures of Mediterranean youths and essentially aims to promote the work of Von Gloeden and Corvo among the English public. In defense of the nude the author invokes the power of the classical tradition. He regrets that the modern art market marginalises the taste for the nude, limited to a set of 'allowable subjects' like bathers, the nursery toilette, and allegorical figures.[21] In open defiance to these conventions, he champions the use of the nude outside the artist's studio, a technique pioneered by Von Gloeden. The intent is clearly to seize on Von Gloeden's use of *natural* settings in order to distance his photographs, and the iconography of the youthful male nude more generally, from discourses of unnaturalness and perversions that are traditionally imagined to go on behind closed doors, in secluded spaces like the studio and the boudoir. Reinforcing the defence of Von Gloeden on grounds of naturalness, the author also argues that the darker skin of Italian men is more suited to nude photography than the paler bodies of the Anglo-Saxons, whose 'artificial colour' is produced by an over-civilised clothing practice (p. 106).

The essay in *The Studio* navigates the difficult territory between the high and the low inhabited by these photographs, which can contemporaneously be viewed as art, pornography, and ethnographic documents. It balances the conflicting desires to publicise their risqué contents with the need to make them appear innocuous to its more prurient readers. So, on the one hand, photographs of the nude are 'not to be considered as pictures, but merely as charts for reference, or working drawings, as it were, for artists' (p. 106). The nude is given a technical or scientific use in order to distance it from an economy of pure enjoyment and from the voyeuristic pleasure that culminates in the pornographic consumption of images. The camera becomes a technical aid for the painter; the photograph a document to be consulted for the purpose of study. On the other hand, to those who could read through the lines, the article publicises the existence of homophile networks, which gathered around the circulation of this material and around the growth of amateur photography more generally.

The article is illustrated with photographs of nude young men and boys *en plein air*, some of them displaying classical or oriental attributes. Among the Von Gloeden photographs reproduced in *The Studio* (Plate 5) the most suggestive shows two provocatively draped youths in a classical setting evoked by the sandals and headband worn by one of the models. The interrupted gesture captured by the artist seems to promise the start of a physical intimacy between the two, a suggestion that is reinforced by the downward gazes of the young men, which are in the direction of each other's genitals. The erotic energy of the photograph is generated by the tension between the naïve sense of fulfilment in the represented scene and the frustration of the scopophilic desires of the viewer. For the sight of the boy's full nudity is teasingly obscured by the momentary positioning of the semi-transparent white drape; and the homoerotic touch must, of course, remain a suggestion. Readers are invited to pause on 'the poise of the bodies, the perfect carriage of the head, and irresistible truth of the arrested movement' (p. 106), ostensibly focusing their attention on the pleasure of photographic realism, rather than homoeroticism. The author concludes that these illustrations are offered 'not merely as graceful studies, but as useful diagrams, and since, for many reasons, the model suitable for the purpose is not always attainable, these photographs may be valuable for designers and others' (p. 108). Poised between the 'graceful' and the 'useful', these photographs are placed within the acceptable boundaries of late-Victorian artistic culture. The amateur artists that constitute the overt readership of *The Studio* are told the practical uses and aesthetic value of nude photography; but the author obviously also addresses the homoerotic readership of the magazine, for whom the illustrations 'need no annotation' (p. 108). His simple objective is to introduce them to the work of Von Gloeden, regretting the exclusion of other photographs which 'entirely admirable as records, were, like many other statistics of science, not suitable for general exhibition' (p. 108). Cautiously but unmistakably, he advertises the existence of more explicit material, obliquely encouraging the homoerotically-inclined readers to look for it. Just like Von Gloeden's photographs and Symonds's travel writings, the article in *The Studio* is also a semi-coded advertisement for the erotic pleasures that the Italian trip could offer to the male homosexual traveller. The illustrations publicise the sexual freedom of the South and offer a sort of fantastic catalogue of the goods available there.

Matching visions

The points of contact between the works of Symonds and Von Gloeden reveal a cosmopolitan network of collaboration and identity formation among homosexual men across countries (England, Italy, and Germany) and artistic media (literature and photography). This instance of intersection between visual and textual cultures documents the parallel early histories of art photography and of the homoerotic male gaze, and records a mode of contact and exchange between Northern and Southern Europe in the nineteenth century. Von Gloeden's photographs nurture a nascent international homoerotic taste of which Symonds is a passive consumer, but also an active proponent both within his private circle and publicly in his writings. In this aesthetic the naked body of the working-class man is idealised through a classicising discourse that elevates it to the status of object of contemplation and study; yet the very same body historicises homoerotic desire firmly within the present through a rhetoric of realism and authenticity. This new taste and the homosexuality that it signifies are based on the resolution of apparently antithetical impulses: libido and disembodiment, materiality and transfiguration, decadence and health, mourning and celebration, idealisation and pornographic fruition. The representation of modern homoerotic desire is riddled with these paradoxes. It is, in Symonds's coded phrase, *'l'amour de l'impossible'*, an eroticism which social and moral customs make impossible, and which has made the concept of impossibility into an erotic ideal.

Von Gloeden's photographs illustrate how classicism operates a successful mediation between the physical and the ideal. His models are young Sicilian peasants and labourers whom he recruited in Taormina and in the neighbouring villages. In the photographs they appear mostly scantily draped or naked; many of them immodestly expose their genitals to the camera. These concessions to the pornographic gaze are counterbalanced by the photographer's classical quotations. Classical settings, props, and poses raise the cultural status, and hence the admissibility, of these images (Plate 6). Von Gloeden's nudes deliberately recall the aesthetic and cultural values that Winckelmann had expounded in his canonical writings on ancient art, where he had praised sculpture as the most perfect among the arts of antiquity. Despite its frequent use of the *tableau*, Von Gloeden's art is in fact more deeply in dialogue with sculpture than with painting.[22] His nude studies emphasise the plasticity and elasticity of the male body, and redeploy onto the photographic image the fundamental ancient canons of simplicity and grandeur that were, according to Winckelmann, best exemplified in the Greeks' treatment of the sculpted male nude.[23] It is this appeal to Winckelmann and the classical tradition that enables Von Gloeden's treatment of the nude to dispense with nineteenth-century photographic conventions such as fig leaves on crotches and strategically-blurred anatomies,[24] without becoming univocally pornographic.

Von Gloeden's choice to move the nude out of the studio and into the open-air belongs to the discourse of Hellenism. For Winckelmann the Greeks' sculptures of the male nude embodied their high ideals of civic and intellectual freedom. Von Gloeden's nude in nature displays a similar ideal or utopian quality. It is not only pagan and homoerotic, but ecological and egalitarian. It is a provocative gesture against the narrow sexual morality of the age; it sets itself in antithesis to industrialisation and modernity; it dreams of a classless society.

Von Gloeden, however, grounds these utopian visions in a specific space and time, evoked by the recognisable Southern Italian landscape and by the inescapable modernity of the photographic medium. Antiquity is a fiction that easily collapses under the heavy *mise en scène*. The amphorae, leopard skins, tunics, and garlands that dot these photographs are the stereotyped encoders of an 'overloaded' antiquity, in Roland Barthes' formulation, 'peopled with little peasant gigolos' dark bodies'.[25] In this reading the naïveté that informs Von Gloeden's aesthetics is in fact a form of *kitsch*, made up of an eclectic mixture of Greek, Latin, and Beaux-Arts academies, created by the simultaneous employment of elevated aesthetics and bad taste. The viewer of these photographs experiences the nudes not as sublime images but rather as fundamentally carnivalesque, enjoying the elements of artificiality and erotic playfulness in the compositions. Distortion and hyperbole are Von Gloeden's dominant aesthetic registers. The statuesque nudes in the open air are like fantastic archaeological findings, regurgitated by the earth, upon which the lucky Northern European tourist might stumble during a stroll in the Italian countryside. These living relics of antiquity simultaneously offer a voyeuristic pleasure and an anthropological interest that makes contemplation more admissible: the boys are shown through the prism of racial difference, emphasised by their inevitable swarthiness and by the outdoor nakedness, which invests them with an air of primitivism. Italy, and Sicily in particular, become Arcadian pleasure landscapes that implicitly denounce the restrictions of modern sexual morality in the North.

It is easy to see how Symonds should be drawn to Von Gloeden's vision, as he found in it the same tension between classical aesthetics and modern homoeroticism that he was keen to explore in his own work. Ever since his early writings on ancient Greek literature, Symonds had been haunted by the question of how he could effectively transmit to modern readers the powerful emotional appeal that classical culture held for him: 'How shall we, whose souls are aged and wrinkled with the long years of humanity, shake hands across the centuries with those young-eyed, young-limbed immortal children?'[26] The impossible handshake yearned for in *Studies of the Greek Poets* (1873) is pent up with emotion and repressed sexual energy. It hides the private narrative, which Symonds recounted many years later in his *Memoirs*, of a homosexuality discovered when he stumbled upon Plato's *Phaedrus* and *Symposium* during his last year at school. Plato's depiction of homoerotic desire between men as natural and noble, the legitimate component of an intellectual and artistic life, provided Symonds with 'the revelation I had been waiting for, the consecration of a long-cherished idealism. It was just as though the voice of my own soul spoke to me through Plato, as though in some antenatal experience I had lived the life of a philosophical Greek lover.'[27] This epiphanic encounter was followed by a period of simultaneous intellectual and sexual awakening, when the adolescent Symonds 'devoured Greek literature and fed upon the reproductions of Greek plastic art with which [his] father's library was stocked'.[28] The culture of ancient Greece would always retain this elemental physical power for Symonds, triggering in him the compulsion to repeat his first encounter with Plato and to share its psychological significance with his readers. In *Studies of the Greek Poets*, the private homoerotic narrative finds the most striking public expression in the visualisation of the Genius of the Greeks as 'a young man newly come from the wrestling-ground, anointed, chapleted, and very calm [...]. The pride and the strength of adolescence are his – audacity and endurance, swift passions and exquisite sensibilities, the alternations of sublime repose and boyish noise, grace, pliancy'.[29] Through the trope of embodiment Symonds recasts, in the form of visual desire, the homoerotic appeal that ancient Greece had transmitted to him.

In his travel writings Symonds uses the landscape of modern Italy, still largely untouched by industrialisation, as a magic zone, rich in sensual appeal, which enables the same emotional connection with a world of antiquity that is no more:

> Everything fits in to complete the reproduction of Greek pastoral life [...]. The narcissus, anemone, and hyacinth still tell their tales of love and death. Hesper still gazes on the shepherd from the mountain-head. The slender cypresses still vibrate, the pines murmur. Pan sleeps in noontide heat, and goatherds and wayfaring men lie down to slumber by the roadside, under olive-boughs in which cicadas sing [...]. Nothing is changed – except ourselves. I expect to find a statue of Priapus or pastoral Pan, hung with wreaths of flowers – the meal cake, honey, and spilt wine upon his altar, and young boys and maidens dancing round. Surely, in some far-off glade, by the side of lemon grove or garden, near the village, there must be still a pagan remnant of glad Nature-worship. Surely I shall chance upon some Thyrsis piping in the pine-tree shade, or Daphne flying from the arms of Phoebus.[30]

The descriptive travel narrative slides into a classicising fantasy in which the erotic element is made transparent through the many references to pagan tales of sexual desire. The Italian landscape is the natural home of a homoerotic or phallic sexuality, conveyed by Symonds's open allusion to the myths of Narcissus, Hyacinth, Priapus, and Pan, and to the song of the cicadas, which recalls the opening of Plato's *Phaedrus*. Homoerotic paganism is portrayed as the integral part of a desirable natural order that was fast being destroyed, and therefore made precious, by the moral and anti-ecological forces of modernity: the change is in 'ourselves'. Symonds writes himself into his pastoral fantasy, as a modern seeker after the remnants of a sensuous paganism, which had disappeared, but was imagined in the forms of Bacchic nature cults, gods in exile, and shepherds and 'wayfaring men' slumbering in the shade.

Symonds and Von Gloeden share a similar lyricism. In Symonds's fantastic landscape, as in Von Gloeden's photographs, the homoerotic gaze is freed from the moral repressions of the North and from its discourses of pathology and criminality. Both visions rely on the trope of the aesthetic encounter. As we have seen, for Symonds this normally takes the form of the encounter with working-class men, who, like Von Gloeden's Sicilian boys, are presented as the natural emanation of the erotic landscape of Italy. The bodies of these young men and boys – reproduced and scrupulously itemised for the readers and view-ers, and transfigured though the agency of aesthetic prose, photography, or classical quotation – are the objects which operate the necessary mediation between the present and the past, home and the foreigner, culture and homoeroticism.

The encounter, though, is a Janus-faced trope that signifies disjunc-tion as much as connection. It relies on imagination, autoeroticism, and on the unavoidable mediation of the artistic medium. This is why melancholia is the dominant mood in these works. For Symonds, the aesthetic encounter with the attractive bodies of working-class Italians reinforces the sense of distance: his homosexual desire is built up through the act of mourning for the long-dead classical age. Von Gloeden's models rarely appear content or engage in a complicit dia-logue with the camera. In order to preserve the fiction of authenticity, their gazes must be averted from all that is modern: the photographer, the camera, the viewer. Their presence in the modern world is acciden-tal. They express the home-sickness of exiles, forced into this fantastic universe to satisfy a modern and foreign homoerotic fantasy which they do not necessarily share. Their silence, aptly immortalised by the photo-graphic medium, creates an entirely non-verbal *eros*, in which the spell of cultural distance between viewer and object must not be broken.

To modern viewers and readers this poetics of melancholia is height-ened by the obvious elements of orientalism in these records of silent Italian men and boys, whose physical traces survive in the form of lists of names and visual records, but whose subjectivity is completely lost in the oeuvres of Symonds and Von Gloeden. Their individual psychol-ogy disappears inside the mass of cultural citation in which the authors immerse them. The relationship between the North and the South cre-ated by these encounters has an imperial and predatory element, in which the Northern European subject is empowered by cultural capital, technology (in the form of the camera), and economic strength, and the Southern man is eroticised through the fictions of primitivism and pas-sivity. The hands of Von Gloeden's models often bear the indelible signs of manual labour, which sit uneasily with the noble classical lineage claimed by their athletic bodies, but which reinforce their authenticity and hence their eroticism: in these moments of aesthetic discontinu-ity within the photographs, the Sicilian peasant boy, with his physical reality and potential availability, takes over the ideal nude, which exists out of time and therefore outside the potential economy of fruition of the late nineteenth-century viewer. The erotic fantasy is, in other words, repeatedly entwined with dormant discourses of cultural superiority and it is sustained by exploitative dynamics, in which the human exchange is always mediated by financial transactions.[31] Von Gloeden paid his models, and many of Symonds's relationships with Italian men, including that with his lover Fusato, explicitly involved elements of financial patronage. The dynamics of these aesthetic encounters arise from the overlap of different histories of sexuality, typified by the interplay of a sentimental discourse of belatedness, voyeurism, and self-conscious 'perversion' of the homosexual authorial subjects and the supposedly pre-modern, naïve sexuality of the Italian peasant boys. Their economic matrix is further re-enacted through the circulation of homoerotic texts and images on the wealthy Northern European photography and book markets.

In Symonds's and Von Gloeden's aesthetic encounters with Italian young men the progressive discourse of homosexual emancipation is aligned to fundamentally conservative desires of objectification and orientalist collecting. Von Gloeden's aesthetic vision is itself based on a collecting impulse which combines eroticism and anthropology, in which the bodies of the young male models are endlessly reproduced as precise anatomical records, body types are itemised, and physical differences captured. There is an aesthetic of compulsive repetition in the photographer's use of the same settings, in which countless male bodies alternate and ultimately come to be almost interchangeable, as the photographer and the viewer search for an impossible ideal.

Barthes called the vast body of Von Gloeden's work a 'hominary', that is, a fantastic taxonomy in the tradition of the medieval bestiary.[32] Von Gloeden's homoerotic art, in other words, is itself the dramatisation of a collecting desire. And it is for this reason that it lends itself well to the acquisitive drive of collectors such as Symonds, who, by 1890, had amassed enough photographs to 'paper a little room'. Reflecting on his own experience as viewer of these photographs, Symonds confessed that they 'become monotonous, but one goes seeking the supreme form & the perfect picture'.[33] This self-analysis of Symonds's own pornographic gaze describes a narrative of desire, aesthetic quest, and periodic frustration that elucidates the psychological condition of the homosexual author as collector. At the end of the nineteenth century Symonds and Von Gloeden endlessly record and confess their own homoerotic desires in their works, dramatising them for public and private audiences. The encounters between their oeuvres illustrate these two authors' parallel exploration of the aesthetics and psychology of homoeroticism, through which their work helped to shape an international homoerotic taste and to build networks of knowledge, tolerance, and desire.

Notes

1. John Addington Symonds, *Italian Byways* (London: Smith, Elder, & Co., 1883), p. 3.
2. Symonds, *Italian Byways*, p. 31.
3. *The Memoirs of John Addington Symonds*, ed. by Phyllis Grosskurth (New York: Random House, 1984), p. 177.
4. *Memoirs of John Addington Symonds*, p. 189.
5. *The Letters of John Addington Symonds*, 3 vols, ed. by Herbert M. Schueller and Robert L. Peters (Detroit: Wayne State University Press, 1967–69), III, 516.
6. Symonds, *Letters* , III, 768.
7. Duke Letter V [Stazione et Posta Vescovana, Stanghella, Provincia di Padova, Friday, 4 April 1890], quoted in John G. Younger, 'Ten Unpublished Letters by John Addington Symonds at Duke University', *The Victorian Newsletter*, 95 (Spring 1999), 1–10: 5.
8. On this see Paul Robinson, *Gay Lives: Homosexual Autobiography from John Addington Symonds to Paul Monette* (Chicago and London: The University of Chicago Press, 1999) and Robert Aldrich, *The Seduction of the Mediterranean: Writing, Art and Homosexual Fantasy* (London and New York: Routledge, 1993).
9. Walter Pater's essay 'Winckelmann' first appeared in the *Westminster Review* in January 1867. In 1873 it was reprinted in *Studies in the History of the Renaissance.*
10. The Kodak camera was launched by the Eastman Company in 1888. The new camera was portable and easy to use. Most importantly, it contained a film that could be sent to the factory to be developed, thereby opening amateur photography also to people who were unable to process negatives.
11. This archive, together with most of Symonds's papers, was destroyed after the death of Horatio Brown, Symonds's executor, in 1926: see John Pemble, *Venice Rediscovered* (Oxford and New York: Oxford University Press, 1996), pp. 67–8.
12. See, for instance, Symonds, *Letters*, III, 683 and 460.
13. Letter to Henry Graham Dakyns, 22 March 1886, Symonds, *Letters*, III, 125.
14. Letter to Charles Kains-Jackson, 18 December 1892, Symonds, *Letters*, III, 791.
15. Symonds had in fact been deeply involved both in sexological research, collaborating with Havelock Ellis in *Sexual Inversion*, and in late-Victorian Hellenism, writing a homosexual apology entitled *A Problem in Greek Ethics* (1873, 1883). Neither of these models proved entirely satisfactory to him. See Joseph Bristow, 'Symonds's History, Ellis's Heredity: *Sexual Inversion*', in *Sexology and Culture: Labelling Bodies and Desires*, ed. by Lucy Bland and Laura Doan (Cambridge: Polity Press, 1998), pp. 79–99.
16. See letter to Edmund Gosse, 17 December 1889, quoted in Younger, p. 2.
17. See Lisa Z. Sigel, *Governing Pleasures: Pornography and Social Change in England, 1815–1914* (New Brunswick and London: Rutgers University Press, 2002), p. 84.
18. Letter to Edmund Gosse, 12 July 1890, quoted in Younger, p. 7.

19. See Laurel Brake, *Print in Transition, 1850–1910: Studies in Media and Book History* (Basingstoke and New York: Palgrave – now Palgrave Macmillan, 2001), pp. 110–27.
20. Timothy d'Arch Smith, *Love in Earnest* (London: Routledge & Kegan Paul, 1970), p. 62.
21. Anon., 'The Nude in Photography: With Some Studies taken in the Open Air', *The Studio* (June 1893), 103–08: 104; hereafter in text.
22. Cf. Italo Mussa, *The Inquisitive Innocence of the Photographic Eye of Wilhelm von Gloeden* (Taormina: Malembrì, 1980).
23. Johann Winckelmann, *History of the Art of Antiquity*, trans. Harry Francis Mallgrave (Los Angeles: Getty Publications, 2006). For a study of desire and homoeroticism in Winckelmann, see Alex Potts, *Flesh and the Ideal: Winckelmann and the Origins of Art History*. Potts concludes with an analysis of Winckelmann's afterlife in post-revolutionary French painting and British Victorian aestheticism.
24. Peter Weiermar, 'Wilhelm Von Gloeden's Arcady: Remarks on an Obsessed Career', in *Wilhelm von Gloeden* (Cologne: Taschen, 1994), p. 10.
25. Roland Barthes' essay on Von Gloeden is reprinted in Jack Woody, ed., *Taormina: Wilhelm Von Gloeden* (Pasadena: Twelvetrees Press, 1986).
26. John Addington Symonds, *Studies of the Greek Poets* (London: Smith, Elder, & Co., 1873), p. 398.
27. Symonds, *Memoirs*, p. 99.
28. Symonds, *Memoirs*, p. 106.
29. Symonds, *Studies of the Greek Poets*, p. 399.
30. Symonds, *Sketches in Italy and Greece* (London: Smith, Elder, & Co., 1874), p. 6.
31. On the conservative social dynamics of Von Gloeden's art, see Sigel, *Governing Pleasures*, p. 118; on Symonds and imperialism, see Robinson, *Gay Lives*, p. 18.
32. See Woody, *Taormina*.
33. Letter to Gosse, 12 July 1890, cited earlier, quoted in Younger, p. 7.

Part III

Illustrations and Latent Images

6
'Latent Preparedness': Literary Association and Visual Reminiscence in 'Daisy Miller'

Graham Smith

> Wherever I walk, I come upon familiar objects in an unfamiliar world; everything is just as I imagined it, yet everything is new.
> (Goethe, *Italian Journey*)

'Daisy Miller: A Study', Henry James's first great success, appeared originally as a two-part story in the June and July issues of the 1878 *Cornhill Magazine*, the pre-eminent Victorian literary periodical.[1] Part 1 was reviewed favourably in June in the *Academy* and in the *Spectator*, two English weeklies, whereas responses to Part II were somewhat ambivalent, largely because of the story's melancholy ending. Harper & Brothers of New York published the first book edition later in 1878, selling in a few weeks more than 20,000 copies in their popular 'Half-Hour Series', and in London in 1879 Macmillan issued the first revised edition. James made extensive revisions in style and emphasis, in addition to changing the title of the story to become simply 'Daisy Miller' when he revised it for publication in The New York Edition thirty years later.[2]

The revisions significantly changed the tenor of the story, especially with regard to the characterisation of Daisy and of her critics.[3] Daisy becomes more charming and sympathetic as her critics become more strident, and Giovanelli, Daisy's beautiful Italian, is treated with increased harshness. For the purposes of the present study, however, these alterations are less fundamental than the changes in reception and structure that resulted from the translation of the story from the two-part magazine story to the novella in four parts.

The magazine format had a great impact on the reader's experience of 'Daisy Miller'. As Michael Lund points out, reading 'Daisy Miller:

A Study' in the summer of 1878, when the two parts of the story were separated physically and by time, required a special type of engagement on the part of the reader, one that was quite different from the flexible and continuous experience offered by the text published in The New York Edition and continued in modern editions.[4] The autonomy of the two parts in the *Cornhill Magazine* is marked by the forceful headings, 'Part I' and 'Part II', and by their physical and temporal separation from each other. Although the sense of a sequence continued in The New York Edition by the insertion of Roman numerals to indicate an organisation in four chapters, this more discreet partitioning softened the original distinction between two parts only. Parts I, II, III, and IV follow each other almost seamlessly, with no physical or temporal breaks.

The physical nature of the original story is also important in separating unambiguously the locations treated by James in the two sections of story. Part I takes place in Switzerland in June, in the grounds and in the environs of the 'Trois Couronnes', a 'grand hotel' on Lake Geneva, at Vevey, not far from the medieval Château de Chillon. Part II, by contrast, occupies a larger stage and is physically and temporally remote from the setting of the first stage: it takes place in Rome some six months after the conclusion of the first part. The month that elapsed between the publication of Part I and the appearance of Part II was, in a sense, a real counterpart to the fictional time that elapsed between the two parts. In effect, the month between the two parts made real the transition from the 'Trois Couronnes' on Lake Geneva to the formidable Mrs Walker's drawing room in Rome.

My primary intention in the present study is to examine the character and functions of the settings that James selected for the two parts of 'Daisy Miller: A Study', but it is necessary first to consider the peculiar nature of travel in the nineteenth century. 'Joyous it is', wrote Virgil in a famous passage in the *Georgics*, 'to roam o'er heights, where no forerunner's track turns by a gentle slope down to Castalia' (III: 292–93). The goals of nineteenth-century travellers were quite different. John Hale, for instance, in his introduction to the journal of Samuel Rogers, who travelled in Italy in 1814 and 1815, observed that the 'greater part of the pleasure of the whole tour [...] consisted not in discovery, but in recognition'.[5] More recently, William W. Stowe has argued that the 'culturally determined' expeditions made by the leisured classes of the nineteenth-century constituted a form of ritual, resulting in behaviour of a kind normally associated with religious, social, or tribal practices. Travel and ritual are both 'conventionally structured', and this structure comprises three stages, each of which leads to 'personal growth and discovery'. The anthropologist Victor Turner defined these stages as: a 'phase of separation', in which neophytes seek a space, knowledge or time that are distinct from their quotidian existence; a transitional or marginal state, 'a sort of social limbo', in which the novices are removed from their ordinary world and have the leisure to collect new impressions and amass cultural treasures; and a final phase, in which the initiates return to ordinary society and are reintegrated into it, having been transformed in some fashion by the previous stages.[6] It was also the case that literary and visual traditions affected the manner in which familiar sites were experienced. In essence, most nineteenth-century travellers journeyed in search of the familiar in order to accrue a form of cultural capital. What they saw was generally already known to them from literature and from representations, first in the form of drawings, paintings, and prints, and then, after the invention of photography, in the form of photographs.

The relationship between travel, convention, and recognition had already been subtly defined by Goethe on 1 November 1786, three days after he arrived in Rome for the first time. 'Wherever I walk', he wrote, 'I come upon familiar objects in an unfamiliar world; everything is just as I imagined it, yet everything is new'.[7] Goethe's 'unfamiliar world' was Rome, of course, and the 'familiar objects' were views of the ancient city that his father had hung in the family home in Frankfurt, the first engravings Goethe remembered seeing. Goethe's feelings of wonder and disorientation stemmed from his need to harmonise the Rome he saw with the vision of the city that he knew from those engravings. Goethe's emotions were in fact not very different from those experienced by the young Henry James, when, a little over one hundred years later, on 30 October 1869, he too arrived in Rome for the first time. In a letter to his brother, written in the evening after his arrival, James reported:

> From midday to dusk I have been roaming the streets. Que vous en dirai-je? At last – for the first time – I live! It beats everything: it leaves the Rome of your fancy – your education – nowhere. [...] I went reeling and moaning thro' the streets, in a fever of enjoyment. In the course of four or five hours I traversed almost the whole of Rome and got a glimpse of everything – the Forum, the Coliseum (stupendissimo!), the Pantheon, the Capitol, St Peter's, the Column of Trajan, the Castle of St. Angelo – all the Piazzas and ruins and monuments. The effect is something indescribable.[8]

James enlarged on the relationship between travel and education in the broadest sense in 'A Passionate Pilgrim', a story he wrote on his return to Cambridge and published in 1871 in the *Atlantic Monthly*.[9] This story is set in England rather than Italy, but James's sentiments, when he expatiated on 'the latent preparedness of the American mind [...] for the most characteristic features of English life' (p. 352), were similar to those expressed in the foregoing letter.

Daisy Miller too engages in the ritual of European travel in so far as she and her mother and brother tour Switzerland and Italy under the stewardship of a professional courier. But Daisy remains an ingénue abroad, for she appears to have done little conventional preparation for her initiation into old Europe and seems immune to the customary desire to accumulate the 'honorific' signs of culture associated with travel. Instead, she follows a ritual of her own, one for which she had been prepared by life in Schenectady and by visits to New York. At the 'Trois Couronnes' she dabbles in the ritual of courtship by flirting with Frederick Winterbourne, a polished but somewhat weary American expatriate residing in Geneva, and in Rome she transgresses more dangerously by 'going about' with 'the beautiful Giovanelli' (p. 48) (we are not told his first name), a handsome young Roman of indeterminate class. This is not to say that Daisy does not 'do' Rome, for she sees and – at least as important in the context of the story – is seen at many of the notable tourist sites. For Daisy, the ritual of travel is subsumed within the conterminous and complementary ritual of courtship, and the renowned sights of ancient and modern Rome become settings for her very public flirtation with Giovanelli. Instead of treating Rome with a seriousness in keeping with the work of cultural improvement, Daisy and Giovanelli appropriate the city casually as the stage for their inappropriate companionship.

This is not to discount the significance of Rome for James and his readers. While Daisy may not have been infused with 'latent preparedness' for Switzerland and for Italy, such preparedness was surely central to nineteenth-century readers' appreciation of the nature and substance of James's story. Indeed, the coexistence in 'Daisy Miller' of the major ritual of the discovery of Rome with the minor rite of Daisy's flirtation with Giovanelli is an important element in the wit of James's story. Furthermore, a significant aspect of the pleasure readers derive from the novella lies in their ability to connect with the sights that Daisy views with her innocent eye.

'Daisy Miller: A Study. Part I'

James placed his American readers on home ground in the first paragraph of Part I by observing of Vevey, on Lake Geneva, that it 'assumes [in the month of June] some of the characteristics of an American watering place. There are sights and sounds which evoke a vision, an echo, of Newport and Saratoga'.

> There is a flitting hither and thither of 'stylish' young girls, a rustling of muslin flounces, a rattle of dance music in the morning hours, a sound of high pitched voices at all times. You receive an impression of these things at the excellent inn of the 'Trois Couronnes' and are transported in fancy to the Ocean House or to Congress Hall.
>
> (p. 678)

But the Trois Couronnes is distinguished from those fashionable American establishments by 'neat German waiters, who look like secretaries of legation; Russian princesses sitting in the garden; little Polish boys walking about held by hand, with their governors; a view of the sunny crest of the Dent du Midi and the picturesque towers of the Castle of Chillon' (p. 678). This last feature, the Château de Chillon, recurs throughout Part I.

Winterbourne, a twenty-seven-year-old expatriate residing in Geneva, first encounters Daisy Miller in the garden of the Trois Couronnes, overlooking Lake Geneva. Having captivated Winterbourne by her 'charming garrulity' (p. 696) and having opined that Europe was 'perfectly sweet' (p. 684), Daisy focuses upon the Château de Chillon:

> 'Have you been to that old castle?' asked the young girl, pointing with her parasol to the far-gleaming walls of the Château de Chillon.
>
> 'Yes, formerly, more than once', said Winterbourne. 'You too, I suppose, have seen it?'
>
> 'No; we haven't been there. I want to go there dreadfully. Of course I mean to go there. I wouldn't go away from here without having seen that old castle.'
>
> 'It's a very pretty excursion', said Winterbourne, 'and very easy to make. You can drive, you know, or you can go by the little steamer.'
>
> (p. 685)

Later that evening Winterbourne even dares to volunteer to row Daisy to the Château de Chillon, 'in the starlight' (p. 694). ' "I don't believe it!" responded Daisy'. Two days later, when Daisy and Winterbourne do make their excursion to the castle, the narrator records that Daisy 'turned a singularly well-shaped ear to everything that Winterbourne told her about the place' (p. 696). Winterbourne, however, 'saw that she cared very little for feudal antiquities and that the dusky traditions of Chillon made but a slight impression upon her'. ' "Well I hope you know enough!" ' was her riposte when he told her the story of 'the unhappy Bonnivard' (p. 697). What might be astonishing is that neither Winterbourne, nor Daisy, nor the narrator mentions Lord Byron, whose 'Sonnet on Chillon' and 'Prisoner of Chillon' had made Bonnivard and the castle household names in America and in Europe:

> Chillon! thy prison is a holy place,
> And thy sad floor an altar – for 'twas trod,
> Until his very steps have left a trace
> Worn, as if thy cold pavement were a sod,
> By Bonnivard! May none those marks efface!
> For they appeal from tyranny to God.[10]

It is no exaggeration to say that Byron's lines became inscribed on the European and American imagination, as James himself shows in 'Four Meetings', another magazine story, published in *Scribner's Monthly* in 1877.[11] 'Four Meetings' tells the story of Caroline Spencer, a school teacher who lived 'in the depths of New England'. The narrator first meets Miss Spencer at a New England tea-party when his hostess asks him to show to her guests some photographs that her son had brought back from Europe. Most of the young women 'were provided with an object of interest more absorbing than the most vivid sun-picture', the narrator observes, 'but there was a person alone near the mantel-shelf, and looking round the room with a small gentle smile, which seemed at odds, somehow, with her isolation' (p. 44). This was Caroline Spencer, who professed herself delighted to be shown the photographs. The narrator proceeded to show her a series of large views of Switzerland, Italy, and Spain, 'landscapes, reproductions of famous buildings, pictures and statues' (p. 45), saying whatever he could about them. Miss Spencer became flushed, rubbed her lip with her paper fan while looking at the first set of photographs, and caressed a second portfolio. Lingering over the photographs with this cosmopolitan young man was evidently an erotic epiphany for her. For the narrator the photographs showed familiar sites, but for Miss Spencer they constituted an irresistible invitation.

When, prompted by a photograph of the Château de Chillon, the narrator stumbled over some lines from Byron, Miss Spencer quoted the poem correctly. 'By the time she had finished, she was blushing' (p. 45), observed the narrator. The young man complimented her, telling her she was 'perfectly equipped' to visit Switzerland and Italy. However, if she hoped to recognise Byron's description, she must go abroad soon, for Europe was becoming 'sadly dis-Byronized'.[12] If it were not for their silence on Byron, Winterbourne and Daisy might be lineal descendants of the narrator and Caroline Spencer in 'Four Meetings'. However, we can be sure that James's omission of Byron was calculated rather than casual. Daisy's innocence of Byron and of Bonnivard, the prisoner of Chillon, provides vivid proof of her lack of 'preparedness' and is also a sign that she belongs to the new generation of travellers that contributed to Europe's 'dis-Byronization'.

By the time James published 'Daisy Miller: A Study', the Château de Chillon had been photographed many times, most notably by Adolphe Braun & Co., an internationally-renowned commercial firm located in Alsace, near the Swiss border.[13] In the 1860s Braun had on his inventory numerous views of Switzerland, including a plate showing the Château de Chillon as Daisy and Winterbourne must have seen it when they approached by steamer (Plate 7).[14] Likewise, Braun's *Vues de Suisse et de Savoie*, a collection of panoramic views of Switzerland and Savoy dating from about 1867, contains one picture showing the Château de Chillon and another representing Lake Geneva from what is very likely the garden of the Trois Couronnes.[15] Braun's views of the Château de Chillon show the castle from the lake, but contemporaneous stereo cards represent the road that Daisy and Winterbourne must have taken when they drove back to Vevey 'in the dusk'.

Had Caroline Spencer accompanied Winterbourne to the Château de Chillon, we can be sure that she would have savoured the castle's literary and historical associations. She might also have read Byron's 'Prisoner of Chillon' 'on the spot', and she would have bought photographs as souvenirs of her visit. Daisy, by contrast, lived in the present, and so, for her, the romance of the place lay in its function as the setting for her flirtation with Winterbourne. It gave her a theatre for her performance; an opportunity to rustle her dresses in the corkscrew staircases of the castle, to find out more about Winterbourne, and to tease him about his 'mysterious charmer' (p. 697) in Geneva. In short, the castle served as a romantic backdrop for her lively femininity and as a stage on which she could discomfit him with 'the frankness of her *persiflage*' (p. 697).

'Daisy Miller: A Study. Part II'

In contrast to Part I, which is confined to the gardens of the Trois Couronnes and to the Château de Chillon, Part II of 'Daisy Miller' traverses a much larger and more varied stage, with Imperial, Baroque, and nineteenth-century Rome providing settings for a series of interrelated episodes. Although the Miller family merely exchanges one grand hotel for another, Daisy finds Rome much less 'poky' (p. 49) than she had expected and, after a penitential week of formal sightseeing with a professional cicerone, foolhardily 'rackets about' (p. 44) the city with Mr Giovanelli, her 'perfectly lovely' (p. 47) Italian 'amoroso'.

The narrative resumes in a hotel in Rome, where Winterbourne's aunt, Mrs Costello, is staying. We learn that the Millers have been in Rome for some time, and that Mrs Costello's distaste for the family is unabated. The next scene is set in the apartment of Mrs Walker, a Genevan acquaintance of Winterbourne. It is there, on the Via Gregoriana, near the top of the Spanish Steps, that Winterbourne renews his acquaintance with Daisy. Later he leaves Mrs Walker's apartment with her, intending to escort her to the Pincian Gardens, where she had arranged to meet Giovanelli. This episode leads to Daisy's unforgivable *faux-pas*, her refusal to abandon Giovanelli and join Mrs Walker in her carriage. Three days later Mrs Walker's drawing room provides the setting for the critical moment in Daisy's ostracism from American expatriate society in Rome. When Daisy approached Mrs Walker to take leave of her, the latter 'turned her back straight upon Miss Miller and left her to depart with what grace she might'. When Winterbourne observes, 'That was very cruel', Mrs Walker responds dramatically: 'She never enters my drawing room again!' (p. 58).

Thereafter James presents Daisy as an outsider in relation to American society in Rome. She is the subject of malicious gossip when Winterbourne and his aunt see her strolling about St Peter's with Giovanelli. The 'mala lingua' continues when Winterbourne learns from a friend that he had spotted Daisy in the Palazzo Doria Pamphili, 'all alone' with Giovanelli, in the 'secluded nook' (p. 60) containing Velásquez's portrait of Pope Innocent X.[16] A few days later, Winterbourne himself encounters Daisy and Giovanelli on the Palatine Hill. The climactic scene in the novella takes place in the Colosseum, late at night, when Winterbourne discovers Daisy and Giovanelli seated together at the centre of the arena, at the foot of the great cross commemorating the Christian martyrs, who, according to legend, had perished there. Daisy is contaminated, in more ways than one, by this nocturnal escapade: Winterbourne loses his respect for her, and Daisy contracts malarial fever and dies. The final episode in the story is set in the Protestant Cemetery of Rome, adjacent to the Pyramid of Caius Cestius, outside the Aurelian Wall at the southern limit of the ancient city. Each of these settings formed part of standard nineteenth-century itineraries of Rome, such as those recommended by Karl Baedeker and by John Murray in their respective handbooks to the city. This being the case, they would have been familiar to those among James's readers who had visited Rome and to those who were intending to do so. In fact, the mere mention of these sites would have conjured up visual, historical, and literary associations in the minds of James's readership. The remainder of this section will examine these sites in more detail, considering their function as familiar backdrops, against which we view successive episodes in Daisy's reckless, ill-advised, innocent, and, ultimately, tragic 'progress' through Rome.[17]

Even more than Part I, Part II of 'Daisy Miller' is concerned with convention and class and is built around a collision of cultures. Paradoxically, however, the misunderstandings and tensions that James brings out in the story result not from a clash between old Europe and new America but from a fissure that separates two American classes. Schenectady is not Boston or New York, and so Daisy and her mother represent a new provincial, moneyed, and uncultured middle class that began to flourish in post-revolutionary America. The Millers and their wealth have still to acquire the patina that comes with age. Despite her immaculate self-presentation, Daisy is characterised by what James would later term a 'general shining immediacy' that is not yet softened by 'the tone of time'.[18] At Vevey Daisy is shunned by Mrs Costello, Frederick Winterbourne's ultra-exclusive aunt, who refuses to be introduced to her; in Rome she comes to be ostracised by a self-appointed American elite made up of expatriates of the 'right' kind. One suspects that Daisy was in the end rejected by her compatriots less because of her social indiscretions than because she and her mother simply did not 'fit'. Most particularly, Daisy is contrasted to Winterbourne, a painfully stiff, thoroughly Europeanised American. Indeed, one of the many overlapping themes in the story is Winterbourne's failure to understand Daisy and, correspondingly, Daisy's inability to comprehend Winterbourne. Unlike Daisy and Giovanelli, who communicate easily and uncomplicatedly with each other, Winterbourne and Daisy are separated by their respective upbringings and by their different social conventions and expectations. In the end, Daisy not only fails in the customary ritual of travel but is also unwilling to submit to the social conventions laid down by her compatriots.

The Pincio

Known in antiquity and during the sixteenth century as the 'Hill of Gardens' ('Collis Hortularum'), early in the nineteenth century the Pincian Hill was transformed by Giuseppe Valadier, Pope Pius VII's architect, into a public park, which was linked to the Piazza del Popolo by a series of terraces and ramps.[19] By mid-century, 'the beautiful and frequented promenade of Monte Pincio', as it was styled by Murray's 1894 *Handbook to Rome*, had become a popular gathering place, much like the Jardin des Tuileries in Paris, where fashionable Romans and visitors to the city would go to see and be seen and to promenade. George Stillman Hillard, a Boston lawyer and friend of Nathaniel Hawthorne, visited Rome in 1847 and, five years later, in his travel book, *Six Months in Italy*, observed of the crowds that swarmed to the Pincio in the evenings:

> The fashionable hour of resort to Monte Pincio is that just before sunset. At this time, the gravelled terrace on the western side begins to be thronged with pedestrians. Carriages arrive in rapid succession, and, wheeling into line, move around in an unbroken succession, and soon are brought so near to each other that no one can stop without deranging the economy of the whole circle.[20]

The popularity of the Pincian Gardens among visitors to Rome is also apparent in 'A Stroll on the Pincian', the twelfth chapter in Hawthorne's *The Marble Faun*, published in 1860. 'The Pincian Hill', wrote Hawthorne, 'is the favourite promenade of the Roman aristocracy'. 'At the present day, however', he continued, 'like most other Roman possessions, it belongs less to the native inhabitants than to the barbarians from Gaul, Great Britain and beyond the sea, who have established a peaceful usurpation over whatever is enjoyable or memorable in the Eternal City'.[21] James would sometimes spend afternoons 'baking' himself in the sun of the Pincio, and so he had ample opportunity to observe the 'staring, lounging, dandified, amiable crowd'. 'Sometimes', he acknowledged, 'I lose patience with its parade of eternal idleness, but at others this very idleness is a balm to one's conscience'.[22] In addition to providing the perfect setting for 'aimless flânerie', as James termed it, the western limit of the Pincian functioned as a belvedere, from which magnificent views over the Piazza del Popolo and the Tiber to the Janiculum and the Vatican could be enjoyed. Indeed, the vista from the Pincian, with its prospect of the dome of St Peter's, was generally recognised to be one of the best general views of Rome.

In addition to being admired by writers, the celebrated view from the Pincio was also captured by painters and photographers during the nineteenth century. In 'Roman Views', Andrew Szegedy-Maszak has shown that views from the Pincio were popular subjects among early photographers such as Fréderic Flachéron, Giacomo Caneva, Robert Macpherson (Plate 8), and James Anderson, all of whom were active in Rome in the 1850s and 1860s.[23] Likewise, Jean-Baptiste Camille Corot in the 1820s and the New York painter Sanford Gifford in the 1860s painted the view from the promenade followed by Daisy and by Winterbourne. The teeming sociability of the Pincio was captured in the 1890s in a series of watercolours by the New England painter Maurice Prendergast.[24]

When compared with earlier literary accounts and with the visual records provided by paintings and photographs, James's account of the Pincio in 'Daisy Miller' can be seen to be accurate in detail. The time is right: 'the afternoon was drawing to a close – it was the hour for the throng of carriages and of contemplative pedestrians'. 'We had better go straight to that place in front, [...] where you look at the view' (p. 49), said Daisy when she and Winterbourne entered the Pincian Gardens. When Daisy spots Giovanelli, he is leaning against a tree, directing at the women in carriages what James in 'From a Roman Notebook' had called the 'practised stare'.[25] 'Did you ever see anything so cool?' asked Daisy of Winterbourne. And when Mrs Walker arrives on the scene, her carriage has to detach itself from the 'revolving train' (p. 51) in order to draw up beside the path where Daisy was walking with her 'two cavaliers'.

St Peter's

Leaving aside the second episode in Mrs Walker's apartment, the next setting that James selected as a stage for Daisy's vagaries was the interior of the great basilica of St Peter's. In fact, the transition from the Pincio to St Peter's is a natural one, for, in an essay of 1877, reprinted in *Italian Hours*, James himself had already linked the two:

> The Pincio continues to beguile; it's a great resource. [...] To be able to choose of an afternoon for a lounge (respectfully speaking) between St Peter's and the high precinct you approach by the gate just beyond the Villa Medici [...] is a proof that if in Rome you may suffer from ennui, at least your ennui has a throbbing soul in it.[26]

'It is something to say for the Pincio', continued James, 'that you don't always choose St Peter's'. Earlier, in 'A Roman Holiday', James had admitted: 'One is apt to proceed [to St Peter's] on rainy days with intentions of exercise [...]. Taken as a walk not less than as a church, St Peter's of course reigns alone'. Entering St Peter's, he observed, 'seems not so much a going in somewhere as a going out'.[27]

The secular and social functions of St Peter's are clearly in evidence in 'Daisy Miller'. One Sunday afternoon, having gone to St Peter's with his aunt, Winterbourne 'perceived Daisy strolling about the great church in company with the inevitable Giovanelli' (p. 59):

> A dozen of the American colonists in Rome came to talk with Mrs. Costello, who sat on a little portable stool at the base of one of the great pilasters. The vesper service was going forward in splendid chants and organ tones in the adjacent choir, and meanwhile, between Mrs. Costello and her friends, there was a great deal said about poor little Miss Miller's going really 'too far'.
>
> (p. 60)

Mrs Costello's peculiar 'at home' in St Peter's confirms an observation made by William Vance, to the effect that St Peter's 'was, in a manner of speaking, [Anglo-Americans'] grandest salon'.[28] 'Winterbourne was not pleased with what he heard', continues the narrator, 'but when, coming out upon the great steps of the church, he saw Daisy, who had emerged before him, get into an open cab with her accomplice and roll away through the cynical streets of Rome, he could not deny to himself that she was going very far indeed' (p. 60). What Winterbourne failed to notice was the parallel between Giovanelli's dalliance with Daisy and his own un-chaperoned carriage-ride with her, at dusk, from the Château de Chillon to Vevey.

'By St Peter's' (Plate 9), Alvin Langdon Coburn's frontispiece to 'Daisy Miller', in volume eighteen of The New York Edition, connects in a general way with these episodes in the church and piazza of St Peter's, without illustrating either in a literal fashion. This is in accord with James's views on the proper relationship between text and image, a matter he addressed in detail in his preface to The New York Edition of *The Golden Bowl*. 'Anything that relieves responsible prose of the duty of being, while placed before us, good enough, interesting enough and, if the question be of picture, pictorial enough, above all in itself', wrote James, 'does it the worst of services, and may well inspire in the lover of literature certain lively questions as to the future of that institution'.

By contrast, Coburn's photographs were distinguished by what James termed 'their discreetly disavowing emulation': their subjects' references were 'exactly not competitive and obvious', but instead made their case 'with some shyness, that of images always confessing themselves mere optical symbols or echoes, expressions of no particular thing in the text, but only of the type or idea of this or that thing'.[29]

Coburn's frontispiece provides an oblique view of St Peter's from the southeast. The shaft of one of the massive Doric columns of Gian Lorenzo Bernini's colonnades dominates the left foreground; a large part of the middle ground is taken up by his fountain, which seems visually to echo the dome in the background, and by the jet of water that it emits. The fountain and its spray largely obscure Carlo Maderno's façade, while also giving unusual prominence to Michelangelo's dome. Coburn's picture minimises those aspects of St Peter's that were held in low regard in the second half of the nineteenth century, while giving prominence to elements that were universally admired.[30] If Coburn approached James's narrative with modesty, it is also the case that he treated St Peter's discreetly and sympathetically, at least from the perspective of American travellers of the second half of the nineteenth century. A comparison of Coburn's image with typical general views produced by Giovanni Battista Piranesi in the 1770s or by Gioacchino Altobelli and Pompeo Molins about 1860 shows immediately the extent to which the photographer departed from the iconographic norm in order to create a picture that would be in accord with the taste of James and his contemporaries.

The Colosseum

Szegedy-Maszak has provided an admirable account of the place occupied by the Colosseum in Anglophone literature and in the American and British imagination.[31] 'Until the end of the [nineteenth] century', he writes, 'two narratives dominate the foreign travellers' accounts of the Colosseum':

> The first has to do with the visitors' experience of the building itself. Mirroring their approach and entry, there is a standard sequence of responses to the Colosseum that includes, *seriatim*, comments on its size, its ruined condition, and the lush vegetation and Christian monuments in the interior of the arena. The second story, paralleling the first, involves the history of the Colosseum itself and of the Roman Empire. The massive size of the Colosseum, the extravagant and often

bloody spectacles it had housed, and its picturesque decay made it the perfect embodiment of the history of the imperial city. Until their removal in the 1870s, even the stations of the cross had their place, symbolizing the victory of Christianity over paganism.[32]

As Szegedy-Maszak demonstrates, these narratives had been inscribed for Anglophone travellers by writing of various kinds, ranging from the romantic poetry of Lord Byron in the second decade of the nineteenth century to the factual handbooks produced about mid-century by Baedeker and by Murray. In 'Manfred' and in the fourth canto of 'Childe Harold's Pilgrimage', in particular, Byron defined how English-speaking travellers approached the Colosseum and primed them to experience the appropriate emotions when they did so. It was Byron in 'Manfred', for instance, who implanted the notion that the Colosseum was best seen at night, by the light of the stars. This romantic view was also embedded in the Victorian pictorial consciousness, as can be seen, for example, in a remarkable nocturnal watercolour of 1819 by J.M.W. Turner.[33]

In 'Miriam's Trouble', an important chapter in *The Marble Faun*, Hawthorne continued the Byronic tradition but superimposed upon it a layer of irony. In the course of a nocturnal ramble in Rome, Miriam, Hilda, Kenyon, and Donatello spend some time in the Colosseum, where, 'as usual, of a moonlight evening', the narrator informs the reader, 'several carriages stood at the entrance of this famous ruin, and the precincts and interiors were anything but a solitude'.[34] 'Byron's celebrated description is better than the reality', he continues. Nevertheless, 'a red twinkle of light [...] ascending to loftier and loftier ranges of the structure [...] indicated a party of English or Americans, paying the inevitable visit by moonlight, and exalting themselves with raptures that were Byron's, not their own'. But Hawthorne dwelt more upon the contemporary nature of the arena as a theatre for the enactment of a lively night life. There was much 'pastime and gaiety', observes the narrator. Young men and 'light-footed', 'frolicksome' girls chased each other across the arena to embrace in the 'duskiness' of the arches, and on the steps of the cross at the centre of the arena, 'sat a party, singing scraps of song, with much laughter and merriment between the stanzas'.[35]

James's account of Daisy Miller's late-night visit to the Colosseum is anticipated in several respects by Hawthorne's description in *The Marble Faun*, but the younger author staged its characters alone in the amphitheatre, implicitly contrasting the intimate nature of their tryst to the rambunctious communal nature of the social gathering described by

Hawthorne. This opposition makes Daisy's moonlight excursion appear more intimate, and, ultimately, more dangerous, morally as well as physically, than that undertaken by Hawthorne's subjects.

But James also situated his episode more sympathetically in relation to the Byronic tradition. When Winterbourne approached the Colosseum he was literally infused with the spirit of the romantic poet. In contrast to his account of the visit to the Château de Chillon, where Byron's presence was latent, at the Colosseum James makes explicit the poet's verbal influence and psychic presence. 'The place had never seemed to him more impressive', observed the narrator, 'one-half of the gigantic circus was in deep shade, the other was sleeping in the luminous dusk' (p. 63). Standing there, Winterbourne 'began to murmur Byron's famous lines out of "Manfred" '.[36] James did not quote these lines, a sign that he took it for granted that his readers would know them:

> I do remember me, that in my youth,
> When I was wandering, upon such a night
> I stood within the Colosseum's wall,
> 'Midst the chief relics of almighty Rome;
> The trees which grew along the broken arches
> Waved dark in the blue midnight, and the stars
> Shone through the rents of ruin.
>
> (3.4. 8–13)

When Daisy and Giovanelli recognise Winterbourne, they too situate his arrival in the context of the gladiatorial combats for which the Colosseum was renowned. ' "Well, he looks at us as one of the old lions or tigers may have looked at the Christian martyrs!" ' (p. 64) exclaimed Daisy. When Winterbourne chastises Daisy for the 'craziness, from a sanitary point of view' of her 'lounging away the evening in this nest of malaria', she responds foolhardily, ' "I was bound to see the Colosseum by moonlight; I shouldn't have wanted to go home without that" ' (p. 65). As she left the arena with Winterbourne, she ventured once more, ' "Well, I *have* seen the Colosseum by moonlight! [...] That's one good thing" '.

As William Vance acutely points out, although Daisy breaks one code, that of decorum, she does so in order to conform to another, 'that of Byronic romanticism'.[37] The pestilential nature of the Colosseum, which was, as Winterbourne emphasised, a notorious breeding ground for Roman fever, results predictably in Daisy's death. But it is significant that, despite Daisy's flouting of societal convention, hers is an innocent's death, not unlike those of the legendary Christian martyrs who were reputed to have died for their faith in what Byron, in 'Manfred', termed the 'bloody circus'. Paradoxically, it is also in this scene that James suggests most directly the likelihood of there having been a sexual relationship between Daisy and Giovanelli, something that Edith Wharton built upon and made implicitly explicit sixty years later in her famous short story, 'Roman Fever'.

The Protestant Cemetery

The Protestant Cemetery, just outside the Aurelian Wall, adjacent to the ancient Pyramid of Caius Cestius, was, for many Anglophone travellers, part of standard nineteenth-century itineraries of Rome, partly because of the Victorian fascination with graveyards, something that had been instilled in the English consciousness in the second half of the eighteenth century by the publication of Thomas Gray's 'Elegy Written in a Country Charchyard'. The cemetery in Rome was notable also because the English Romantic poets, John Keats and Percy Bysshe Shelley, were buried there. In fact, Jeffrey Meyers has argued that Keats and Shelley, as well as Byron, 'create a rich context for [James's] tale of a charming young innocent abroad'.[38]

'The cemetery is an open space among the ruins covered in winter with violets and daisies', wrote Shelley, in his preface to 'Adonais: an Elegy on the Death of John Keats', which he published in 1821. 'It might make one in love with death', he added, 'to think that one should be buried in so sweet a place'. In the poem itself Shelley likewise mentioned 'a slope of green', where a 'light of laughing flowers along the grass is spread'. More generally, because the cemetery was also the resting place of many ordinary British and American travellers, who, like Daisy Miller, had died in Rome, it served as a catalyst for musings on the transience of life, prompting romantic meditations on the intermingling of past and present. The cemetery also engendered sentiments of pleasurable melancholy and produced what might be styled an 'Et in Arcadia Ego' effect. For James, writing in 'The After-Season in Rome', the Protestant Cemetery was 'tremendously, inexhaustibly touching', 'one of the solemn places in Rome', and 'a mixture of tears and smiles, of stones and flowers, of mourning cypresses and radiant sky, which gives us the impression of our looking back at death from the brighter side of the grave':

> The cemetery nestles in an angle of the city wall, and the older graves
> are sheltered by a mass of ancient brickwork [...] Shelley's grave is

here, buried in roses – a happy grave every way for the very type and figure of the Poet. Nothing could be more impenetrably tranquil than this little corner in the bend of the protecting rampart, where a cluster of modern ashes is held tenderly in the rugged hand of the Past. The past is tremendously embodied in the hoary pyramid of Caius Cestius, which rises hard by, half within the wall and half without, cutting solidly into the solid blue of the sky and casting its pagan shadow upon the grass of English graves – that of Keats, among them – with the effect of poetic justice.[39]

The Protestant Cemetery was also embedded in the Victorian pictorial imagination, for J.M.W. Turner in 1833 had executed a watercolour of it that was published as the frontispiece to volume thirteen of John Murray's *Life and Works of Lord Byron*.[40] Consequently, Turner's image would have been known almost universally among what John Pemble in *The Mediterranean Passion* termed the 'travelling classes'.[41] In 1873 William Bell Scott painted companion watercolours depicting Keats's grave, in the Old Protestant Cemetery, and Shelley's, in the New Cemetery.[42] Furthermore, by the 1860s photographic views of the Protestant Cemetery were available from Robert Macpherson, James Anderson, and others commercial firms.

James treated Daisy's burial in only a few lines, mentioning that her grave was 'in an angle of the wall of imperial Rome, beneath the cypresses and the thick spring flowers', a description that might have suggested to readers that she had been buried not far from Shelley. Winterbourne took his final leave of Daisy, 'staring at the raw protuberance [of her grave] among the April daisies' (p. 67).

It has not been sufficiently emphasised that Daisy's name was correctly 'Annie P. Miller', as her odious young brother informed Winterbourne at the 'Trois Couronnes'. In retrospect, it is apparent that the name 'Daisy' was carefully chosen, for it links Miss Miller, thematically and symbolically, to several of the sites in which James placed her in his story. If Florence was 'a city planted in a garden',[43] then the Rome that Daisy inhabited was in large part a city of gardens. This was evidently the case with the Protestant Cemetery, but the Pincian and Palatine Hills and the Colosseum were also perceived in writings of the period to be, in some senses, pastoral settings. In 'Daisy Miller' James himself described the Palatine as 'that beautiful abode of flowering desolation known as the Palace of the Caesars' (p. 61). The Colosseum likewise was often described as if it were a work of nature rather than a construction by man, an Alpine valley encircled by towering mountains. The pastoral aspect of the area was also heightened by the profusion of flowers, plants, and trees that grew in the amphitheatre before its defoliation in the 1870s. Indeed, in some photographic views, as Szegedy-Maszak felicitously observes, 'the Colosseum resembles a *hortus conclusus*, an enclosed and enchanted garden that is set apart as a refuge from the agitation of daily life'. Expressed in these terms, it too was evidently an appropriate setting for a 'Daisy'.[44]

In America and in Great Britain during the nineteenth century, flowers came to provide a secret language that could be used for intimate forms of communication. This custom was codified in numerous books devoted to the subject, and it was given popular form in 1884 with the publication of a *Language of Flowers* illustrated with colour prints by Kate Greenaway, the author of children's stories.[45] In that volume the daisy is listed as signifying 'Innocence', precisely the quality that is for much of James's story in doubt with respect to Daisy. It was also the case that the daisy, or marguerite, was distinguished by its ability to flower in wintertime and by its 'eternal vigour', which enabled it to bloom 'even in the most inclement weather'.[46] These characteristics give it a nice appropriateness to Daisy and to Winterbourne. Daisy's blooming in Rome took place in winter and early spring. Furthermore, Winterbourne (Winterborn or Winter-borne), her absent admirer from Geneva came to her in Rome in winter.

Conclusion

This essay has been concerned essentially with what Henry Fox Talbot, the English inventor of negative-positive paper photography, termed, in a letter of 22 September 1849, 'a kind of *latent* picture'. My thesis has been that because James could reasonably presume that the sites he mentioned would be familiar to his readers, any literal description of them would have been superfluous. In essence, latent or 'sleeping' pictures, to adopt the poetic adjective employed by Sir John Herschel, of the Château de Chillon, the Pincio, St Peter's, the Palatine, the Colosseum, and the Protestant Cemetery pre-existed in the minds of James's readers, needing only to be agitated gently in 'exciting liquid', to borrow another of Talbot's terms, in order to be 'appear *spontaneously*'. In practice, James's subtle evocations of these sites served as an 'exciting liquid' that stirred these dormant images into wakefulness in receptive readers' minds.[47]

Notes

1. Henry James, 'Daisy Miller: A Study', Part I, *The Cornhill Magazine*, 37 (January to June 1878), 678–98; Part II, *The Cornhill Magazine*, 38 (July to December 1878), 44–67; hereafter in text.
2. On the publication history of 'Daisy Miller: A Study' and of 'Daisy Miller', see Philip Horne, 'Henry James at Work: the Question of Our Texts', in *The Cambridge Companion to Henry James*, ed. by Jonathan Freedman (Cambridge: Cambridge University Press, 1998), pp. 63–72.
3. Violet R. Dunbar, 'The Revision of Daisy Miller', *Modern Language Notes*, 65:5 (May 1950), 311–17.
4. Michael Lund, 'Henry James's Two Part Magazine Stories and "Daisy Miller"', *The Henry James Review*, 19 (1998), 126–38.
5. *The Italian Journal of Samuel Rogers*, ed. by John R. Hale (London: Faber and Faber 1956), p. 94.
6. 'Travel as Ritual' is the title of the second chapter in William W. Stowe's *Going Abroad: European Travel in Nineteenth-Century American Culture* (Princeton: Princeton University Press, 1994), pp. 16–28: 16, 19–21.
7. Goethe, *Italian Journey*, p. 129.
8. Henry James, *Letters*, ed. by Leon Edel, 4 vols (Cambridge, MA: The Belknap Press of Harvard University Press, 1974–84), I, 160.
9. Henry James, 'A Passionate Pilgrim', *The Atlantic Monthly*, 27 (March 1871), 352–71, and *The Atlantic Monthly* (April 1871), 478–99.
10. George Gordon, Lord Byron, *Byron, Complete Poetical Works* (Oxford: Oxford University Press, 1970), p. 336.
11. Henry James, 'Four Meetings', *Scribner's Monthly*, 15:1 (November 1877), 44–57.
12. This and the preceding passage are adapted from the chapter on Henry James in my book, *'Light that dances in the mind': Photographs and Memory in the Writings of E.M. Forster and his Contemporaries* (Oxford: Peter Lang, 2007), pp. 119–22.
13. A search of 'Photography Collections Online' at the George Eastman House, Rochester, produced: a calotype negative from 1852 by the Irish photographer John Shaw Smith; an albumen print from a collodion negative taken in September 1855 by the Irish photographer, Joscelyn Coghill and published in 'The Photographic Album for the Year 1857' together with the text of Byron's poem 'Prisoner of Chillon'; and two stereo cards from the 1860s, produced 'Under the Special Patronage of The Alpine Club by William England'. On Braun, see Maureen C. O'Brien and Mary Bergstein, *Image and Enterprise: the Photographs of Adolphe Braun* (New York: Thames & Hudson, 2000).
14. Reproduced in O'Brien and Bergstein, *Image and Enterprise*, p. 69; see also page 71 and notes.
15. O'Brien and Bergstein, *Image and Enterprise*, checklist 49, p. 54.
16. On this motif, see Jeffrey Meyers, 'Velásquez and "Daisy Miller"', *Studies in Short Fiction*, 16 (1979), 170–8.
17. On the sites of James's and Daisy Miller's Rome, see William L. Vance, *America's Rome*, 2 vols (New Haven and London: Yale University Press, 1989).
18. 'Crapy Cornelia', in *Henry James: Complete Stories 1898–1910* (New York: The Library of America, 1996), p. 839.

19. For the history of the Pincian Hill in the sixteenth century, see David R. Coffin, *The Villa in the Life of Renaissance Rome* (Princeton: Princeton University Press, 1979), pp. 215–38.

20. Quoted in Theodore E. Stebbins, *The Lure of Italy: American Artists and the Italian Experience 1760–1914* (Boston and New York: Museum of Fine Arts, Boston, and Abrams, 1992), p. 252.

21. Nathaniel Hawthorne, *The Marble Faun: or, the Romance of Monte Beni*, The Centenary Edition of the Works of Nathaniel Hawthorne, IV (Columbus: Ohio State University Press, 1968), 99.

22. Henry James, *Italian Hours* (New York: Penguin Books, 1995), pp. 183–5.

23. Andrew Szegedy-Maszak, 'Roman Views', in *Six Exposures: Essays in Celebration of the Opening of the Harrison D. Horblit Collection of Early Photography* (Cambridge, MA: The Houghton Library, Harvard University, 1999), pp. 89–106, figures 27–9.

24. One of these is reproduced in Stebbins, *The Lure of Italy*, p. 253.

25. James, *Italian Hours*, p. 183.

26. James, *Italian Hours*, p. 184.

27. James, *Italian Hours*, p. 134.

28. Vance, *America's Rome*, II, 98.

29. Henry James, *The Golden Bowl*, p. xlvii.

30. Vance, *America's Rome*, II, 80 and 96–100.

31. Andrew Szegedy-Maszak, 'A Perfect Ruin: Nineteenth-Century Views of the Colosseum', *Arion: A Journal of Humanities and the Classics*, 2:1 (1992), 115–42.

32. Szegedy-Maszak, 'A Perfect Ruin', p. 122.

33. Reproduced in *Imagining Rome: British Artists and Rome in the Nineteenth Century*, ed. by Michael Liversidge and Catharine Edwards (London: Merrell Holberton Publishers, 1996), p. 21.

34. *Marble Faun*, p. 153.

35. *Marble Faun*, pp. 154–5.

36. See also Jeffrey Meyers, ' "Daisy Miller" and the Romantic Poets', *The Henry James Review*, 28 (2007), 94–100.

37. *America's Rome*, I, 62.

38. Meyers, ' "Daisy Miller" and the Romantic Poets', p. 94.

39. James, *Italian Hours*, p. 172.

40. Reproduced in *Imagining Rome*, p. 80.

41. John Pemble, *The Mediterranean Passion* (Oxford: Clarendon Press, 1987), p. 1.

42. Reproduced in *Imagining Rome*, pp. 119–20.

43. For William Hazlitt's famous characterisation of Florence, which appeared in the *Morning Chronicle* in 1825, see Cecilia Powell, *Turner in the South: Rome, Naples, Florence* (New Haven and London, Yale University Press 1987), p. 92.

44. Szegedy-Masak, 'A Perfect Ruin', pp. 122 and 125.

45. Kate Greenaway, *Language of Flowers* (London: George Routledge and Sons, 1884). See also Robert Tyas, *The Language of Flowers: or, Floral Emblems of Thoughts, Feelings, and Sentiments* (New York: George Routledge and Sons, 1865); Henrietta Dumont, *The Language of Flowers: the Floral Offering: a Token of Affection and Esteem, Comprising the Language and Poetry of Flowers*

(Philadelphia: T. Bliss & Co., 1863); and Beverly Seaton, *The Language of Flowers: a History* (Charlottesville: University Press of Virginia, 1995).
46. See Sylvia Hunt, 'The Daisy and the Laurel: Myths of Desire and Creativity in the Poetry of Jean Froissart', *Yale French Studies*, 80 (1991), 246–9: 249.
47. For Talbot's first uses of these terms, see Larry J. Schaaf, *Out of the Shadows: Herschel, Talbot & the Invention of Photography* (New Haven and London: Yale University Press, 1992), p. 104.

7
A Modern Illustrated Magazine:
The Yellow Book's Poetics of Format

Lorraine Janzen Kooistra

> The writer's work is merely a kind of optical instrument which he offers to the reader to enable him to discern what, without this book, he would perhaps never have perceived in himself.
>
> (Marcel Proust)[1]

The Yellow Book is the most familiar of fin-de-siècle objects. Everybody knows its distinctive cover, its symbolic status as the epitome of decadent aesthetics, its association with scandal and the firing of art editor Aubrey Beardsley after Oscar Wilde was arrested while carrying a yellow-backed French novel, mistakenly thought to be a volume of the notorious periodical at the time.[2] Despite the brevity of its print run – the quarterly only appeared thirteen times between April 1894 and 1896 – *The Yellow Book* remains inextricably linked with the decade it coloured, 'the yellow nineties', and central to the study of fin-de-siècle literature and visual culture. However, as *The Yellow Book*'s contemporary creation, Sherlock Holmes, might have said, we have seen but not observed. The periodical has become strangely dematerialised, its critical afterlife concerned more with what it represents than what it is, its literary history restricted to a handful of extracted prose and art works. The significance of these pictures and texts as objects sequenced and stitched together in contiguous relationship within the printed pages of a bound book has gone largely unnoticed. If, as Matthew Arnold reminds us, the first aim of criticism is 'to see the object as in itself it really is',[3] what comes into our critical sights when we shift our optics to see *The Yellow Book* as the material object it is rather than the symbol it represents?

This chapter focuses on the physical features of format as a lens through which we can understand the uniqueness of what it is we see when we really look at *The Yellow Book* – when we hold the square octavo in our hands and turn its wove-paper pages. As I hope to demonstrate, the first volume of *The Yellow Book* self-consciously calls attention to itself as an object whose physical features must be read. Through its poetics of format Volume I directs readers to an organising thematics of looking, reading and performance – thematics, as we shall see, that deliberately extends beyond the printed pages of the bound book into the world of objects, makers and users. *The Yellow Book's* significance as a modern illustrated magazine lies in the way its contents are expressed in the editorial policies shaping its making and marketing and in the vehicular forms of its design. In what follows I argue that *The Yellow Book's* poetics of format requires a materialist hermeneutics attentive to the complex relations among image, text, book and world.[4]

When *The Yellow Book* set out to be a modern illustrated magazine it did so by establishing a distinctive format separating 'pictures' from 'letterpress', an editorial decision that must be viewed within the context of visual culture and publishing history. Painting and poetry had been identified as sister arts more remarkable for their similarities than their differences from classical times, with the palm given to poetry as the superior sister since at least the Middle Ages.[5] The Horatian maxim, *ut pictura poesis* – 'as is painting so is poetry' – reverberated through centuries of codex culture to reach a new apotheosis in nineteenth-century Britain. As Gerard Curtis and Richard Altick have shown, 'The relationship between the sister arts was never closer than in the mid-Victorian period', when a strong narrative tradition in the arts combined with technological advances to make the joining of image and text on the printed page seem a natural coupling.[6] In fact, the second half of the nineteenth century marks a significant shift in the history of visual culture – the moment in which picture and word entered the daily lives of ordinary people through the products of the illustrated press. Newspapers, periodicals, and books were multi-media events combining columns or lines of letterpress with inset or full-page black-and-white pictures. As time went on, vehicles of visuality – including the printed picture and the display of type – assumed greater importance in an increasingly image-centred world.[7]

By the end of the century, not only were more books than ever before being mass-produced in illustrated form, but a revival in printing and book design, and a new understanding of the book as an art form, resulted in the publication of beautiful limited editions at John Lane and Elkin Mathews' Sign of the Bodley Head. Designed by innovative book artists such as Charles Ricketts, Laurence Housman and Beardsley, Bodley Head books were produced to be beautiful objects catering to the contemporary craze for collecting first editions as prized for their physical features as their contents.[8] As Michael Hatt's chapter in this collection demonstrates, Ricketts' inspired design for John Gray's *Silverpoints* (John Lane and Elkin Mathews, 1893) marked a tour de force in the poetics of design, integrating typography, layout and the long, narrow 'saddle book' format to provide the vehicular structure for Gray's poetry. In the same year, Laurence Housman used a similarly elongated format to house the short lines of Christina Rossetti's *Goblin Market* for Macmillan; for The Bodley Head, Housman concentrated on the architectural, pictorial, and decorative details of bindings, title page, and frontispiece for Francis Thompson's *Poems*. One of the most beautiful of Bodley Head book designs was produced the following year by Beardsley for Oscar Wilde's *Salome*. Beardsley's elegant and distinctive cover design opened onto nine full-page illustrations in black-and-white that enacted a performative commentary on Wilde's poetic drama.[9]

The Bodley Head's Book Beautiful provides the context in which publisher John Lane and editors Henry Harland and Beardsley set out to redefine the illustrated magazine as established by Victorian publishing practice. It was John Lane's genius to connect the book-as-object to middle-class desire for cultural status by merging the features of the limited collectible with the techniques of mass communication. As Karl Beckson notes, Lane was able to market Bodley Head books 'to a wide public who still believed they were an artistic minority'.[10] When Henry Harland and Beardsley proposed themselves as joint editors of a new periodical in early 1894 John Lane enthusiastically agreed to support the venture.[11] Like the Belles Lettres series produced at The Bodley Head, *The Yellow Book* was targeted at consumers who wished to be seen as culturally *au courant* and who valued the display value and sensuous qualities of beautiful books. *Yellow Book* buyers were therefore encouraged 'to read every detail of its appearance as a sign of the manufacturers' commitment to actualizing an aesthetic ideal'.[12]

Linda Dowling has called *The Yellow Book* a 'proto-modernist periodical',[13] and the Prospectus issued in advance of the first volume in April 1894 certainly announced the intention to 'make it new':

> The aim of the Publishers and Editors of THE YELLOW BOOK is to depart as far as may be from the bad old traditions of periodical literature, and to provide an Illustrated Magazine which shall be beautiful as a piece of book-making, modern and distinguished in its letter-press and its pictures, and withal popular in the better

sense of the word. The pictures will in no case serve as illustrations to the letterpress, but each will stand by itself as an independent contribution.[14]

The Yellow Book, in short, was to be an illustrated magazine with no illustrations, a magazine that was no magazine – a beautiful book rather than an ephemeral periodical.

With its editorial policy that 'The pictures will in no case serve as illustrations to the letterpress, but each will stand by itself as an independent contribution', *The Yellow Book* set out to challenge the outmoded convention that gave the word supremacy and the image secondary, referential status. This toppling of the hierarchy by asserting the autonomy of the image was celebrated by Walter Sickert, who contributed two drawings to the inaugural *Yellow Book*: 'The Old Oxford Music Hall' (*Yellow Book*, Plate IV) and 'A Lady Reading' (*Yellow Book*, Plate XIII). At a dinner honouring the launch of Volume I Sickert gave a speech in which he 'looked forward to the day when authors would be compelled to write stories and poems around pictures'. According to Simon Houfe, 'that such a remark could be made at all shows the heights that illustrative art had attained in this gilded decade'.[15]

In fact, Sickert's toast reveals a startling ignorance of both nineteenth-century visual culture and *The Yellow Book's* modern challenge to the Victorian illustrated magazine. In addition to the ekphrastic tradition practiced in Shelley's poem on the Medusa, which evokes an art object invisible to the reader, many poems in the period were printed beside the reproduced art works they had been commissioned to describe.[16] Pictures had been 'written up' by poets in this way throughout the century, most frequently during the heyday of the literary annuals in the 1820s through 1850s, but also in the gift books and illustrated magazines that accompanied the emergence of wood-engraving as the dominant mode of pictorial reproduction at mid century.[17] By the 1890s, process engraving, in halftone and line, had become the principal means of mechanical reproduction, valued for its relative speed, cheapness and fidelity to the original. All of Beardsley's work as an artist was drawn in black-and-white for reproduction by process on the printed page. Even when it was not composed to accompany a specific literary text, his art is inextricably bound up with books, as evident in the Book Plate design (*Yellow Book*, Plate XIV) he selected to complete the volume.[18]

Beardsley's lifelong fascination with literature and art made the joint editorship of *The Yellow Book* an exciting opportunity for him to experiment with a new approach to visual/verbal relations focused more on connections developed spatially, temporally, and thematically than on correspondence. As art editor Beardsley was not after an inverted hierarchy of power relations for picture and word but – to use an expression from Canadian politics – a new kind of sovereignty association. *The Yellow Book*'s separation of the sister arts into 'letterpress' and 'pictures' emphasises that they are both objects to be read while simultaneously asserting the independent, non-referential and increasingly dominant status of the visual in the modern age of print culture – the age of the image.

The Yellow Book, in fact, was all about image in the modern sense of branding and marketing. From the pre-publication poster, prospectus, advertisements, interviews, and publicity dinner to the thing itself, the editors and their publisher were intent on making the periodical represent the bold and the modern rather than the staid and Victorian – to give it, in short, a public profile and persona, an *image*, in the popular imagination through the offices of the public press. They therefore cultivated the press on both sides of the Atlantic for extensive pre-release coverage and post-publication commentary. As the *National Observer*'s reviewer remarked of this 'star of modernity', 'Never was the way of a magazine made so plain before it as *The Yellow Book*'s: judicious advertisements planted and injudicious interviews watered'.[19] In an interview in *The Sketch* Harland and Beardsley declared, 'The time has come for an absolutely new era in the way of magazine literature [...] Distinction, modernness – these, probably, so nearly as they can be picked out, are the two leading features of our plan'.[20]

One way to achieve distinction and modernity was to be a *cause célèbre* – the focus of print coverage and conversation. The editors milked this for all it was worth in the Prospectus to Volume II, which contained excerpts (good and bad) from the press's reception of the first volume. They followed up on this strategy in Volume II itself with P.G. Hamerton's lengthy critique of the pictures and letterpress (or, as he preferred, art and literature) of Volume I. Given their modern view of the market value of publicity of all kinds, the editors must have been delighted when *The Westminster Gazette*'s review of Volume I called for 'a short Act of Parliament to make this kind of thing illegal' in response to two of Beardsley's pictures, 'Portrait of Mrs. Patrick Campbell' and 'L'Education Sentimentale'. The *Gazette*'s hysterical reception of Beardsley's artwork implicitly blends the notion of image as public profile with its other connotation of visual art. In so doing, its critique touches precisely on two of the most modern features of *The Yellow Book*: its insistence on the act of reading and interpretation as constitutive of all human/object relations, and its contestation of putative boundaries in art and life through its poetics of format.

The result, according to *The Spectator*'s critic, was 'an indigestible monster, half-book, half-magazine'.[21] While digestibility is always a matter for the individual palate and stomach to determine, *The Yellow Book* certainly did require consumers to adjust their taste to an offering that was neither fish nor fowl – neither book nor magazine. *The Yellow Book* may be viewed as a three-dimensional form of one of Beardsley's ubiquitous pictorial monsters, its hybrid body enacting a challenge to traditional expectations of permanent and ephemeral objects, popular and elite art, the relative values of pictures and words, and the roles of editors and readers. If the hybridity of a new artform is precisely the come-on the editors and their publisher were aiming for, its liminal market was materialised in the price stamped in black on its yellow bindings. As Laurel Brake points out, the 5 shilling price poised *The Yellow Book* 'between the periodical press and the book' at a time when quarterlies were becoming outdated:

> By this time in the century, when monthly reviews were selling for about 2 shillings to 2s. 6d, magazines for 1 shilling, and old (expensive) quarterlies for 6 shillings, the 5 shillings of *The Yellow Book* is toward the upper end of the market for periodicals. However, as a cloth bound *book*, it was priced at 1 shilling less than cloth bound, one-volume novels at 6 shillings. Neither the old quarterlies nor the one-volume novels were likely to be copiously illustrated, and if they were, neither the quality and quantity of their illustrations were likely to match those of *The Yellow Book*.[22]

With its high-quality illustrations, its cloth-covered format, its quarterly production and its pricing, *The Yellow Book* positioned itself in a niche market between books and periodicals, a market Harland and Beardsley hoped would appeal to contemporary consumers' collecting spirit. As Margaret Stetz comments, 'for a mere five shillings a copy, a middleclass consumer would supposedly enjoy cheap and immediate access to the world of collectibles, with all its upper-class associations'.[23]

Apart from the aesthetic and decadent associations conjured by the colour, the name chosen, '*Yellow* Book,' asserted the magazine's claim to permanence and its goal to be valued as an object worthy of purchase, preservation and display. As Beardsley explained in a press interview, 'The quarterly is to be a *book*, a thing to be put in the library just like any other volume, a *complete book*' (my italics).[24] The Prospectus to Volume I bore witness to this bibliographic aspiration of sight and touch, drawing attention to paper quality, typography and layout in a way typical of limited editions for collectors rather than of the ephemeral periodical for casual readers:

> In point of mechanical excellence THE YELLOW BOOK will be as nearly perfect as it can be made. The present announcement shows the size and shape of the paper (now being especially woven) on which it will be printed, as well as the type that will be used, and the proportion of text and margin. It will contain 256 pages, or over, and will be bound in limp yellow cloth.

As 'a book beautiful to see and convenient to handle' (Prospectus), *The Yellow Book*'s target audience extended beyond committed bibliophiles with an aesthetic passion for surrounding themselves with beautiful objects. With a 5000 copy print run in its first edition, it was hardly a limited issue even if its unusual design features displayed the deliberate appeal of the unique, the rare, and the beautiful to the collector. *The Yellow Book* set out to be 'popular in the better sense of the word' – that is, to appeal to the mass audience of periodical readers by being 'a book that will make book-lovers of many who are now indifferent to books' (Prospectus). The success in meeting this goal may be measured by the fact that the first edition of 5000 copies sold out within a week of publication and ongoing demand necessitated the release of a further three editions.[25]

As we have seen, some critics strongly objected to *The Yellow Book*'s deliberate confusion of the fields of restricted and large-scale cultural production.[26] The reviewer from the *Spectator* who opened his column with the vitriolic attack on *The Yellow Book*'s monstrosity went on to describe the cover design in compelling detail as evidence for his claim (Plate 10):

> All that this literary cackling [i.e., the advance advertising] has produced is a jaundiced-looking, indigestible monster, half-book, half-magazine, its contents indicated on its cover by a comic muse who surely represents the buffoonery of farce rather than the delicate humour of genuine comedy, and a tragic muse with alert eyes and blubber lips, while the sacred fire that was to illuminate and dazzle the world is curtailed to the modest proportion of a guttering candle.[27]

What the critic fails to notice is that his review performs precisely the kind of reading deliberately invoked by *The Yellow Book*'s distinctive format. To begin with, his critique opens in a reversal of the usual procedures of book-reviewing practice with a sustained commentary on the cover, thus upsetting time-honoured hierarchies of value and priority in the world of print culture. Secondly, by giving the features of the design such close attention, the critic implicitly admits that *The Yellow Book* must be assessed as an object whose material features contribute to its meaning: that one must, in fact, 'judge a book by its cover'. This is just what Beardsley and Harland are after in their identification of the object – a bright yellow and black square octavo – with its name and nature. And thirdly, by analysing the cover's visual/verbal relations, the critic engages in precisely the kind of materialist hermeneutics this 'magazine book' requires.

Beardsley designed the back cover to announce *The Yellow Book*'s new relation of picture and word by merging the two contents pages (printed separately inside the magazine) into a single layout in which 'Letterpress' and 'Pictures' are divided by a lighted candle, a motif that recurs throughout the volume (Plate 11). A visual pun on the concept of 'illumination' that resides within the meaning of 'illustration', the candle throws some light on the periodical's deliberate division of picture and word. The candlestick literally draws the line between them in order to assert both their independence and their contiguity. Separate but joined, picture and text appear as visual objects on the printed pages of a bound volume whose poetics of format enact its meanings. To emphasise the performative – and, hence, arbitrary and playful – nature of the volume's letterpress and pictures, Beardsley presents the list of contents as a playbill under a curtained stage or window featuring a Harlequin flanked by two women in large hats. The repeating motifs of candle, hatted women and costumed men, link the front and back cover designs with the contents they introduce. Taken together, the bindings emphasise the volume's organising themes of looking, reading and performance. Inside the volume, Beardsley rings the changes on these themes by manipulating pictorial selections, visual motifs, and image/text sequences.

Beardsley elaborates on the editorial plan announced by the bindings in his decorated title page, which immediately follows the two Contents pages that initiate the volume (Plate 12). Reading in the usual left-to-right progression, we can see that the pictorial vignette squeezes the verbal matter into a vertical column, thus neatly dividing the page between image and text and emphasising the visual quality of lines of type. As so often happens with both Beardsley's own designs and the pictures by other artists he places before and after the volume's stories, poems and essays, the title-page image is connected to the typeset words by the self-reflexive figuration of a look. The woman playing a piano in a windy field looks at neither the keyboard she plays on nor the landscape she stands in. Rather, she looks past a candlestick and across the barrier of the frame to the lines of title and publishing information – out of the pictorial world she inhabits and into the 'alphabetic textuality'[28] of print culture with which she is inextricably linked. The picture does not illustrate the text displayed on the same page in any traditionally referential way, and in this sense it is an autonomous work of art. At the same time, however, the title-page vignette, by virtue of its status as a printed object in a bound book, has an associative and relational connection to the letterpress it accompanies and introduces. Moreover, the vignette is clearly illustrative in terms of its artistic style and subject matter, implying a story that the reader must discern from its pictorial features and its textual context, but without reference to any immediate narrative.

Beardsley did, however, provide a fictitious source for the image in one of the many para-texts to *The Yellow Book* circulating in the popular press. In a high-spirited letter to *The Pall Mall Budget* written in response to the many objections he had received, 'both by the Press and by private persons, to my title-page of *The Yellow Book*', the artist offered the following ground for the title-page figure:

> Christopher Willibald Ritter von Gluck, in order to warm his imagination and to transport himself to Aulis or Sparta, was accustomed to place himself in the middle of a field. In this situation, with his piano before him, and a bottle of champagne on each side, he wrote in the open air his two *Iphigenias,* his *Orpheus,* and some other works. I tremble to think what critics would say had I introduced those bottles of champagne. And yet we do not call Gluck a *decadent.*[29]

Beardsley's invention of an imaginary composer's eccentricities as ground for his design is both a comic and a self-promoting intervention into the popular press and its readership. While mocking the notion that art imitates life in any uncomplicated way Beardsley simultaneously draws attention not only to his own artistic work and the book it introduces, but also to the columns of printer's ink it has occasioned in editorial columns, critical reviews, and readers' letters. Like the Prospectus, this letter in a popular newspaper functions as an advertisement for an innovative illustrated magazine, one whose appeal to touch and sight requires a new kind of handling and a new kind of looking and reading.

Like the cover designs, the title-page is a practical application of *The Yellow Book*'s modern theory of visual/verbal relations. It asserts distinct, non-referential identities, giving the image equal status with the word, while working with larger associations, both intra- and extra-textual, common to both. This editorial approach guides the structure and format of the volume itself. Printing each image on special art paper suitable to high quality reproduction by process engraving,[30] Volume I alternates pictures and letterpress to form a sequence that self-reflexively comments on its thematic concerns and editorial priorities. In each case the image is doubly separated from the verbal text by two intervening pages: a half-title page identifying the artist, the title of the work, and the engraver; and a tissue-paper guard that protects the process engraving itself. The significance of the independent image is reinforced by an artful sequencing of picture and letterpress that is incorporated in the poetics of format adumbrated by Volume I as a whole.

William Watson, a reluctant and somewhat staid contributor to *The Yellow Book*, complained to John Lane that Volume I had 'no "editing" apparent at all – nothing but the mere fortuitous raking together of a number of heterogeneous items, having no unity or community or cohesion or bond of any kind'.[31] In fact, the editing was both invisible and in plain view – unapparent, perhaps, to those with traditional expectations, but available to anyone looking at *The Yellow Book* steadily and seeing it whole. After all the verbiage that preceded its publication in advertisements, interviews, and press releases, Volume I of *The Yellow Book* makes its argument for being a 'new Illustrated Magazine' entirely visually, in the material features of its format. The pictorial statements made by the decorative bindings and title page are immediately followed by the first full-page plate, the frontispiece by Sir Frederic Leighton entitled 'A Study' (Plate 13). Located immediately after the title page and just before the magazine's first story, the frontispiece acts in place of the missing Editorial Introduction one would normally expect to see in this location, particularly in the first volume of a new magazine.

Nothing could be farther, in artistic style and pictorial impact, than Beardsley's title-page design and the picture he chose for the frontispiece. As the President of the Royal Academy and a peer, Sir Frederick Leighton's appearance as the introductory artist in the aggressively modern magazine may seem strange. In fact, Beardsley chose to represent Leighton in two of the fifteen pictures for the inaugural *Yellow Book*, strategically placing them at the opening and mid-way point

(*Yellow Book*, Plates I and VII) of the volume. Leighton's contributions, both studies for future paintings – 'fine art' rather than the illustrative, poster-style art of Beardsley – also seem out of place on first blush.[32] However, the sequencing of the pictures and letterpress reflects the editors' plan to balance the traditional and the new. Just as Leighton's frontispiece is connected to Beardsley's title-page design through immediate proximity, his second picture is carefully positioned between works from the hands of each editor. Beardsley's atmospheric 'Night Piece' (*Yellow Book*, Plate VI) is the visual text that immediately precedes Leighton's second 'Study' (*Yellow Book*, Plate VII), which in turn introduces Harland's contribution, 'Two Sketches' (135–48). Positioned at the heart of Volume I, Leigton's second study is a rapid life drawing of a female and male dancer emphasising movement. Significantly, the title for the two prose pieces by *The Yellow Book*'s literary editor draws on visual culture for its effect. Like Leighton's study, Harland's sketches are rapidly drawn evocations taken from life: the first, an autobiographical glimpse of a child and his performing theatre of white mice; the second, the story of an old man who dies remembering his lost love. As in Leighton's study, Harland's emphasis is on capturing the moment's intensity, in all its movement and emotional charge.

In contrast to Leighton's life drawing study at the volume's centre, the frontispiece is a study from the antique, focusing not on movement but on stasis. A classical study of draperies on two human forms, the drawing shows a foreground figure in profile facing left, and a background figure facing full front (Plate 13). Beardsley's selection of Leighton's study of draperies for the frontispiece image is crucial to understanding how the poetics of format work in *The Yellow Book* – physically, visually and hermeneutically. As the eye reads from left to right and the hand turns back the right-hand corner to reveal the next page, there is a momentary glimpse of the draped figure at left of the frontispiece facing the piano-player of the title page, whose image lingers on the reader's retina. This visual juxtaposition of pose and figure implies association, an association that insists on a counterpoint between new and old, avant-garde and traditional. It is also significant that the principal draped figure of the frontispiece has its back to the story that begins after the next page turn: Henry James' 'The Death of the Lion' (7–52). The other draped figure of the frontispiece is sightless and featureless, holding an admonitory finger up to invisible lips in a ghostly, undrawn face. In the narrative context of James' story, the two draped figures of Leighton's chalk study perform a kind of valedictory inviting mourning for the death described in the ensuing pages.

Significantly, the first story of Volume I focuses on the death of an author in the modern world of the interview and the new journalism, precisely the world that *The Yellow Book* editors manipulated in their aggressive creation of an image in the popular press through advertisements, interviews and letters to the editor.[33] Volume I artfully juxtaposes the work of its two most lionised artistic and literary contributors, Leighton and James, in its lead pieces as a means of increasing *The Yellow Book*'s own celebrity. But as the opening text, James' 'The Death of the Lion' also functions as a touchstone for the thematics bound up in the volume's physical features and the editorial policies implicit in them but not stated in any textual introduction.

Identifying the literary contents as 'letterpress' is, of course, itself a way of decentring the authorial word (if not killing the author) by suggesting that text is a verbal object displayed in visual form, the outcome of social and material processes. In fact, the design of *The Yellow Book* paid a very modern attention to the look of the page, deploying a generous amount of white space in the header, margins and footer, as well as between the lines of the clean and elegant Caslon old-face type selected for printing, using a dropped, asymmetrical title placement and byline, and beginning the first line with a dropped initial capital. The catchword at the bottom of each page is a typographical feature coming out of the fine-printing revival, probably inspired by Charles Ricketts' use of it in his designs for Bodley Head books like Oscar Wilde's *The Sphinx* (1894). It therefore represents a design feature calculated to make the page itself an object of beauty and rarity desirable to collectors. But the catchword also has a role to play in the materiality of the reading experience itself. It calls attention to the fact that the text has been displayed in type, that the story has been assembled on folded leaves of paper in a printed book, that the words on the page have no meaning without the mediation of human bodies.[34] Positioned at the extreme bottom of the page, flush right under the last line, the catchword directs the necessary choreography between eye and hand. As the eye travels down the text, the hand hovers at the right-hand corner, ready to turn the page so that the reader loses neither syntax nor semantics in the momentary blur. As both the last word read on one page and the first read on the next, the catchword catches the eye and throws it forward over the page turn to achieve an uninterrupted reading experience, a mental continuity that overrides movement and change to produce an ongoing pleasure of the text.

Significantly for the social and material processes we are considering, the author in this particular case, Henry James, played a role in the editors' policy of keeping text and image separate. Beardsley and Harland were very aware that their innovative approach to the illustrated magazine would be an incentive to James to include his work in *The Yellow Book*.[35] Concerned that Victorian illustration practices had a negative effect on the future of writing, James would not have been keen to publish in a periodical in which commissioned artists illustrated a writer's words with representational pictures. According to Charles Harmon, James feared 'that the illustration of books and literary magazines had become, at the fin de siècle, 'part [...] of an increasingly visually oriented system' that seemed 'designed to relieve writers of the duty of making strong appeals to readers' through words alone.[36] In fact, as Harmon goes on to point out, early twentieth-century literature – modern literature – is distinguished not by being overwhelmed by pictures, but rather 'by the near-absolute absence of illustration', and by the stark emphasis on clean typography, good paper, and good binding.[37] While *The Yellow Book's* commitment to including pictures connects it to the visual/verbal interests of the nineteenth century, its insistence on the autonomy of the image and its deployment of a poetics of format link it more closely to the modern approach of the twentieth.

Beardsley's 'L'Education Sentimentale' immediately follows James' 'The Death of the Lion' and provides another example of *The Yellow Book's* distinctive poetics of format (Plate 14). Described by Kenneth Clark as 'the archetypal Beardsley drawing' focusing on corruption, the figures in this picture are often identified as an aging Madam educating a young but already knowing ingénue.[38] Reading a book she holds in her right hand, the large woman in a flamboyant hat seems barely present, her form traced by the lightest of lines. In contrast, her companion stands out in the solid black shapes formed by the cut of her evening dress and her masses of hair. Both figures appear to be standing on a curtained stage, thus connecting the composition to the volume's thematics of performance, reading and looking. These thematics, moreover, extend into the world of objects and people outside the yellow bindings that contain Beardsley's image. While the scene invites a variety of possible narratives, its caption actually makes an explicit extra-textual allusion to Flaubert's 1869 work of the same title. Flaubert's story focuses on a young countryman coming of age in Paris who misses every opportunity that comes his way. The juxtaposition of this picture and its allusive title with 'The Death of the Lion' effects a retrospective pictorial commentary on Henry James' story. From the ironic perspective of 'L'Education Sentimentale', 'The Death of the Lion' may be viewed as the tale of a countryman, the author Neil Paraday, whose sojourn in London destroys him and his work precisely because he cannot escape the opportunities that overwhelm him. The connecting link is, of course, the book that features so prominently in both James' story and Beardsley's subsequent picture, and the figuration, once again, of the acts of looking and reading.

This self-reflexive commentary is not only elaborated throughout Volume I but is also signalled in the para-textual Prospectus that heralded it. Beardsley's cover design for the Prospectus depicts an elegant urban woman in black gloves and feathered hat, standing alone at night outside a bookseller's shop while the proprietor, in the costume of Pierrot, observes her riffle through his bin of discounted books (Plate 15). Said to be a parodic representation of the dour Elkin Mathews, who maintained a dim view of *The Yellow Book* during his short association with it,[39] the Pierrot of the Prospectus also connects to the harlequin figure on Volume I's back cover, where he appears flanked by two women, and to Beardsley's Book Plate design in the volume itself.[40] With Mathews of The Bodley Head in the doorway, and *The Yellow Book* on offer inside, the cover design of the Prospectus draws attention to its editors' concern for prestige and posterity, a concern evident in the pre-publication publicity, in the claims to permanence and beauty manifested by the material object, and in the themes and motifs repeated throughout the selections of Volume I. In Fred Simpson's 'The Dedication', for example (159–84), the character Harold Sekbourne apostrophises his first book in a way that seems deliberately invoked by Beardsley's design for the Prospectus:

> Will you one day adorn the shelves of libraries, figure in catalogues of 'Rare book and first editions', and be contended for by snuffy, long-clothed bibliomaniacs, who will bid one against the other for the honour of possessing you? Or will you descend to the tables of secondhand book-stalls marked at a great reduction; or lie in a heap, with other lumber, outside the shop-front, all this lot sixpence each, awaiting there, uncared for, unnoticed, and unknown, your ultimate destination, the dust-hole? (163)

Far from lying in a heap in a book-seller's discount bin, *The Yellow Book* did indeed become the prized object of collectors. Catalogued in lists of first-editions and contended for by bibliomaniacs around the world, its thirteen distinctive yellow-and-black spines line up on shelves in rare books rooms and private libraries alike. But *The Yellow Book* was also an immediately valued commodity for the contemporary middle-class consumer of the 1890s who wished to acquire an object beautiful to the touch and appealing to the sight, an object that would also confer on its owner a reputation for being in the forefront of culture. For just as assiduously as *The Yellow Book* cultivated an image for itself, it promised an image for its owner.

The Yellow Book's separation of letterpress and pictures into two distinct and ostensibly unrelated categories does much, much, more than assert their equal value and importance and their non-referential relationship. Like Dr Johnson's metaphysical conceit, the heterogeneous picture and letterpress are yoked by violence – or at least, by stitching and book glue – together. As art editor, Beardsley selects and sequences the pictures in such a way that they work in a poetic relationship with each other and with the verbal texts they are interleaved among. Meaning in the 'complete book' that is Volume I depends on the connections between form and content and develops, as it does in a poem, by association and juxtaposition, allusion and symbol, image and figure, and, above all, by repetition and a musical rhythm of alternation. That alternation of duration and pacing is achieved visually and sensually by the regular sequencing of picture, story, poem, and picture. In this poetics of format, the visual and the verbal are connected by repeating motifs like those of looking, reading, and performing, as well as by the constant reminder that every object, in art as in life, is a composition that demands to be read.

Notes

1. Marcel Proust, *Time Regained*, trans. Andreas Mayor (London: Chatto & Windus, 1970), p. 283 ('En réalité, chaque lecteur est, quand il lit, le propre lecteur de soi-même. L'ouvrage de l'écrivain n'est qu'une espèce d'instrument optique qu'il offre au lecteur afin de lui permettre de discerner ce que, sans ce livre, il n'eut peut-être pas vu en soi-même', *A la recherche du temps perdu*, 3 vols, ed. by Pierre Clarac and André Ferré. Bibliothèque de la Pléiade. Paris: Gallimard, 1954, III, 911)
2. Although Oscar Wilde's work was never published in *The Yellow Book*, some of the periodical's contributors and public deemed Beardsley's decadent art guilty by association and publisher John Lane was forced to fire his art editor.
3. Matthew Arnold, 'The Function of Criticism at the Present Time', *The Complete Works of Matthew Arnold*, III, 258.
4. I am indebted to Jerome J. McGann's approach to materialist hermeneutics as described in *The Textual Condition* (Princeton: Princeton University Press, 1991).

5. See Henryk Markiewicz, 'Ut Pictura Poesis... A History of the Topos and the Problem', *New Literary History*, 18:3 (1987), 535–58, who surveys the tradition and its counter discourse from classical times through to the end of the nineteenth century.

6. Gerard Curtis, *Visual Words: Art and The Material Book in Victorian England* (Aldershot: Ashgate, 2002), p. 118; Richard Altick, *Paintings from Books: Art and Literature in Britain, 1760–1900* (Columbus: Ohio University Press, 1985), p. 57.

7. See Herbert Tucker, 'Literal Illustration in Victorian Print', in Maxwell, *Victorian Illustrated Book*, pp. 163–208, and Kate Flint, *The Victorians and the Visual Imagination* (Cambridge: Cambridge University Press, 2000).

8. See James G. Nelson, *The Early Nineties: a View from the Bodley Head* (Cambridge: Harvard University Press 1971), chapter 3.

9. For an extended analysis of Beardsley's illustrations in relation to Wilde's *Salome*, see chapter 5 in Lorraine Janzen Kooistra, *The Artist as Critic: Bitextuality in Fin-de-Siècle Illustrated Books* (Aldershot: Scolar, 1995).

10. Karl Beckson, ed., *Aesthetes and Decadents of the 1890s: an Anthology of British Poetry and Prose* (Chicago: Academy Chicago Publishers, 1993), p. 7.

11. Nelson, *The Early Nineties*, p. 298.

12. Margaret Stetz and Mark Samuels Lasner, *The Yellow Book: a Centenary Exhibition* (Cambridge: The Houghton Library 1994), p. 8.

13. Linda Dowling, 'Letterpress and Picture in the Literary Periodicals of the 1890s', *Yearbook of English Studies*, 16 (1986), 117–31.

14. Throughout this chapter I quote from the Prospectus to Volume I of *The Yellow Book* held in the miscellaneous printed matter of the John Lane Company Archives in the Harry Ransom Humanities Research Centre at the University of Texas at Austin.

15. Sickert's anecdote is recorded in Karl Beckson, *Henry Harland: His Life & Work*, and quoted in Simon Houfe, *Fin de Siècle: the Illustrators of the Nineties* (London: Barrie & Jenkins, 1992), p. 87.

16. For an enlightening examination of Shelley's Medusa within the ekphrastic genre, see Sophie Thomas's essay in this volume.

17. For an introductory overview of pictures and poems in Victorian annuals and books, see my article on 'Poetry and Illustration', in Richard Cronin, Alison Chapman and Antony H. Harrison, eds, *A Companion to Victorian Poetry* (Oxford: Blackwell, 2002), pp. 392–418.

18. Beardsley's Book Plate design for John Lumsden Propert (*Yellow Book*, Plate XIV) appears on the same page as Robert Anning Bell's Book Plate design for Matt Gosset (*Yellow Book*, Plate XV).

19. Review of *The Yellow Book*, Vol. I, *National Observer* (21 April 1894), 588–80.

20. Qtd. in '*The Yellow Book*', *Critic*, 5 (May 1894), 301.

21. Review of *The Yellow Book*, Vol. I, *Spectator*, 19 (1894), 695.

22. Laurel Brake, 'Endgames: The Politics of *The Yellow Book* or, Decadence, Gender and the New Journalism', *Essays and Studies*, 48 (1995), 38–64:60.

23. Stetz and Lasner, *The Yellow Book*, p. 9.

24. '*The Yellow Book*', *Critic* (5 May 1894), 301.

25. Stetz and Lasner, *The Yellow Book*, p. 11.

26. I draw on Pierre Bourdieu's explanation of these fields in 'The Market of Symbolic Goods', in D.H. Richter, ed., *The Critical Tradition: Classic Texts and Contemporary Trends* (Boston: Bedford, 1998), pp. 1232–53.
27. Review of *The Yellow Book,* Vol. I, *Spectator,* 19 (1894), 695.
28. Tucker, 'Literal Illustration', 166.
29. Letter to the Editor of the *Pall Mall Budget,* dated 3 May 1894, in *The Letters of Aubrey Beardsley,* ed. by Henry Maas, J.L. Duncan and W.G. Good (Rutherford: Fairleigh Dickinson University Press, 1979), p. 68.
30. See Harland's letter to Lane, early April 1894: '[Joseph Pennell] says, by our system of printing each picture separately on art-paper we will get results far and away better than those of any other periodical', in '*The Yellow Book* and Beyond: Selected Letters of Henry Harland to John Lane', ed. by Karl Beckson and Mark Samuels Lasner, *English Literature in Transition (1880–1920),* 42:4 (1999), 406.
31. William Watson to John Lane, May 20 [1894], Box 52, Folder 3, Letters from William Watson, 1892–1894, in the John Lane Company Records, Harry Ransom Humanities Research Centre, University of Texas at Austin.
32. On this point, see Linda Dowling's illuminating discussion of commercial versus fine art.
33. For an excellent analysis of *The Yellow Book* in relation to the new journalism see Brake, 'Endgames', 38–64.
34. See Dowling, 'Letterpress and Picture in the Literary Periodicals of the 1890s', pp. 125–8 and A.J.A. Symons, 'An Unacknowledged Movement in Fine Printing: the Typography of the Eighteen-Nineties', *Fleuron* (1930), 83–119:101.
35. Katherine Lyon Mix, *A Study in Yellow: the Yellow Book and Its Contributors* (Lawrence: University of Kansas Press, 1960), p. 73.
36. See also Graham Smith's discussion of James' attitude to illustration in his chapter in this collection.
37. Charles Harmon, 'Alvin Langdon Coburn's Frontispieces to Henry James's New York Edition: Pictures of an Institutional Imaginary', in Maxwell, ed., *The Victorian Illustrated Book,* p. 298.
38. Kenneth Clark, *The Best of Aubrey Beardsley* (New York: Doubleday, 1978), p. 106.
39. Clark, *The Best of Aubrey Beardsley,* p. 104. Elkin Mathews dissolved his partnership with John Lane after Harland and Beardsley failed to invite him to the dinner the editors hosted for the contributors to the first volume of *The Yellow Book* in spring 1894 (Nelson, *The Early Nineties,* p. 271).
40. The Book Plate design features a woman in profile, wearing an elaborate black dress with lacy flounces; in the foreground, a ruffed harlequin, who appears to be the same figure depicted on the back cover of *The Yellow Book,* prays before a lighted candle.

Part IV
Precious Objects

8
Dandyism, Visuality and the 'Camp Gem': Collections of Jewels in Huysmans and Wilde

Victoria Mills

> I love this word decadent – all shimmering in purple and gold
> [...] it throws off bursts of fire and the sparkle of precious
> stones.[1]

Paul Verlaine uses the optical and opulent qualities of jewels as an image of literary decadence.[2] Jewels appear in the work of a range of fin-de-siècle authors including Henry James, Arthur Symons, Oscar Wilde and Joris Karl Huysmans, where they represent luxury, strangeness and desire, often in relation to aspects of male subjectivity.[3] Walter Pater's exhortation 'to burn always with this hard, gem-like flame' also suggests the role of jewels in late nineteenth-century aestheticism.[4] Critical attention to the symbolism of jewels in Victorian fiction has so far focused on women: Dorothea's bracelets and cameos, Gwendolen Harleth's necklace, and Lizzie Eustace's diamonds.[5] In contrast, this article foregrounds the relationship between men and jewels as represented in Huysmans' *Against Nature* (1884) read alongside Wilde's *Picture of Dorian Gray* (1890).[6]

According to British comedian and writer Kenneth Williams, 'Camp is a great jewel, 22 carats'. Fabio Cleto extends the metaphor to define 'camp as diamond'.[7] The gem functions as a way of thinking about queer visuality. Cleto explores definitions of camp by listing gemmological properties that include multifacetedness (the many faces of camp), a susceptibility for falsification (the need for a discerning eye in order to detect camp), instability and excess (camp's resistance to definition, its semiotic excess), the ability to refract and reflect (camp's ability to distort), and the capacity for refinement (the critical *'carving'* of camp).[8] Ideas relating to camp remain important in my use of the gem metaphor. Indeed, the triangulation of camp, jewel and visuality is suggestive of the triangular facets of a diamond. However, I also foreground other properties of the jewel, including brilliance, transparency and opacity, the relationship between surface and substance, and the capacity to inflame desire. These properties characterise the representation of jewels and the way they are experienced in the visual worlds of Des Esseintes, the anti-hero of Huysmans' *Against Nature*, and of Dorian Gray.[9]

I begin with an examination of the dissident collecting practice of Dorian Gray and Des Esseintes. In the depiction of their house-museums, the gem (in particular the diamond) is a metaphor for queer visuality. Secondly, I explore acts of reading, writing, viewing, and collecting in Wilde and Huysmans. Both authors use the form of the catalogue to represent jewels and both are interested in lapidary language, which is particularly prominent in Huysmans' ekphrastic depictions of Gustave Moreau's 'Salomé' paintings. Finally, I examine the visual qualities of the gem as a symbol of a dandy's identity. In Wilde and Huysmans, collections of jewels have a particular symbolism; they mediate transpositions between different art forms, gender identities, and subject/object relations.

Queering the collection

> I remember so well how, with a strange smile on his pale, curved lips, he led me through his wonderful picture gallery, showed me his tapestries, his enamels, his jewels, his carved ivories, made me wonder at the strange loveliness of the luxury in which he lived.[10]

Baron Arnheim's striking collection in *An Ideal Husband* (1895) exhibits the Victorian collector's insatiable appetite for acquisition. 'Strange loveliness' also characterises the collections of the dandy, who lives through and by objects. Loveliness, or an aesthetic ideal, can be 'differenced'. Recent studies of contemporary collecting have emphasised the gendered nature of collecting, which 'may not be limited to expressing the dichotomy of male and female biological sex or the socially prescribed masculine and feminine gender roles pertaining to a culture and time period'.[11] Theories of collecting that sideline women have also come under attack. For instance, Naomi Schor challenges the phallocentrism inherent in Jean Baudrillard's theory of collecting: 'lacking the phallus', women 'cannot collect'.[12] In this essay, I show how the collections of

Dorian Gray and Des Esseintes undermine models of collecting based on the heterosexual male.

It has become a critical commonplace to talk about the instability of gender identity at the fin de siècle. Recent work rightly insists on a variety of identity positions available to men,[13] but few have looked at the discourse of collecting or taken an object-orientated perspective as a way into these debates.[14] For both Huysmans and Wilde collecting plays a central role in the figuring of gender identities linked to dandyism. Whitney Davis shows that there were a number of nineteenth-century collectors interested in homoerotic art. John Addington Symonds described Lord Ronald Sutherland Gower's collection as 'saturated in urningham' and Edward Perry Warren furnished Lewes House in Sussex with a collection of bronzes, vases, and carved gems with homosexual motifs.[15]

But 'queer collecting' defines the 'queer reception of visual material', rather than collections of objects linked to a particular sexual orientation.[16] For instance, Des Esseintes and Dorian Gray reject those collections that could be found in the typical bourgeois male household (insects, stamps, coins) and prefer gender-bending accumulations of flowers, jewels, perfumes and textiles. Such objects participate in the creation of 'new life narratives' by single male occupants who dedicate their lives to the pursuit of pleasures that disregard 'reproductive time'.[17] 'In opposition to the institutions of family, heterosexuality, and reproduction', their collections articulate 'alternative relations to time and space'.[18] In other words, they participate in a 'queer phenomenology', a term Sara Ahmed uses to address questions of orientation towards objects in space. Her analysis of disorientations in the arrangement of things and between objects and the body has interesting implications for the study of collecting.[19] For Des Esseintes this disorientation is deliberate. In a purposeful attempt to create a queer space, his dining room resembles a ship's cabin and it contains an organ which dispenses liqueurs instead of music from its stops.[20] Yet neither Des Esseintes nor Dorian Gray collect objects that are explicitly homoerotic. As I will go on to argue, their collecting of jewels suggests a way of 'seeing things differently'. Their ocular perspective on the gem constructs non-conventional forms of male identity.[21]

The house-museums of Des Esseintes and Dorian Gray foreground and problematise the visual economy of the collector's gaze. In the Victorian period, the dominant discourse on collecting privileged a scientific mode of seeing based on classification and systematic ordering.[22] Wilde makes it clear that such a model no longer prevails via a derogatory reference to the dull Duke of Monmouth who bores the company with a description of 'the last Brazilian beetle that he had added to his collection'.[23] Rejecting traditional, entomological collections like Camden Farebrother's in *Middlemarch* (1871), Dorian's collection has to appeal to his sense of beauty and satisfy his appetite for 'strange loveliness'.[24] The novel engages in what Regenia Gagnier has called a 'protest against [...] scientific factuality' with its insistence on a reductive single world view.[25] Both Huysmans and Wilde use collecting to show modes of seeing that are as multiple and multifaceted as gems. In their house-museums, rules of classification are not imposed from outside, the authentic is not always privileged over the inauthentic, and curatorial imperatives are motivated by desire.

Aspects of the gem as a model for queer visuality emerge in chapter four of *Against Nature*, in which Des Esseintes takes us through a catalogue of jewels, all possible candidates for the camp adornment of his tortoise. Refinement, refraction, multifacetedness, and the potential for falsification are all critical to Des Esseintes' discerning eye. His inspection emulates the act of carving, in which facets of a gem emerge out of a process of *refinement*. His view *refracts* the traditional point of view of the gemmologist: going against traditional criteria, Des Esseintes rejects highly prized jewels.[26] Rubies and emeralds evoke a sullying association with modernity, because they are 'too much like the green and red eyes of certain omnibuses'; diamonds conjure the common tradesman who 'sports one on his little finger', while topazes are suggestive of tawdry jewel cases stored in the cheap mirrored wardrobes of the middle classes (p. 36). In his view, the association of jewels with bourgeois consumerism has led to their falsification. Instead of diamonds, rubies, sapphires, he chooses chrysobels, peridots, olivines, almandines, ouvarovites – jewels both artificial and real, whose names conjure strangeness. Chosen for their 'more unusual, more bizarre qualities' (p. 37), Des Esseintes' fake jewels form part of a larger parodic collection, which includes flowers and perfumes. These choices destabilise stereotypically gendered collecting as well as the authentic/inauthentic binary.[27] In a nod to the multiple visual possibilities suggested by the multifacetedness of the gem, Des Esseintes chooses a mixture of opaque and transparent stones. Yet, rather than standing for straightforward clearness, transparency here suggests a more refracted, deviant quality. The cymophanes and sappharines glint 'with morbid, vitreous, lights' and emit 'mysterious and perverse scintillations'. The cat's eyes are 'striped with concentric veins that constantly appear to shift and change position, depending on the way the light falls'. Opacity is provided by western turquoises 'whose blue-green is clogged, opaque, sulphurous, as though yellowed with bile' (p. 37). In viewing Des Esseintes's jewel collection we are 'down the rabbit hole',[28] where nothing is as it seems and the boundaries between transparent and opaque, artificial and real are distorted. This deliberate distortion suggests a different way of seeing and 'being in the world'.[29]

Des Esseintes' decadent collecting is associated with a perversion of the natural order. Emblematic of such perversion is the artistic overload which causes the death of Des Esseintes' tortoise as a result of its encrustation with jewels. The optical excess of the collector's desiring gaze is also evident in the *crescendo* with which Wilde presents the catalogue of jewels in chapter eleven of *The Picture of Dorian Gray*:

> On one occasion he took up the study of jewels [...] This taste enthralled him for years, and, indeed, may be said never to have left him. He would often spend a whole day settling and resetting in their cases the various stones that he had collected [...] He loved the red gold of the sunstone, and the moonstone's pearly whiteness, and the broken rainbow of the milky opal. He procured from Amsterdam three emeralds of extraordinary size and richness of colour, and had a turquoise *de la vieille roche* that was the envy of all the connoisseurs.
>
> (p. 282)

Compare John Ruskin's description of a visit to a jeweller's shop in Geneva (1885–8):

> You told what you wanted: it was necessary to know your mind, and to be sure you *did* want it; there was no showing of things for temptation at Bautte's. You wanted a bracelet, a brooch, a watch – plain or enamelled [...] There were no big stones, nor blinding galaxies of wealth [...] Absolutely just and moderate price; wear, – [*sic*] to the end of your days. You came away with a sense of duty fulfilled, of treasure possessed, and of a new foundation to the respectability of your family.[30]

While Dorian relishes in the description of jewels (their 'extraordinary size', 'richness of colour'), desire is anaesthetised Ruskin's passage. Ruskin's emphasis is on knowing your mind and not deviating from this position. There is nothing tempting in the shop. Everything is controlled. Ruskin privileges the eternal over the possibility of change; he roots the purchase of gems in the middle-class heterosexual household, in which jewels are a family heirloom. By contrast, Wilde shuns such an approach in which life imperatives are based on family and the production of children.[31] Instead, in the private domain of the dandy the relationship between collector and objects is governed by the desiring gaze. Jewels are coveted for their capacity to give pleasure and add kudos to his status as connoisseur.

Desire is a motivating factor in his collecting, but Dorian also recognises what lies beneath the surface of the gem and thus challenges the alignment of the dandy with mere superficiality.[32] As part of his research for Dorian's jewel collection, Wilde read A.H. Church's handbook on the precious stones in the South Kensington Museum, which shows that the properties of diamonds relate to both surface *and* substance.[33] These substantive concerns appear in *The Picture of Dorian Gray*. The 'gilded threads' of Dorian's hair, his amethyst-like eyes, and his gold-tipped cigarette boxes convey preciousness and luxury (p. 185), but jewels have very different connotations when they are associated with the lower classes. The Jewish theatre manager has 'fat jewelled hands' and sports 'an enormous diamond' which 'blazed in the centre of a soiled shirt' (pp. 238, 211). Sybil Vane's mother has 'false-jewelled fingers' in contrast with the carefully chosen rings worn by Lord Henry Wotton and Dorian Gray (p. 221). While Eliot's Dorothea worried about the 'miserable men' who make the jewels,[34] both Des Esseintes and Dorian Gray worry about the miserable men and women who wear them. Such a shift reveals the fear that lower middle-class prosperity might encroach on the aesthetic territory of the dandy. However, Wilde's interest in the political economy behind aestheticism emerges in his concern for the labour involved in mining the gold, witness the exchange between Sybil Vane and her brother prior to his departure for Australia. Sybil 'prattled on [...] about the gold he was certain to find' but later rejects this fantasy because the gold-fields are 'horrid places, where men got intoxicated, and shot each other' (p. 226).[35] Wilde's 'young king' in the *House of Pomegranates* (1892) expresses similar concerns, seeing 'blood in the heart of the ruby and death in the heart of the pearl' when the appalling conditions endured by those obliged to physically collect jewels are revealed to him.[36] Despite his famously negative take on sentimentality, in the *Happy Prince* (1888) Wilde uses jewels as part of an argument for the redistribution of wealth to the poor.[37] His ability to see through the jewel's glistering surface reminds us of the dandy's often ignored ability to go beyond the superficial, positioning him as a more socially engaged figure.

Museums of words

[…] in its special mode of handling its given material, each art may be observed to pass into the condition of some other art.

> (Walter Pater, 'The School of Giorgione', 1877)[38]

Huysmans goes to my soul like a gold ornament of Byzantine workmanship.

> (George Moore, *Confessions of a Young Man*, 1887)[39]

The style in which it was written was that curious jewelled style, vivid and obscure at once.

> (Oscar Wilde, *Picture of Dorian Gray*, 1890)[40]

The house-museums of Des Esseintes and Dorian Gray do more than just represent groups of objects. They are themselves figured using the language of museums, of viewing, collecting and arranging. Both authors use the catalogue form in their writing. The museum also influences their ideas about the materiality of language and its jewel-like qualities. Wilde's use of handbooks on the jewel collections of the South Kensington Museum shows that museum culture is a direct source of inspiration for his writing.[41] Similarly, Huysmans draws our attention to the 'showcase' of *Against Nature* and to the arrangement of his 'little museum', which includes his ekphrastic descriptions of Moreau's Salomé portraits.[42] (He also comments that his representation of religious art is based on 'the odds and ends I found in museums').[43] As Huysmans and Wilde metamorphose museum exhibits into the queer space of their homes, their parodic appropriation is a 'challenge and transformation' of the cultural form of the museum, as Jonathan Dollimore would argue.[44]

In their preoccupation with lists, both authors utilise the catalogue, a literary form coincident with the rise of the museum and the department store, in which visible consumer choices are verbalised. Criticised by Georg Lukács for privileging description over narration, the catalogue form in fact has its own textuality and structuring impetus: it gives order to *Against Nature* in the same way that a museum catalogue or guidebook provides a way of organising a collection.[45] With its selection, classification, juxtaposition and listing of objects, the catalogue inspired French writers including Flaubert, Balzac, and especially the Goncourts, whose *Maison d'un Artiste* (1881) is often cited as an influence on Huysmans' novel.[46] In the ekphrastic passages on 'Salomé Dancing before Herod', Huysmans describes Salomé's jewels through a long catalogue of verbs and adjectives:

> she begins the lubricious dance [...] her breasts rise and fall, their nipples hardening under the friction of her whirling necklaces; the diamonds adhering to her moist skin glitter; her bracelets, her belts, her rings, flash and sparkle; on her triumphal gown – pearl-seamed, silver-flowered, gold-spangled.
>
> (p. 45)

This accumulative listing conveys the growing frenzy of the dance and the rising surge of sexual desire. Similarly, when he visualises the death of Salomé, an extension of his ekphrasis of Moreau's painting 'The Apparition', Huysmans lists the female body parts to be gilded and purified. Functioning like a pornographic gaze that moves across her body enjoying and enumerating, the act of listing brings about a crescendo of desire and reaches satisfaction through the 'naming of pleasures' in what amounts to an 'eroticism' of the catalogue.[47]

Such inventory, as Roland Barthes suggests, is never neutral. In these texts, lists of jewels are part of a chain of borrowing between the verbal and the visual, which involves the reworking of an original text. Museum guidebooks such as those used by Wilde in his research are themselves a verbalisation of a past viewing experience.[48] According to Streeter, 'when a ray of light enters a diamond, it is turned from its original path to a much greater extent than if it had entered [...] any other material'.[49] Wilde draws on this refractive power, the eschewing of a 'straight' visual path, in his reworking of William Jones' *History and Mystery of Precious Stones* (1880), which describes some of the jewels that could be found in the South Kensington Museum. In his 'performance' of this text, Wilde constructs a queer genealogy based around key figures from British history associated with homosexuality.[50] Following a section in Jones' text which describes the jewels owned by British monarchs, Wilde refers to Piers Gaveston, one of Edward II's favourites, a reference not included in the original. He emphasises features such as the earrings that James I gave to his favourites, which Jones calls 'effeminate ornaments'. Jones describes Richard II as 'the greatest fop of his day' and Wilde duly pays homage to this foppery with a reference to his bejewelled coat. His campy rewrite of *History and Mystery* includes the exaggeration of the number of diamonds on Charles II's stirrups (from 320 in Jones' text to 421 in Wilde's novel) and ends with the

excessively adorned gloves of Henry II and the pearl and sapphire stud-
ded hat of Charles, Duke of Burgundy.[51] Wilde's plagiarism is creative,
transformative, and camp; his excessive quoting of Jones' guide sub-
stantiates Susan Sontag's claim that 'camp sees everything in quotation
marks'.[52]

Lists are a way of forging a relationship between words and things,
between texts and objects. So too does ekphrasis establish a relationship
between writing and the art-object.[53] Ekphrasis might be compared to
a jewel, its substance constantly refined through a process of recurring
dialogue between author, artist, and reader/viewer. This relationship is
triangulated like the facets of a diamond. In Huysmans, ekphrasis is part
of a chain (necklace?) of artistic transpositions that begin with a text
rather than a work of art. Moreau is inspired by Flaubert's *Salambô* (1862)
to produce 'Salomé Dancing' and 'The Apparition', which then inspire
Huysmans' descriptions.[54]

These descriptions participate in a long trajectory of interest in the
gendered discourse of ekphrasis. The paragonal struggles of ekphrasis
have often been seen as a battle between the masculine word and the
feminine image.[55] W.J.T. Mitchell seeks to downplay the binary opposition of male and female; for him ekphrasis stands in a triangular relation
to two othernesses (the conversion of the visual into the verbal and the
reconversion of the verbal into the visual in the mind of the reader). By
describing this relationship as a 'menage à trois', he retains a sexualised
language suggestive of deviance and transgression, as does Bryan Wolf
in his essay 'Confessions of a closet ekphrastic: literature, painting and
other unnatural relations'.[56]

That ekphrasis can be compared to a 'camp gem' is suggested by early
definitions that emphasise its excessive description and frivolity. An
1814 *Edinburgh Review* article on the writings of the Early Church Fathers
associates 'ecphrasis [*sic*]' with 'florid effeminacies of style', which make
it unsuitable 'when applied to sacred topics'. Thomas Moore, the author
of this piece, implies that the rhetorical excess inherent in ekphrasis
is linked to the efforts of the Fathers' female pupils, who went over-
board in 'spreading their words'.[57] Ekphrasis is associated with feminine
excess, superfluous ornamentation, an interpretive device highly suitable to dandy fiction, which, as Rita Felski has shown, relies partly upon
the feminisation of writing.[58] Conceived as the epitome of pure artifice
(the representation of representation), ekphrasis, like the dandy, dwells
in the relationship between original and copy and in the imitation or
borrowing of different artistic styles.

In *Against Nature* ekphrasis is highly sexualised, as Huysmans makes
jewels blur the boundaries between male and female gender identities

and thus complicate the idea of the silent female image and the speaking male viewer/writer. Much as Shelley averts Medusa's returned gaze by objectifying her through the indirect form of the third person,[59] Huysmans' Salomé has no visual agency outside the frame. Des Esseintes chooses to ignore the strong symbolic implications of the pendant hanging from her left arm, an open eye suggestive of female spectatorship. Instead, he subverts gender stereotypes by regendering the jewel wearer. In his description of 'Salomé Dancing' it is Herod who is adorned with jewels. He wears a tiara and gold robe embroidered with precious stones and sits on a throne that shines with 'fiery brilliants'. Herod is also feminised in Wilde's *Salomé*, which echoes Dorian's appearance to his guests as the bejewelled Anne de Joyeuse, Admiral of France. The partial feminisation of Herod mirrors the description of Salomé's jewels in which masculine attributes are no longer the exclusive domain of the male body, but identify a queered 'female masculinity', to use Judith Halberstam's term.[60] Salomé's 'breastplate of jewellery' points to a male propensity for war. In chapter fourteen of *Against Nature*, she is described as being drawn out, like a sword 'from the sheath of her jewels' as they fall away to reveal her nakedness' (pp. 45, 159).[61] Moreover, there are clear phallic resonances in the description of the 'gigantic pendant [...] spilling over with rubies and emeralds', hanging in the upper part of her thighs (p. 48). Salomé's masculinised body is not of the emancipatory 'new woman' type, but a creation of the (queer) desiring gaze of the collector, whose collection of mistresses displayed earlier in the novel demonstrates a preference for manly women. Jewels suggest masculine traits and a recuperation of the masculine from what is usually seen as a dissident female sexuality.[62]

Manliness is also suggested by Huysmans' use of fire imagery. Again, in 'The Apparition', Salomé burns with a flame that is not just gem-like, but fuelled by gems: 'all the facets of [her] jewels catch fire; the stones come to life, tracing out in incandescent contours the body of the woman; catching her at the neck, the legs, the arms, with sparks of fire, bright red like glowing coals' (p. 48). Salomé's 'burning' is masculine in that it draws on the Paterian idea that young men should lead passionate, fulfilled lives ('burn with a gem-like flame').[63] However, if attempted by women, such behaviour will meet with a Joan of Arc style punishment, foregrounding the tension between the attractions and repulsions of female masculinity and destabilised gender binaries. A man gazing on a woman who is regendered as male can be read through Eve Sedgwick's erotic triangle, in which a woman acts as conduit for the desire between two men. Here the 'other' man could be Herod, the male reader or even Salomé herself as an androgynous figure.[64]

This kind of gender transmutation mirrors ekphrastic 'transpositions of art', a phrase used by Huysmans in his book on modern art. Boundaries between the arts are blurred just as those that demarcate gender identities. Yet these transpositions are not confined to the verbalisation of images. Despite a dominant critical focus on Huysmans and 'l'écriture peinture', his writing suggests a broader phenomenological engagement with objecthood. In *Against Nature*, the jewel-object remediates both writing and painting. In an essay on Moreau, Huysmans writes: 'these paintings no longer seemed to belong to painting in the strict sense of the term [...] the methods he uses to make his dreams visible seem to have been borrowed from the techniques used by German engravers [...] and from jewellery'.[65] Moreau renders painting thing-like through the skilful remediation of the jewel. Similarly, in chapter five of *Against Nature*, Des Esseintes argues that Moreau's Salomés go 'beyond the confines of painting', borrowing from the art of the enameller, the lapidary, and from 'the art of writing its most subtle evocations' (pp. 49–50).[66] Reminding us of the intermedial dimensions of the chain of ekphrasis, the initial artistic 'borrowing' may be *from* writing that is transformed into paint and then back to writing via verbal description. As a result of the triangulation of word, image, and object, the paintings blur subject-object boundaries to become hybrid 'living things'.

This tag game of artistic transposition continues in both authors' use of the language of gems and in their interest in gem-like language. Huysmans describes 'Salomé Dancing' through a language of light specific to the gem. The jewels 'glitter', 'flash', 'sparkle' and 'dazzle'. He draws on a language of jewelled adornment ('gorgerin', 'girdle', 'fastner') to visualise 'The Apparition' (p. 48).[67] By recurring to strange words ('cymophane', 'chrysobel'), Huysmans turns his jewels into strange objects. When later criticised for his inaccurate descriptions, Huysmans downplays the importance of scientific literalness[68] and invokes synaesthesia as a further transposition in the sensory perception of objects. His words become 'the colours for the ear, the hues which one sees with closed eyes. With these syllables can be created miraculous gems which have no form and which one can hear shining'.[69] Such words are part of an imaginative transformation whereby the gem acquires eccentric sensory properties.

In addition to the 'curious jewelled style' of Huysmans' novel, Dorian Gray reads Théophile Gautier's *Emaux and Camées* (Enamels and Cameos, [1852]) and quotes lines that refer to gold, pearls, amethysts, and amber. Gautier's work appeals to the senses through a refined aesthetic experience, which later characterised the symbolist movement in literature. Commenting on *Emaux and Camées*, Gautier writes that 'every poem was to be a medallion fit to be set in the cover of a casket, or a seal to be worn on the finger'. He also uses the jewel trope to define poetic form in a discussion of the lapidary style of poet Théodore de Banville, who 'feels the beauty of words; he loves to have them brilliant, rich, and rare and he sets them in gold round his thought as it might be a bracelet round a woman's arm'.[70] Des Esseintes also takes pleasure in the work of Gautier 'just as he took pleasure in rare gemstones and precious minerals' (p. 154).[71] His interest in the lapidary style of writers across the ages is part of a process of critical distillation, in which the true value of a work can be ascertained by attention to its refined 'essence'. He admires the 'gem-like' clarity of literature: Lucan's verses are 'brightly-enamelled, gem-studded' and those of Petronious are 'splendidly wrought and 'highly polished' (p. 25).[72] This preference for artistic distillates pays homage to the durability of the diamond, its hardness and purity, characteristics which problematise the camp gem through their association with essentialism. In *Against Nature*, gems have the properties of both substance and surface; like dandy identity, they are both fixed and dispersed. No binary can escape as Huysmans challenges what might be seen as the essentialism of an anti-essentialist stance which is itself part of a binary opposition.[73]

The dandy as gem

> 'The world is changed because you are made of ivory and gold.'
> (Wilde, *Picture of Dorian Gray*, p. 355)

As well as gender transmutations and 'transpositions d'art', depictions of jewels in Huysmans and Wilde suggest a transformation of the dandy-collector into a jewel-object. In his essay on the 'dandiacal body', Thomas Carlyle writes that a dandy wants to be seen as 'a visual object, or thing that will reflect rays of light'.[74] Both Des Esseintes (before he closets himself away) and Dorian Gray are concerned with high visibility. Dorian is repeatedly likened to a jewel. In the course of the novel he changes from a shining brilliant into a 'cunningly-wrought' enamel (p. 290). Furthermore, 'as jewel', Dorian has the capacity to change other peoples' ways of seeing; 'I see things differently' says Basil Hallward in response to Dorian's 'merely visible presence' (p. 177).

Georg Simmel's 1908 essay on adornment highlights the link between jewels, visibility, and personality, drawing on Paterian figures of heat and light. Adornment operates 'as a sort of radiation', which enlarges the personality: 'by virtue of this brilliance, its wearer appears as the centre of a circle of radiation in which every close-by person, every seeing eye, is caught'.[75] Such is the visibility of the dandy at the height of his powers. Consider, for instance, in William Powell Frith's 'Private View at the Royal Academy' (1883) where Wilde himself appears at the centre of such a circle of radiation. Simmel presents the relationship with the public in highly visual terms: 'as the flash of the precious stone seems to be directed at the other – like the lightning of the glance the eye addresses to him – it carries the social meaning of jewels – the being-for-the-other, which returns to the subject as the enlargement of his own sphere of significance'.[76] The dandy's visibility, his 'adamantine lustre' relies on the public in a similar way; as Albert Camus would later write, the dandy 'can only be sure of his existence by finding it in the expression of others' faces'.[77]

The high visibility of the dandy is problematised by the authors' interest in the refractive qualities of gems. Pater's model of the crystalline man presupposes a harmonisation of soul and body effected through heat and light. Crystals and crystallography permeate Pater's work. At first glance, his crystal images seem to be rooted in ideas of clarity and purity. They appear in relation to the writing style of Wordsworth: 'the heat of his genius, entering into the substance of his work, has crystallised a part'. A 'clear crystal nature' also characterises the diaphanous type.[78] In *Plato and Platonism* (1893), Pater compares Plato to the 'impassioned glow' of Dante's conceptions: 'the spiritual and the material are blent and fused together [...] in that fire and heat, what is spiritual attains the definite visibility of a crystal, what is material, on the other hand, will lose its earthiness and impurity'.[79] Yet, as we have seen, a crystal is multi-faceted and refractive. When traced to its Greek roots, the term 'diaphanous' means 'a state of shining through', which suggests something rather more translucent, than transparent. Pater's opaque use of the crystal figure is compounded by his subversion of scientific connoisseurship in his use of heat and light imagery in relation to jewels. A flame cannot be 'gem-like', because it flickers and flares. However, Pater's play with paradox reveals a deliberate attempt to problematise the crystal, rather than scientific inaccuracy.[80] In his *Life of Goethe* (1855), G.H. Lewes compared the development of Goethe's character with the crystallising process, arguably a source for Pater's 'diaphaneite':[81] Instead of a 'clear, crystal nature', however, both Des Esseintes and Dorian Gray have (and relish) the flaws in their crystals.

Drawing on the tropes already discussed, Huysmans and Wilde use the gem to suggest a diffuse personality and a fragmented visual perspective.

The dandy-collector is represented through the polarities of hard and soft, concentration and dispersal, transparency and opacity, collector and collected. This positioning between binaries figures the dandy, like Moreau's paintings, as a hybrid of both agent and object. As 'thing', the dandy takes on gem-like properties. Linking the idea of possession with the concept of ownership of the self, Des Esseintes and Dorian Gray collect, but also become objects in their own collections.[82] This hybridity gestures to the fin-de-siècle interest in hermaphroditism and androgyny, blendings of male and female which inspired a number of writers. Indeed, Gautier's *Emaux et Camées* contains a poem titled 'Contralto' which compares the indeterminately sexed beauty of a Greek statue to that of a singer with a contralto voice.

In a further elision, Kit Andrews points to the ability of both the collector and Pater's 'diaphanous type' to 'perceive fine distinctions'.[83] According to Simmel, jewels provoke 'an enlargement or intensification' of the personality which is gathered 'in a focal point' in an attempt to garner 'sensuous attention'.[84] Attention was a key area of study in the late nineteenth-century, as Jonathan Crary shows. A lack of attention might signify non-normative masculine behaviour. For Max Nordau, the degenerate's lack of attention results in 'false judgements respecting the objective universe, respecting the qualities of things and their relations to each other'.[85] In his exploration of the subject, John Dewey uses an optical language linked to the gem: 'In attention we focus the mind, as the lens takes all the light coming to it, and instead of allowing it to distribute itself evenly concentrates it in a point of great heat and light. So the mind, instead of diffusing consciousness over all the elements presented to it, brings it all to bear upon some one selected point, which stands out with unusual brilliancy and distinctness'.[86] Similarly, jewels draw the eye to a focal point by means of the polarisation of light. However, the dandy 'as jewel' accentuates the gem's ability to diffuse light and embodies Crary's thesis that there exists no separation between useful attention and a potentially threatening distraction.[87]

The type of attention that Dorian Gray and Des Esseintes exert as collectors involves selection, narrowing and focusing. They exemplify Walter Benjamin's idea that the collector's key motivating factor is 'the struggle against dispersion' and they operate, in part, within the socially acceptable realm of attention described by Crary.[88] On the other hand, the constant movement of their gaze from one set of objects to another and the unorthodox arrangement of their house-museums, in which things are displayed against the grain of the 'objective universe', are also evidence of a capacity for distraction. The dandy's attention and distraction extends to his perception of the self as jewel-object. 'I am too much concentrated on myself', states Dorian, critiquing his own self-absorption and desiring to divert the gaze (p. 342).

Conclusion

Today, the advent of 'bling' draws attention to the relationship between men and jewels in ways which echo the role of gems in the construction of late-Victorian masculinities, particularly dandyism. Many Rap and Hip Hop artists destabilise the gender binary, albeit unwittingly. They appear dandiacal in their display of large rings, necklaces, gem-studded canes and yet maintain a homophobic stance in their lyrics. Likewise, but to clearly different ends, Huysmans and Wilde show that the interpretive possibilities of jewels are not solely confined to the construction of female identity. Jessica Feldman writes of the dandy's interest in human identity as 'vapor or diamond'.[89] Her use of the diamond to suggest hardness and inflexibility ignores the multiple and refractive qualities of the camp gem. A focus on dandy jewel collections reveals the queer dimensions of the museum and facilitates an exploration of the gender blurring emerging in ekphrastic transpositions. The representation of the dandy 'as gem' equates the visual qualities of the jewel with the dandy's penchant for both high visibility and opacity and grants the gem an important place in the carving and refinement of masculine identity. Through the jewel, the dandy carves out his own role and hopes like Dorian, who longs to refashion the world anew (p. 279).[90]

The dandy's relationship with jewels suggests a simultaneous and ultimately unsustainable dispersion and concentration of personality. By the end of *Against Nature*, Des Esseintes appears as burnt-out diamond, reduced to carbon, degenerated. Wilde's novel ends with Dorian's death. I began this essay with Verlaine's triangulation of jewels, decadence and visuality. *The Picture of Dorian Gray* ends with a similar triangulation in which jewels linger as the only visible signifier of Dorian's identity. His death signals the end of the dandy's dominance of the visual field. Instead, a working-class gaze takes over as his servants force open the room at the top of the house and view their master, victim of an excessively decadent lifestyle, slumped next to his portrait in its original state: 'lying on the floor was a dead man [...] He was withered, wrinkled, and loathsome of visage. It was not till they had examined the rings that they recognized who it was' (p. 357).[91]

Notes

1. J.K. Huysman, quoted in George A. Cevasco, *Breviary of the Decadence: J.K. Huysmans's A Rebours and English Literature* (New York: AMS Press, 2001), p. 18.
2. See Joseph Bristow's discussion of the terms 'decadent', 'aesthetic' and 'symbolist' in *The Fin-de-Siècle Poem* (Athens, Ohio: Ohio University Press, 2005), pp. 7–12.
3. An interest in jewel-like writing was not confined to men. Olive Custance, wife of Lord Alfred Douglas and thus on the fringes of Wilde's circle, wrote a book of poems entitled *Opals*: see Olive Custance, *Opals* (London and New York: John Lane, 1897).
4. Walter Pater, *The Renaissance*, p. 236.
5. See Jean Arnold, 'Cameo Appearances: the Discourse of Jewellery in Middlemarch', *Victorian Literature and Culture*, 30:1 (2002), 265–88; Aviva Briefel, 'Tautological Crimes: Why Women can't Steal Jewels', *Novel*, 37:1/2 (2003), 135–57.
6. This is a common pairing, given that *Against Nature* is a likely candidate for the infamous 'yellow book' Dorian receives from Lord Henry Wotton.
7. Fabio Cleto, ed., *Camp: Queer Aesthetics and the Performing Subject: A Reader* (Ann Arbor: The University of Michigan Press, 1999), p. 1.
8. Cleto, *Camp*, pp. 1–9.
9. For its ability to generate meanings through technologies of duplication the mirror has long been privileged as the main site for visuality in *The Picture of Dorian Gray*: see Christopher Craft, 'Come See About Me: Enchantment of the Double in *The Picture of Dorian Gray*', *Representations*, 91 (2005), 109–36. Yet Isobel Armstrong writes that 'once the idea of the mirror is relinquished, glass is confounding'. The 'reflecting and refracting powers of glass' are optimised in the gem, particularly in the diamond. See Isobel Armstrong, 'Transparency: Towards a Poetics of Glass in the Nineteenth Century', in Francis Spufford and Jenny Uglow, eds, *Cultural Babbage: Technology, Time and Invention* (London: Faber and Faber, 1996), pp. 123–48. For its greater refractive index than both glass and the plane mirror, the gem is an ideal way into the visuality of Wilde's novel.
10. Oscar Wilde, *An Ideal Husband* (Oxford: Oxford University Press, 1998), p. 192.
11. Russsell W. Belk and Melanie Wallendorf, 'Of Mice and Men: Gender Identity in Collecting', in *Interpreting Objects and Collections*, ed. by Susan M. Pearce (London, Routledge, 1994), p. 246.
12. Naomi Schor, 'Collecting Paris', in John Elsner and Roger Cardinal, eds, *The Cultures of Collecting* (London: Reaktion Books Ltd., 1994), p. 257.
13. See Richard Dellamora, *Masculine Desire: the Sexual Politics of Victorian Aestheticism* (Chapel Hill: University of North Carolina Press, 1990), Herbert Sussman, *Victorian Masculinities: Manhood and Masculine Poetics in Early Victorian Literature and Art* (Cambridge: Cambridge University Press, 1995), James Eli Adams, *Dandies and Desert Saints: Styles of Victorian Masculinity* (Ithaca and London: Cornell University Press, 1995).
14. For an exception, see Neil Bartlett, *Who Was That Man? A Present for Mr Oscar Wilde* (London: Serpent's Tail, 1988), pp. 173–89.

15. Whitney Davis, 'Homoerotic Art Collection from 1750–1920, *Art History*, 24 (2001), 247–77. See also James M. Saslow, *Pictures and Passions: a History of Homosexuality in the Visual Arts* (New York and London: Viking Penguin, 1999).
16. Peter Horne and Reina Lewis, eds, *Outlooks: Lesbian and Gay Sexualities and Visual Cultures* (London: Routledge, 1996), p. 1.
17. Ibid., p. 2.
18. Judith Halberstam, *In a Queer Time and Place: Transgender Bodies, Subcultural Lives* (New York and London: New York University Press, 2005), pp. 1–2.
19. Sara Ahmed, *Queer Phenomenology: Orientations, Objects, Others* (Durham and London: Duke University Press, 2006), p. 162.
20. Joris Karl Huysmans, *Against Nature*, trans. Margaret Mauldon and ed. by Nicholas White (Oxford: Oxford University Press, 1998), p. 17; hereafter in text. Des Esseintes' 'ship cabin' dining room also creates a sense of queer time in which 'without ever leaving his home, he was able to enjoy the rapidly succeeding, indeed almost simultaneous, sensations of a long voyage' (p. 18).
21. I follow Halberstam's definition of queer as a 'nonnormative logics and organizations of community, sexual identity, embodiment and activity in space and time'. Halberstam, *In a Queer Time and Place*, p. 6.
22. For example, Charles Darwin's research was based on his collecting practice, as was that of Augustus Pitt Rivers.
23. Oscar Wilde, *The Picture of Dorian Gray: the 1890 and 1891 Texts*, ed. by Joseph Bristow (Oxford: Oxford University Press, 2005), p. 334; hereafter in text.
24. George Eliot, *Middlemarch* (Oxford: Oxford University Press, 1999), p. 194.
25. Regenia Gagnier, *Idylls of the Marketplace: Oscar Wilde and the Victorian Public* (Stanford: Stanford University Press, 1986), p. 1. However, the dandy should not be denied the ability to collect in a scientific *mode*, if not to scientific ends. Des Esseintes, for instance, is quite systematic in his approach to collecting.
26. Such as those discussed in Edward Streeter, *Precious Stones and Gems: Their History and Distinguishing Characteristics* (London, 1882).
27. For Camp's similar deconstruction of the opposition between original and copy, see 'camp as diamond, camp as zircon', *Camp*, p. 8.
28. I am suggesting the idea of Wonderland as a 'queer space'.
29. Des Esseintes celebrates the kind of 'queer' moments of disorientation that Merleau-Ponty wishes to overcome (see Ahmed, *Queer Phenomenology*, pp. 65–7).
30. John Ruskin, *Praeterita* (London: George Allen, 1907), II, 129–30.
31. Lee Edelman, *No Future: Queer Theory and the Death Drive* (Durham and London: Duke University Press, 2004), p. 2.
32. For 'surface' views of the dandy, see Jessica R. Feldman, *Gender on the Divide: the Dandy in Modernist Literature* (Ithaca: Cornell University Press, 1993), p. 13 and Rita Felski, *The Gender of Modernity* (Cambridge, MA: Harvard University Press, 1995), p. 91, and Ellen Moers, *The Dandy: Brummell to Beerbohm* (London, Secker & Warburg, 1960), p. 13.
33. A.H. Church, *Precious Stones* (London: Chapman and Hall Ltd., 1883), pp. 4–5.
34. Eliot, *Middlemarch*, p. 15.

35. Cleto associates camp with exclusivity and luxury, but the camp gem can also operate in a working class setting, see Sybil's 'drag act' (PDG, p. 233).

36. Oscar Wilde, *The House of Pomegranates, Oscar Wilde: Complete Shorter Fiction*, ed. by Isobel Murray (Oxford: Oxford University Press, 1998), p. 180.

37. See Gagnier, *Idylls of the Marketplace*, p. 63.

38. Pater, *The Renaissance*, pp. 133–4.

39. Quoted in Cevasco, *Breviary*, p. 36.

40. Wilde, *Picture of Dorian Gray*, p. 274.

41. Wilde also refers to other museum handbooks such as Daniel Rock, *Textile Fabrics* (London: South Kensington Museum, 1876).

42. Huysmans, 'Preface, "Written Twenty Years After the Novel" ', *Against Nature*, pp. 192, 189.

43. Huysmans, 'Preface', *Against Nature*, p. 186.

44. See Dollimore, *Sexual Dissidence* (Oxford: Clarendon Press, 1991), p. 52.

45. Georg Lukács, 'Narrate or Describe?', in *Writer and Critic and Other Essays*, trans. and ed. by Arthur Kahn (London: Merlin Press, 1970), pp. 110–48. In *Against Nature*, cataloguing acts bring the reader out of dream-like memory sequences and drive the narrative forward.

46. For further discussion of the catalogue form in French literature see Janell Watson, *Literature and Material Culture from Balzac to Proust* (Cambridge: Cambridge University Press, 1999).

47. Bartlett, *Who was that Man?*, p. 182. See also Herod's listing of his jewel collection in Wilde's *Salome*: 'I have topazes yellow as are the eyes of tigers', see *Oscar Wilde: The Importance of Being Earnest and Other Plays*, ed. by Peter Raby (Oxford: Oxford University Press, 1998), p. 88.

48. 'Inventory is never a neutral idea; to catalogue is not merely to ascertain … but also to appropriate', see Roland Barthes, 'The Plates of the Encyclopaedia', in Susan Sontag, ed., *A Barthes Reader* (London: Cape, 1982), pp. 218–35: 222.

49. Streeter, *Precious Stones*, p. 52.

50. Wilde's canon-forming project gives a voice to a homosexual experience that did not emerge solely in response to pressure from what Foucault identifies as regulatory apparatus. See Michel Foucault, *History of Sexuality: 1* (London: Penguin, 1998) and Michael F. Davis, 'Walter Pater's "Latent Intelligence" and the Conception of Queer "Theory" ', in Laurel Brake, Lesley Higgins and Carolyn Williams, eds, *Walter Pater: Transparencies of Desire* (Greensboro, NC: ELT Press, 2002), pp. 261–85.

51. William Jones, *History and Mystery of Precious Stones* (London: Richard Bentley and Son, 1880), pp. 325, 359, 343.

52. Susan Sontag, 'Notes on "Camp" ', *Against Interpretation* (New York, Picador, 2001), pp. 275–93: 280.

53. For further discussion of the concept of an artwork as object or 'thing' see Esther Pasztory, *Thinking with Things: Towards a New Vision of Art* (Austin: University of Texas Press, 2005), pp. 7–15.

54. See Françoise Meltzer, *Salome and the Dance of Writing: Portraits of Mimesis in Literature* (Chicago and London: Chicago University Press, 1987). The chain continues as Flaubert views the paintings and is then inspired to write his *Herodias*.

55. For further discussion see James Heffernan, *Museum of Words: the Poetics of Ekphrasis from Homer to Ashbery*, pp. 108–12. 'A paragon' (without an 'e') is a perfect diamond of 100 carats plus.

56. See W.J.T. Mitchell, *Picture Theory*, p. 164 and Bryan Wolf, 'Confessions of a Closet Ekphrastic: Literature, Painting and other Unnatural Relations', *Yale Journal of Criticism*, 3 (1990), 181–203.

57. See Grant F. Scott, *The Sculpted Word: Keats, Ekphrasis and the Visual Arts* (Hanover, NH, and London: University Press of New England, 1994), pp. 31–2.

58. Felski, *The Gender of Modernity*, p. 91.

59. See Benveniste, *Problems in General Linguistics*, pp. 198, 200, 217, 221–2.

60. See Judith Halberstam, *Female Masculinity* (Durham and London: Duke University Press, 1998).

61. It is not entirely clear whether in this passage Huysmans is referring to Salomé or Herodias, her mother. The two names are often mistakenly conflated.

62. On the dandy's paradoxical relationship with women, see Jessica Feldman, *Gender on the Divide*, p. 6.

63. Pater, *The Renaissance*, p. 236. Pater states 'This brief "Conclusion" was omitted in the second edition of this book, as I conceived it might possibly mislead some of the young men into whose hands it might fall' (p. 233).

64. See Eve Kosofsky Sedgwick, *Between Men: English Literature and Male Homosocial Desire* (New York: Columbia University Press, 1985), pp. 21–8. A similar triangulation occurs in Henry James' revamped version of *Roderick Hudson* (1905) in which Christina Light's links to the tradition of Salomé are clearly inspired by the representations of Moreau, Huysmans and Wilde.

65. J.K. Huysmans, 'Modern Art', in Rosemary Lloyd, ed., *Revolutions in Writing: Readings in Nineteenth-Century French Prose* (Indiana University Press, 1996), p. 33.

66. For the link between the art of painting and the goldsmith, see also Mary Haweis, 'Jewels and Dress, or the Philosophy of Jewels', *Contemporary Review*, 56 (July–December 1889), 95–6.

67. Meltzer makes a similar point in *Salome and the Dance of Writing*, p. 25.

68. On the difficulties inherent in the symbolism of gems Huysmans later wrote: 'the hermeneutics of gems are uncertain', see J.K. Huysmans, *The Cathedral* (New York: Dedalus, 1989), p. 136.

69. J.K. Huysmans, quoted in Christopher Lloyd, *J.K. Huysmans and the Fin-de-Siècle Novel* (Edinburgh: Edinburgh University Press, 1990), p. 23 (my translation).

70. Théophile Gautier, 'Progress of French Poetry since 1830', *The Works of Théophile Gautier*, ed. by F.C. de Sumichrast, 24 vols (London: George Harrap, 1900–3), XVI, 267 and 243.

71. However, Des Esseintes criticises Gautier for being too impersonally precise in his description.

72. There are many other examples: the monks of the seventh and eighth centuries whose 'eccentric adjectives' were 'roughly shaped out of gold after the uncouth and charming style of gothic jewellery' (p. 33).

73. For further discussion of the 'stand off' between essentialism and anti-essentialism see *The Essential Difference*, ed. Naomi Schor and Elizabeth Weed (Bloomington and Indianapolis: Indiana University Press, 1994).
74. Thomas Carlyle, 'The Dandiacal Body', *Sartor Resartus* (Oxford: Oxford University Press, 1999), p. 207.
75. Georg Simmel, 'Adornment', *The Sociology of Georg Simmel*, trans. and ed. by Kurt H. Wolf (New York: Free Press, 1950), pp. 338–44: 342.
76. Simmel, 'Adornment', p. 342.
77. Albert Camus quoted in Eli Adams, *Dandies and Desert Saints*, p. 213.
78. Pater, *The Renaissance*, p. xi; Walter Pater, 'Diaphaneitè', *Miscellaneous Studies* (1895; London: Macmillan and Co., Ltd., 1910), p. 253. Composed in 1864, the essay was published posthumously in *Miscellaneous Studies* (1895).
79. Walter Pater, *Plato and Platonism* (1893; London: Macmillan and Co., Ltd., 1910), p. 135. Harold Bloom dubs Pater 'The Crystal Man' in his introduction to the *Selected Writings of Walter Pater* (New York: Columbia University Press, 1974), p. vii.
80. See Whitney Davis, 'The Image in the Middle: John Addington Symonds and Homoerotic Art Criticism', in Elizabeth Prettejohn, ed., *After the Pre-Raphaelites: Art and Aestheticism in Victorian England* (Manchester: Manchester University Press, 1999), pp. 188–217: 207.
81. See Ann Varty, 'The Crystal Man' in Laurel Brake and Ian Small, eds, *Pater in the '90s* (Greensboro, NC: ELT Press, University of North Carolina, 1991), pp. 205–15: 208.
82. Gilbert Osmond in James' *Portrait of a Lady* is a further example of the collector as part of the collection.
83. Kit Andrews, 'Walter Pater and Walter Bemjamin: the Diaphanous Collector and the Angel of History' in *Walter Pater: Transparencies of Desire*, p. 251.
84. Simmel, 'Adornment', p. 340.
85. Max Nordau, *Degeneration*, quoted in Jonathan Crary, *Suspensions of Perception*, p. 16.
86. John Dewey, *Psychology*, quoted in Crary, *Suspensions of Perception*, p. 24.
87. Ibid., p. 47.
88. Walter Benjamin, *The Arcades Project*, quoted in *Walter Pater: Transparencies of Desire*, p. 257.
89. Feldman, *Gender on the Divide*, p. 5.
90. For a discussion of carved jewels and the ascription of gender identities see Arnold, 'Cameo Appearances'.
91. A working class gaze is also foregrounded at the end of *Against Nature* when the removal men pack up Des Esseintes' collection.

9
The Book Beautiful: Reading, Vision, and the Homosexual Imagination in Late Victorian Britain

Michael Hatt

How else might the world be?

It is a question that lies at the root of what one might call the homosexual imagination. In late Victorian Britain, as now, many homosexual men asked, in both Utopian and practical modes, how the world would be, such that it could be fully inhabited by a homosexual man. And to imagine an alternative world entails imagining what it would be like to be in it. In this essay, I want to explore three inter-related case studies which ask: to what extent could reading provide the conditions for such imagining? In discussing reading, I shall not be addressing the explicit content of books, but reading as a *practice*. I shall speculate, perhaps recklessly, about the experience of reading, the relationships between the visual and the verbal it can engender, and the ways in which these helped readers to imagine other ways of inhabiting the world. Most important, I want to explore how reading enabled homosexual men to address that crucial question: How else might the world be?

Beauty is Truth (Plate 16) was made in 1896 by the American photographer and publisher, Fred Holland Day. Day lived in and around Boston, but was deeply involved in transatlantic aesthetic and homosexual cultures. His company, Copeland and Day, published the American editions of Wilde, Beardsley and *The Yellow Book* (as well as a range of tamer volumes), and he exhibited widely in London and Europe as a photographer. He was a friend of Charles Ricketts, who designed bookplates for Copeland & Day, of Edmund Gosse, of Gleeson White, editor of the *Studio*, and many other figures central to both the British art world and its homosexual subculture. His image brings together a beautiful male body with a Keatsian subject, signalled by the title. When the photograph was exhibited in London in 1898 it was displayed in a frame inscribed with the final two lines of the *Ode on a Grecian Urn*: 'Beauty is truth, truth beauty – that is all / Ye know on earth, and all ye need to know'. It is hard to know exactly what the subject of the photograph is. It seems to be as meaningful and meaningless as the poetic lines that inspired it. In one respect, the choice of a Keatsian subject is utterly conventional. The late nineteenth-century Royal Academy is littered with Lamias, hung with hordes of belles dames all without merci, and much has been said about Victorian artists' use of romantic English poetry, particularly in its medievalising and proto-aesthetic guises.[1] Unlike these painters and sculptors, Day eschews narrative; there is nothing illustrative about his work. In this, he is highly unconventional. It is as if he seeks to express the experience of reading and the notional space in which reading takes place. And unlike other artists, Day had a specific attachment to the poet. He had the largest collection of Keats volumes and memorabilia in the USA, much of which was collected at great expense and no small amount of personal trouble. In his study hung Keats' death mask, so, working at his desk, Day would be in visual contact with his hero. Day was instrumental in the creation of the Keats memorial in Hampstead parish church. Unveiled in 1894, Day gave a small speech before Edmund Gosse delivered the main address. Such was Fred's devotion to the poet, that each year he would celebrate Keats' birthday with his great friend, the poet Louise Guiney.

But how did Day actually read Keats? And what is the relationship between reading and his artistic practice? There are two factors which might help answer these questions. The first line of inquiry is the use of Keats as a means of thinking about homosexuality. James Najarian has argued in a recent book that Keats was important for Victorian homosexual men as a resource for articulating alternative sexual and gendered positions.[2] Certainly, in mid-century, many frowned on the poet, agreeing with Hazlitt's famous verdict of effeminacy. Hopkins declared Keats unmanly; for Swinburne and Matthew Arnold this was confirmed by the publication of the letters to Fanny Brawne in 1878. Monckton Milnes's biography of 1848 and the work of the Pre-Raphaelites had started to recuperate the poet, and by the 1880s explicit bids were made to return him to the masculine fold. In 1883, the four-volume edition of the works edited by Henry Forman (which Fred Holland Day reviewed) claimed for the poet a 'male robustness'; Sidney Colvin, in his biography of 1887, insisted on Keats's 'manly spirit'.[3] Even so, the ghost of effeminate Keats continued to haunt late Victorian literature. The other biography of 1887, by William Michael Rossetti, could not help but agree that the poet 'tended to the namby-pamby' and had 'a certain want of virility'.[4] Matthew Arnold's battle with Keats is palpable, both in his criticism and in his own verse; in a poem like *Thyrsis*, for instance, which betrays both an attraction to Keats and a need for moral distance from him.[5] In the midst of this anxiety, Wilde, in his sonnet on Keats' tomb, casts the poet as Guido Reni's Saint Sebastian, overtly homosexualising him. All this might support Najarian's notion that a passion for Keats represented an attack on heterosexual masculinity. As seductive as this thesis is, we need to be very careful. We must not confuse effeminacy with homosexuality. Indeed, Keats's effeminacy is decisively heterosexual, often exemplified by his relationship with Fanny Brawne. The issue is not sexuality, but sensuality; the fact that Keats privileges sensation over volition (which is, in a sense, what effeminacy means for many Victorians). For Keats, the world is not simply given, available to sight and dutiful agency, but comes into being through experience, formed as it is felt, felt as it is formed. This is what he refers to as 'snail horn perception', the way the body touches and recoils from the world.[6] It is this concern for sensuous experience that underpins the Victorian wish for a greater robustness in the poetic character. The recasting of Keats as manly and conventionally moral is a means of making the snail draw in his horns, leaving only the hard shell.

For Day, photography functions precisely as the medium of snail horn perception, visualising a relationship with the world in its sensual particularity. This is not simply to remark the rendering of, say, cloth or skin or glass or metal in an image like *Beauty is Truth*; it is about the insistence on one thing touching another; the shadowy recession of the body that invites the touch of the eye; the delicacy of the tonal variations across the image demanding that each component is subject to a distinct scopic engagement; the way the folds of fabric and folds of flesh become metaphors for each other; the need to approach closer to turn blurry shadow into knowable body. Day's photographic practice understands that seeing is not a distancing from the world, but a bringing close, a reaching out. In this way he does open up a connection between Keats and his sexuality. This is not a reductive notion of Keats as a private code for homosexuality. Rather, Keats's snail horn perception describes a way of inhabiting the world where sexuality is inevitably part of a continuum of experience; it arises as a necessary consequence of touching, of making the world.

There is a second factor that may help elaborate Day's reading of Keats. This is the nature of collecting and the relationship between the collector and his books or objects. If Day's enthusiasm were purely for the poems themselves, he would need no more than the simplest pocket edition. Walter Benjamin explains that the collector's books constitute a history of how they came to be acquired, and are hence a repository of experience: where one was, the surroundings, the path that led one there, the dual roles of choice and chance, the narratives of getting, losing, finding. For the collector, the history of acquiring the volume is also a history of acquiring oneself.[7] But, Benjamin argues, there is also a childlike aspect to collecting. To collect a book is a means of renewing it, by conjuring it into a private world. Benjamin compares the collector to a child sticking stickers on to something or colouring in, or touching, naming, absorbing an object into a fantasy. This is less about the archiving of experience, and more about imagining alternatives. So on the one hand, collecting is about a desire for totality. The collector is concerned with order, with a totalising narrative where objects, including the self, acquire meaning through their relationship with other objects in the collection. Collecting is about the production of a self-contained, fixed framework for making experience coherent. On the other hand, there is also an allegorical impulse. The allegorist dislodges things from their context in order to find their meaning; he is concerned with the dispersed, the arbitrary, the discontinuous. The meaning of any object, or any self, is found in a distant world with which it shares an affinity. There is, as Benjamin says, a collector in the allegorist and an allegorist in the collector. The collector is aware that he never achieves completeness, and that he too is compiling fragments under the sign of order. The allegorist is aware that any fragment yearns to return to wholeness, and as such 'he can never have enough of things'. This paradox describes well Day's relationship with Keats. If Day's study shows us the collector, his photographs reveal the allegorist.

The photograph, *Hypnos* of 1896–7 (Plate 17) is another example of Day's unconventional Keatsian tendency. The same beautiful male body is at the centre of the work, this time as Hypnos, the god of sleep, in his winged headdress, inhaling the drowsy perfume of the poppy. The Keatsian connections are multiple and self-evident. Sleep is a favourite topic of Keats', and the poppy a familiar symbol in his verse. In addition to these thematic and iconographic connections, *Hypnos* also envisions a more conceptual Keatsian principle: namely, that art is an escape to an elsewhere, an elsewhere that can be found on the boundary between sleeping and waking. Hypnos stands, eyes closed, poised at exactly this spot, the poppy a threshold to this revised world. As well as being a conventional sign of death or sleep, and as well as being a Keatsian symbol, the poppy had personal associations for Day. Day experimented liberally with opium, and the flower is a clear sign of a chemically altered consciousness. The poppy as an aesthetic or chemical portal to another world is also connected to Day's interest in spiritualism. He was involved with the American Psychical Society, and established his own group called the Visionists (formed in 1891, they read Keats together that year). A network of affinities between the textual and the psychic starts to emerge from the vapouring lair of photography. One crucial qualification is needed here: this emphasis on personal experience is not to be confused with narcissism. The aesthete, and by extension or association, the homosexual is characterised as a narcissist in late Victorian Britain and America. In caricatures like 'An Aesthetic Midday Meal' from *Punch* by George Du Maurier, the aesthete looks out on the world and sees only his own ineffable beauty looking back; he and the lily are mirror images in their perfect form and desirability. Fred Holland Day was not one for narcissism. In condemning certain photographic images that are insufficiently poetic, he writes they are:

> Incapable of drawing our dreams to lovelier shores [...] they send us back pitilessly our own faces.[8]

For Narcissus, his face is that lovelier shore; the world is reduced to desire. For Day the Keatsian, desire should open up the world; it is the passage to elsewhere.

If the pictorial fulcrum of *Hypnos* is the face and the poppy, the eye is continually drawn away to the clavicle and the hollow at the base of the throat, perhaps the moment of greatest clarity and density in the image. This is the point of sensuous focus around which the edges of the body start to dissolve (look at the right shoulder or nipples for instance). Here at the throat, the viewer is encouraged to meet the world with his snail horns, to imagine lip and finger not on the cold hard metal of the flower but on the warm soft flesh. Just as Hypnos has his poppy as a threshold, so the viewer has the body. If, in the photograph, Hypnos dreams of another world and orientation coming into being, this dreaming is enacted or mimicked in the viewing of the image. Analogous to both is the dream of another world enabled by the reading of Keats. There are three analogous and supervenient relationships here: Hypnos and the poppy; the viewer and the body; the reader and Keats. In each, in contrast to the narcissist's distance from the world, there is proximity. In each, to touch is to be touched, not just the snail horn on the flesh, but the flesh or text or image pressing back. In each, we stand on a threshold, floral or fleshly, poetic or photographic; a threshold to a lovelier shore.

My account of Fred Holland Day rests on the notion that reading is more than the garnering of knowledge of information or ideas. This is hardly an insight. Every reader will recognise the fact that to read, say, Keats is not merely to acquire some thoughts, an argument about melancholy or art or autumn, but is to be plunged into the intensity of sensation, as if an excess of imagination is leaching from the page to the reader. Day's images, too, remind us that there is not always a direct and instrumental connection to be made between text and reader. Of course, homosexual men may have read a writer like Walt Whitman and recognised the poet as articulating their sexual interests, but rather than simply understanding a text as a bald description of the self, as a kind of mirror reflecting one's desires, reading can allow the conjuring of a different world where everything, including oneself, might be transformed. I now want to turn to a more literal consideration of reading, and to locate this visual strategy in relation to Victorian theories of readership.

Scholars have long asked questions about homosexual reading, in the sense of what homosexual men read, what books were currency in the subculture, what could be coded or decoded to represent a certain kind of sexual desire. As will by now be apparent, what interests me is something rather different: namely, *how* these books were read. Reading as a practice is notoriously hard to deal with – indeed, there is a sense in which it is irrecoverable and beyond the reach of history. We can identify where books came from; we can identify audiences; we can identify what was popular and what was not. But this still leaves little clue to the very experience of reading, of what it was like for the reader, of how a reader may have immersed himself in a book, or resisted; how he may have read in a prescribed way, or against the grain. More ephemeral still, what of the sense of pleasure, of boredom, of affinity, of comfort or discomfort? At this point, I would like to sketch two modes of reading, which we might call the textual and the visual. These are only labels of convenience and are not to be taken too seriously, but they will help to establish a framework for addressing this question of readerly behaviours.

The most important work on reading for the Victorian context is Ruskin's *Sesame and Lilies*, two lectures delivered in Manchester in 1864 and published the following year.[9] It was an extraordinarily popular work, selling tens of thousands of copies, and going through many editions; the thirteenth edition was printed in 1892. In the first of the two lectures, 'Of Kings' Treasuries', Ruskin offers a series of instructions as to how to read, emphasising the need for the reader to suspend their own thoughts in order to enter those of the writer. He describes the engagement with literature as a 'conversation' with the great minds of the past, but his prescription is clearly more like his own Manchester lectures, with an audience mutely sitting and soaking up the wisdom of the author. The reader's self-abnegation is achieved by paying attention to the smallest part of the text, to reading word by word. This is both a philological exercise – Ruskin cites the great philologist Max Müller – and an etymological one. Ruskin recommends the use of a Greek dictionary. One should learn the Greek alphabet even if one does not know the language, to enable the recognition of the roots and sources of words. Thus, the reader understands a word's meaning as archaeological, accruing over time, with an abstract or conceptual history condensed in it. The opposite of this correct mode of reading is exemplified by novel reading, with its superficial, demoralising thrills, encouraging the magnification of self rather than its annihilation.

The other key text with regard to the practice of reading in the late Victorian period is Matthew Arnold's essay 'The Study of Poetry', written as the introduction to MacMillan's anthology *The English Poets*, published in 1880.[10] Arnold's argument resembles Ruskin's in certain respects. In particular, Arnold asks that the reader avoid two fallacies: the historic fallacy, which is reading a work in terms of its historical significance and not its inherent value, and the personal fallacy, a reading wholly governed by personal taste. The antidote to these is expressed in Arnold's best-known pronouncement about how to read: the idea of the touchstone. These are lines, moments, quotations which should remain in the mind as exempla of high style and moral strength, an internal index by which any other work should be measured.

Against this framework of literary didacticism, other writers have suggested what one might call a visual approach to reading, one that can be understood in terms of an imaginative or experiential blossoming. Keats famously articulates this in the sonnet on reading Chapman's Homer; how he becomes a watcher of the skies, or stands like Cortez on a peak in Darien, not just improved, but transformed. A fuller and more theorised argument emerges in the work of Proust, who is characteristically sensitive to the nature of reading and its possibilities:

In reality every reader is, while he is reading, the reader of his own self. The writer's work is merely a kind of optical instrument which he offers to the reader to enable him to discern what, without this book, he would perhaps never have perceived in himself.[11]

It is important to note that this optic instrument is not a mirror. Again, it is not a question of narcissism, but the transformation of self and social space. The significance of the visual imagination is evident in graphic examples too. Beardsley described his illustration as the embroidering of a text. He did not seek to represent narrative or event, but, like Day, to spin out patterns of thought, imagine where else the text might go.[12]

So there we have two opposed theories of reading. In one, the text is given, there to be excavated (in Ruskin's metaphor) or mapped (think of Arnold's touchstones as landmarks in a textual geography). In the other, text and reader come into being through the act of reading. I must emphasise that these are not to be thought of the literal and the imaginative. Nor are they a stable pair – they certainly break down with someone like William Morris. But there is a difference here between the hermeneutic and the transformative, between the collector and the allegorist, the one proceeding word by word, the other metaphor by metaphor. As a concrete example of this distinction I want to visit two Victorian men, both of whom are reading Plato. First, John Addington Symonds, who exemplifies the transformative mode. In his memoirs, detailing much of his life and struggle as a homosexual man, there is a telling passage where Symonds recounts what is, to all intents and purposes, an epiphany. The seventeen-year-old Harrovian had to read Plato's *Apology* and so bought himself a copy of Plato's works:

> I went to bed and began to read my [...] Plato. It so happened that I stumbled on the *Phaedrus*. I read on and on, till I reached the end. Then I began the *Symposium*; and the sun was shining on the shrubs outside the ground-floor room in which I slept, before I shut the book up. [...] Here in the *Phaedrus* and the *Symposium* [...] I discovered the true *liber amoris* at last, the revelation I had been waiting for, the consecration of a long-cherished idealism. It was just as though the voice of my own soul spoke to me through Plato, as though in some antenatal experience I had lived the life of a philosophical Greek lover. Harrow vanished into unreality. I had touched solid ground.[13]

His own voice speaks back to him from the book. Plato's works constitute a point at which the world dissolves into an alternative. Harrow is now only a mirage, and the real Symonds is the reincarnated Greek lover, remembering, through the act of reading, his true nature and the world to which he truly belongs.

A very different way of reading Plato emerges in Benjamin Jowett's great translated edition of the philosopher's work, first published in 1871 (with subsequent editions in 1875 and 1892). Like all classicists of the day, Jowett could not duck the issue of homosexual desire; to do so would have been an unscholarly and unscrupulous bowdlerisation of Plato. Thus, in the long and detailed introductions to the *Phaedrus* and to the *Symposium* he explains how one should read these dialogues in order to dispense with the problem and, in his terms, approach the pure philosophical content of Plato. The corollary of this insistence on the abstract is that desire between men is no more than a rhetorical figure. Socrates's second discourse in the *Phaedrus*, for example, is 'only an allegory, or figure of speech'.[14] Similarly, Pausanias's speech in the *Symposium* is 'more words than matter'.[15] The implication of Jowett's account here is that while homosexuality is undoubtedly the subject, its presence is for reasons of argument; that there is a transformation of homosexual desire into rhetoric which dematerialises the somatic desire itself.

There are two further manoeuvres Jowett makes which bring us closer to the actual practice of reading, and throw into relief the antinomian nature of Symonds's reading. In relation to the *Phaedrus*, the great classicist writes:

> What Plato says of the loves of men must be transferred to the loves of women before we can attach any serious meaning to his words. Had he lived in our time he would have made the transposition himself.
>
> (p. 406)

While Symonds projects himself back into time, Jowett pulls Plato into the Christian era and reads him from the moral position of the present. This does not mean that Jowett is unaware of history, or gives up any sense of the historical context and construction of Platonic philosophy. Far from it. While proselytising for a Christian era reading, he adds that 'it is not to be denied that [...] nameless vices were prevalent at Athens and in other Greek cities' (p. 415). The point is that such historical knowledge should not be allowed to get in the way of finding the philosophical essence, the trans-historical morality which is better exemplified by Christian practice than Greek. Symonds's imaginative historicisation of himself, casting himself in his own classical costume drama and screening it on the pages of his Plato, does the very opposite, insisting that these historical facts are exactly the point. Jowett's other clue as to how to be a reader of Plato also occurs in the discussion of Socrates' second discourse in the *Phaedrus*. In reading the dialogue, we must not

> call up revolting associations, which as a matter of good taste should be banished, [...] These and similar passages should be interpreted by the Laws, book viii, 36.

> (p. 415)[16]

He prescribes a scholarly mode of reading where a text must always be understood in relation to other texts, in this case a precaution against unnatural love in the Laws. In order to read properly one must cross-reference, reading not in relation to one's own experience, as Symonds does, but in relation to other Platonic ideas. One should abstract oneself from the process except as the point through which different texts pass and collide. What I want to emphasise here is that these are not simply different interpretations of Plato, but that they point to different modes of reading: in the library or in the bedroom; to exercise the mind or to quicken the pulse; to find the letter of the text or to find alternatives in the margin; sitting upright or lounging; a hand with pen and paper, or a hand touching the page, urgently wanting to turn it. At the same time, there is a point at which these readings meet, and it would be wrong to be too dogmatic about the differences. Jowett's search for a given non-metaphorical truth at the heart of the text requires metaphor to find it. Symonds' ekphrastic reading insists on a literal account of certain textual elements. This resembles the paradox of the collector in the allegorist and the allegorist in the collector, as word dissolves at the edges into metaphor, and metaphor hardens into word. The two readings also meet at the boundary of the homoerotic. Jowett marks the limits of what can be said about Greek love; he stakes out a limit for the noble and abstract lessons that male relations can provide, beyond which 'they are liable to degenerate into fearful evil' (p. 529). Symonds, on the other hand, begins at that boundary and strays into the land beyond, finding not evil but joy, not monsters but his true self.

The book itself can function, like a body, like a text, as transport to this beyond. Having moved from image to text, I now want to move from text to book, and speculate on how the book as a thing can provoke the kinds of reading practice we have seen in Day and Symonds. And beyond this, I want to suggest that the book can serve as a *representation* of this kind of reading. Bibliophiles will understand at once that a book is more than a text. It can be a desirable object, beautiful in itself, luxurious or rare or imbued with a sentimental aura. Whether a weighty tome or a slim volume of verse, all aspects of the book can seduce: the binding, the cover, the weight, the quality and kind of paper, the typeface. For the book lover, the physical matter of the book is often inseparable from its contents. These material characteristics somehow become signs of the book's promise, what it has to offer once opened, or they are a visual memento of the pleasures garnered from it. The book's objecthood is not reducible to a physical description.

The late nineteenth century is a moment of particular significance in the history of book design. William Morris's Kelmscott Press is only the best known of a range of book designers and producers who attempted to recreate the book as a beautiful art object, in opposition to the commercial, commodified and often shoddily produced books churned out for the widening reading public. A new attention was brought to bear on what books looked like, what they were like to handle, their visual appearance in every detail from the binding to the layout of the margins. Hugh Kenner points out that the Kelmscott Chaucer was less a book and more a sacred object. The typography, he continues, made it difficult to read, requiring effort on the part of the reader. It is as if the reader is like a Burne-Jones knight, slashing his way through the briar wood of margin and densely woven type. In effect, to use Kenner's brilliant metaphor, Chaucer was not just stories, but a remote place to be attained.[17] If this casting of the book in terms of space and matter is one concern of the bibliographic world of late Victorian Britain, another is the book as a moral, and often erotic object. While there has always been a suspicion of books, the 1880s and 1890s magnify this. *The Yellow Book* is the most widely discussed symptom of this suspicion. While the journal is largely characterised by the highbrow decency of its contributors (Henry James, Lord Leighton), it was viewed by many as murky territory. The garish cover with its perverse Beardsley illustration may not point to any definite moral failing, but it was seen to have an air of the unhealthy, decadent or morally suspect.

What is being acknowledged is not so much the immoral content of a particular publication, but the ways in which morals can slip from the decent to the indecent. There are geographical and personal analogues: think of Holywell Street where antiquarians and bibliophiles are also pornographers: think of Leonard Smithers, the literary avant-gardiste, who was also the brains behind the Erotika Biblion Society, publishing volumes like Casanova's memoirs and the homosexual pornographic novel, *Teleny*; or think of Sir Richard Burton whose ethnographic scholarship ends with his famous essay, appended to his *Arabian Nights*, about 'the sodatic zone'.[18] The book can remove one from the world of temptation or can provoke and provide proscribed solitary pleasures. Books are no longer simply good or bad. Instead they become a place where thresholds are opened up and crossed, a place where the most legitimate culture can be transfigured into the most debased. As the example of *The Yellow Book* demonstrates, the physical appearance of the book is very much part of this moral nexus.

One of the best-known books of the 1890s, certainly from a design point of view, is the first volume of verse by John Gray, a slim and exquisite volume called *Silverpoints* (Plate 18). Published in 1893, the book was designed by Charles Ricketts, and the publication was originally to have been funded by Wilde. In the early 1890s, Gray was Wilde's protegé, and is still perhaps best known for the fact that his name is the same as that of Wilde's most infamous creation. Gray, Ricketts and Wilde were all homosexual. Is this important? On the one hand it is a very striking fact. On the other, it might be a misleading detail given the wealth of other contexts in which the book might be read, such as the decadence of 1890s verse, the Rhymers' Club, or the growth of small presses. What I want to suggest here is not that *Silverpoints* is homosexual in any straightforward way, but that it offers a template for the book that is consonant with the bourgeois homoerotic reading practice we saw in Day and Symonds. (I want to emphasise the bourgeois, since this is not to be understood as a generic homosexual reading. It has, needless to say, a powerful class dimension).

One has only to see a copy of *Silverpoints* to recognise at once that this book is more than the actual verse. So distinct is the design, it has, since its publication, threatened to upstage the poetry. Frank Harris, in a review in the *Saturday Review*, declared the poem 'The Barber' to be 'the only piece that comes up to the binding'.[19] Soon after its publication, Ricketts wrote to Fred Holland Day that ' "Silverpoints" is achieving quite a success of excoriation for which the eccentric book shape and printing come in for a small share'.[20] Rather than to stage a contest between binding and content, though, the design of *Silverpoints* is intended to complement the poems. Late Victorian writing on bibliographic matters makes frequent reference to what one critic calls 'a physiognomy in books', and it was widely acknowledged that a relationship should pertain between binding and content.[21] Victorian books are often banally literal about this, with covers frequently illustrating the contents in a direct manner: editions of Shakespeare often have a portrait of the author on the cover. Ricketts is subtler in ensuring that the physical appearance of the book prepares the reader for a certain kind of poetry. One might even say that the design of the book is a representation of Gray's verse. The stamped cover with its fine repeated pattern points to a certain small-scale decorativeness, a preciousness (in both senses of that word). More importantly, the *design is also a representation of a certain way of reading*, and I want to defend this claim by attending to the book's format, its typography, and its layout.

The format is unusual. Ricketts, on one occasion, claimed a Renaissance prototype for it – a Virgil once owned by Isabella d'Este[22] – but it has been more usually identified as a saddle book, a Persian format. This in itself offers up a host of associations. Persia and the sensual are often taken to be synonymous in the late nineteenth century. Gleeson White connects them in an article on Moreau in *The Pageant* in 1897 (also designed by Ricketts).[23] One might cite Sir Richard Burton and his interest in Persia, or the poet Hafiz, whose homosexual verse was much translated and discussed in the nineteenth century. The format is also a disavowal of paper's ubiquity. If the growth of print media now means that all Victorian Britain is plastered with pages, this book revisits a world where paper is a luxury. This is evident in the form, in the quality of the paper used, and in the profligacy signalled by the margins, which I shall come to in a moment. The saddle book offers bibliographic intimacy, too. Unlike, say, the Kelmscott Chaucer, which needs a desk, this book is to be carried, held, brought close to the body.

The typography, like Morris's, is not so easy to read (Plates 19 and 20). William S. Peterson points out that for the Victorians fineness of type was a hallmark of refinement;[24] this is exactly what Morris was protesting when he thickened the Golden type to its blocky proportions or fashioned the weighty Chaucer type, so redolent of concrete labour. In contrast, Ricketts retains the fine strokes, the refined and slender characters, but by italicising produces a similarly dense effect. Unlike the heavily-inked Kelmscott types, Ricketts thins the density and blackness of print. One still becomes aware of the words as visual matter, but here the transparency of typography is replaced with, if not the thorny briar, then a knot of ornamental grasses. The title of the volume resonates here; the pen is a silverpoint; the poetry scratched lines in a surface rather than forms stamped on the page. One might think again of the Beardsley embroiderer's needle, of his design for the cover of Ernest Dowson's *Verses* of 1896. The cover shows mere lines, but these arabesques suggest something more. They are incised like a scar on flesh, a mark of being or having been in the world, of a membrane where world and body meet. If Victorians regularly discussed the binding as the book's clothing, this is the binding as skin; like the skin, a site of subjectivity, of touching back. And like skin, pages might be scarred rather than tattooed, scraped by experience rather than reified by ink.

Perhaps the most striking aspect of *Silverpoints'* design is the relationship of the lyric to the page (Plate 19). The poems are printed in small type, and titles and shorter verse are positioned high on the page. Given the shape of the book, this can result in expansive margins; though this is less notable with the longer verse, there is still generous marginal space.[25] Percy Fitzgerald, writing a few years before the publication of *Silverpoints*, sees such margins as affectation:

> Vast margins are often ridiculous exaggerations [...] and present a greater superficial surface of blank paper than does the type itself, as though the fringe or border of the garment were broader than the garment.[26]

Similarly, Emory Walker, who co-designed Morris's typefaces, argued in a lecture to the Arts and Crafts Exhibition Society in 1888 that one failure of modern books was too much space on the page (that lecture became an essay co-authored by Walker and Morris in *Arts and Crafts Essays* in 1893, the year of *Silverpoints'* publication).[27] Ricketts' design prompted a more favourable and more famous remark by Ada Leverson, Wilde's Sphinx: she said that someone should produce a book that is all margin.[28] This is not merely clever or witty, although it is both. It points to a rethinking of the book's design and how it relates to the practice of reading. It makes one aware of the nature of the margins in Morris's books, and how they prescribe the place to be attained in the process of reading. It also prompts the question: what difference does the empty margin make? In certain musical scores, one finds empty bars at the end of pieces or movements, whereby the final chords are followed by rests, or by a rest with a pause mark over it to extend the final silence, making it clear that the piece continues after the final notes have been struck.[29] The composer creates a marginal space in which both the final notes and the listener's response resonate; a reflection, aural and imaginative, that is part of the piece itself. I wonder if this is an appropriate analogy for Ricketts's and Gray's margins. The slender lyric resonates across the blank spaces of the page, unbound from the dense and didactic margins of touchstones and philology and comparative texts.

As an aside, I wonder if there is a more general pattern to be glimpsed here. Increasingly in the period, we see the polarisation of blankness as a space of possibility against insistent and obsessive plenitude as a prescription. In the blank margins of *Silverpoints*, there is a screen for projection; in the Kelmscott Chaucer, the reader is mired in the web of pattern (Plate 20). The empty margin provides a forum for the assembling of fragments; the filled page provides a fantasy of completeness. In decoration one could place the Aesthetic Interior with its eye-boggling detail, its wish to fill every surface with pattern, line, and colour, next to the radically white, blank walls of Keats House, the Godwin house where Wilde and the painter Frank Miles lived. Or think of skin. In Leighton's portrait of Richard Burton time is an aesthetic decorator, covering the surface with proof of a life lived, in the scar, the wrinkling and mottling of the epidermis. In a painting like Henry Scott Tuke's *The Bathers* of 1885, by contrast, we are presented with the dream of a skin which is yet to meet the world. One could also trace this distinction in sculpture, between the white surface of the endlessly mutable ideal and sculpture as the accretion of matter; on the one hand, an attempt to turn substance into pure, blank form, as in a work like Thomas Brock's *Eve* (1900), on the other, the transformation of form into substance as in Gilbert's *St. Elizabeth of Hungary* of the same year. All these pairs, like the margins, are less about marked and unmarked skins, and more about the marked and the not-yet-marked. This distinction is not to be understood as good and bad, as modern and Victorian; I certainly do not want to claim that blankness is to be more highly valued. Often it is the reactionary position, as demonstrated by Morris's radicalism and the conservatism of Gray and Ricketts. Moreover, as with collector and allegorist, they are not wholly separable. Both plenitude and blankness are ways of thinking about the future; in the former an orientation is already there, in the latter one's orientation in space, in selfhood, in the world, is yet to be determined. None the less, blankness does wait to be touched, to be marked by the snail horns of the imagination.

It may seem as if I have strayed far from the question of homoeroticism, and it may be that I have. But while *Silverpoints* resists labelling as a 'homosexual book' it embodies a strategy of design and encourages a mode of reading that lends itself to an ekphrastic homosexual imagination. It bears something of the same character as Day's Keats and Symonds' Plato in that it represents a threshold to the imagining of an alternative world. It suggests that, even in London, with its possibilities for cruising, its baths and brothels, its guardsmen and gentlemen, there were other ways for homosexual desire to find a home in the world. My final image shows Charles Ricketts, sitting with a pile of books from his own Vale Press. The one point of focus in the photograph, the one point of presence, is Ricketts' hand, weighted, lying across the page, the fingers curled round to touch the binding. Ricketts himself is absorbed, a modern Hypnos, but instead of a poppy held to the lips, a book touches the hand. Like Hypnos, his body dissolves as another body forms in the space of the text. In his influential essay 'The Phenomenology of Reading', Georges Poulet describes the book as a thing waiting for the reader to liberate it from its materiality.[30] But I wonder if the opposite pertains; the book can free the reader from his or her materiality; or, at least, allow him to re-imagine his materiality. As Proust remarks in his essay on Ruskin's *Sesame and Lilies*:

> Reading is for us the inciter whose magic keys open to our innermost selves the doors of abodes into which we would not have known how to penetrate.[31]

This is not the 'Open Sesame!' of Ruskin's theory, a door into a world that already exists. Like Day, like Symonds, Ricketts has found the optic instrument that allows him to read another world into existence.

How else might the world be? The answer can be read in the melting edge of a body, in the quickening of the pulse; it is inscribed on the binding and written on the blank page.

Notes

1. See, for example, Julie F. Codell, 'Painting Keats: Pre-Raphaelite Artists between Social Transgression and Painterly Conventions', *Victorian Poetry*, 33:3/4 (1995), 341–70.
2. James Najarian, *Victorian Keats: Manliness, Sexuality and Desire* (Basingstoke: Palgrave – now Palgrave Macmillan, 2002).
3. *The Poetical Works and Other Writings of John Keats*, ed. by Henry Buxton Forman, 4 vols (London: Reeves and Turner, 1883), I, xxviii; Sidney Colvin, *Keats* (London: MacMillan, 1887), p. 212.
4. William Michael Rossetti, *Life of John Keats* (London: Walter Scott, 1887), p. 206.
5. For another case study linking Arnold, vision, and homosexuality, see Michael Hatt, 'Near and Far: Homoeroticism, Labour, and Hamo Thornycroft's *Mower*', *Art History*, 26:1 (February 2003), 26–55.
6. Keats uses the phrase in a letter to Benjamin Haydon of 8 April 1818: *The Letters of John Keats, 1814–1821*, ed. by Hyder Edward Rollins, 2 vols (Cambridge, MA and London: Harvard University Press, 1958), I, 265.
7. For Benjamin's account of collecting see: 'Convolut H' in Walter Benjamin, *The Arcades Project*, ed. by Rolf Tiedemann, trans. Howard Eiland and Kevin McCoughlin (Cambridge, MA and London: The Belknap Press, 1999), pp. 203–11; Walter Benjamin, 'Unpacking My Library,' *Selected Writings, Vol 2: 1927–1934*, ed. by Michael W. Jennings, Howard Eiland, and Gary Smith,

trans. Rodney Livingstone et al. (Cambridge, MA and London: The Belknap Press, 1999), pp. 486–93.

8. Fred Holland Day, 'Is Photography an Art?', unpublished essay, Fred Holland Day papers, Norwood Public Library, Reel 3565.

9. John Ruskin, *Sesame and Lilies*, ed. Deborah Epstein Nord (New Haven and London: Yale University Press, 2002).

10. Republished in *The Complete Prose Works of Matthew Arnold*, IX, pp. 161–88.

11. Marcel Proust, *Time Regained*, p. 283.

12. Nicholas Frankel has written brilliantly on this: Nicholas Frankel, 'Aubrey Beardsley "Embroiders" the Text,' in Maxwell, *The Victorian Illustrated Book*, pp. 259–96.

13. *The Memoirs of John Addington Symonds*, p. 99.

14. *The Dialogues of Plato*, trans. with analysis and introduction by Benjamin Jowett, 5 vols (Oxford: Clarendon Press, 3rd edn, 1892), I, 415; hereafter in text.

15. *Dialogues of Plato*, I, 529.

16. In fact, Jowett means paragraph 836, a precaution against unnatural loves.

17. Hugh Kenner, *The Pound Era: the Age of Ezra Pound, T. S. Eliot, James Joyce, and Wyndham Lewis* (London: Faber & Faber, 1972), p. 24.

18. On Holywell Street, see Lynda Nead, *Victorian Babylon: People, Streets and Images in Nineteenth-Century London* (New Haven and London: Yale University Press, 2000); on Smithers see James G. Nelson, *Publisher to the Decadents: Leonard Smithers in the Careers of Beardsley, Wilde, Dowson* (High Wycombe: Rivendale Press, 2000); Richard Burton, 'Terminal Essay', *The Book of the Thousand Nights and a Night*, Vol. 10 (Benares: Kamashastra Society, 1885).

19. Frank Harris, review of *Silverpoints*, The *Saturday Review*, 75:1958 (6 May 1893), 493.

20. Letter from Ricketts to Fred Holland Day, undated, Fred Holland Day papers, Reel 3566.

21. Percy Fitzgerald, *The Book Fancier, or The Romance of Book Collecting* (London: Sampson Low, Marston, Searle & Rivington, 1886), p. 123.

22. Letter from Ricketts to Day, op. cit.

23. Gleeson White, 'The Pictures of Gustave Moreau,' *The Pageant*, 2 (1897), 3–16.

24. *The Ideal Book: Essays and Lectures on the Arts of the Book by William Morris*, ed. by William S. Peterson, p. xx.

25. At this point, I must acknowledge the work of Nicholas Mirzoeff whom I first heard raise this question of margins in a lecture he gave at the University of Nottingham in 2001 about Jewish-homosexual relations and visual culture in late nineteenth-century London. While Professor Mirzoeff's use of this trope is very different to my own, his elaboration of the margin is at the root of my analysis here and I am deeply indebted to him.

26. Fitzgerald, *The Book Fancier*, p. 121.

27. Peteron, *The Ideal Book*, p. xvii; Oscar Wilde reviewed Walker's lecture in the *Pall Mall Gazette*, 16 November 1888.

28. Ada Leverson, *Letters to the Sphinx from Oscar Wilde with Reminiscences of the Author by Ada Leverson* (London: Duckworth, 1930), p. 19.

29. See, as one example of very many, the end of Beethoven's String Quartet, op. 18, no. 3.
30. Georges Poulet, 'The Phenomenology of Reading,' *New Literary History*, I:1 (1969), 53–68: 53.
31. Marcel Proust, *On Reading Ruskin*, trans. and ed. by Jean Autret, William Burford, and Phillip J. Wolf (New Haven and London: Yale University Press, 1987), p. 118.

Select Bibliography

Abrams, M.H., *The Mirror and the Lamp* (New York: Oxford University Press, 1953).

Adams, James Eli, *Dandies and Desert Saints: Styles of Victorian Masculinity* (Ithaca and London: Cornell University Press, 1995).

Ahmed, Sara, *Queer Phenomenology: Orientations, Objects, Others* (Durham and London: Duke University Press, 2006).

Aldrich, Robert, *The Seduction of the Mediterranean: Writing, Art and Homosexual Fantasy* (London and New York: Routledge, 1993).

Altick, Richard, *The Shows of London* (Cambridge, MA and London: Belknap/Harvard University Press, 1978).

—— *Paintings from Books: Art and Literature in Britain, 1760–1900* (Columbus: Ohio University Press, 1985).

Appadurai, Arjun, ed., *The Social Life of Things: Commodities in Cultural Perspective* (Cambridge: Cambridge University Press, 1986).

Armstrong, Isobel, 'Transparency: Towards a Poetics of Glass in the Nineteenth Century', in Francis Spufford and Jenny Uglow, eds, *Cultural Babbage: Technology, Time and Invention* (London: Faber and Faber, 1996), pp. 123–48.

Armstrong, Nancy, *Fiction in the Age of Photography: the Legacy of British Realism* (Cambridge, MA and London: Harvard University Press, 1999).

Arnold, Matthew, 'The Function of Criticism at the Present Time', *The Complete Works of Matthew Arnold*, ed. by E.H. Super, 11 vols (Ann Arbor: University of Michigan Press, 1960–77), III.

Ashwin, Clive, 'Graphic Imagery 1837–1901: A Victorian Revolution', *Art History*, 1:3 (1978), 360–70.

Baker, Jeffrey, 'The Deaf Man and the Blind Man', *Critical Survey*, 8:3 (1996), 259–69.

Bann, Stephen, *The Clothing of Clio: a Study of the Representation of History in Nineteenth-Century Britain and France* (Cambridge and New York: Cambridge University Press, 1984).

—— *The True Vine: on Visual Representation and the Western Tradition* (Cambridge: Cambridge University Press, 1989).

Barthes, Roland, *Camera Lucida: Reflections on Photography*, trans. Richard Howard (New York: Hill and Wang, 1981).

Beer, Gillian and George Levine, *Literature and Medicine in Nineteenth-Century Britain: From Mary Shelley to George Eliot* (Cambridge: Cambridge University Press, 2004).

Benjamin, Walter, 'Paris – the Capital of the Nineteenth Century' (1935), *Charles Baudelaire: A Lyric Poet in the Era of High Capitalism*, trans. Harry Zohn (London: NLB, 1973), pp. 155–76.

—— 'The Work of Art in the Age of Mechanical Reproduction' (1936), *Illuminations*, trans. Harry Zohn (London: Fontana/Collins, 1973), pp. 219–53.

—— 'A Small History of Photography', *One Way Street and Other Writings*, trans. Edmund Jephcott and Kingsley Shorter (London: Verso, 1985), pp. 240–57.

—— 'Convolut H', *The Arcades Project*, ed. by Rolf Tiedemann, trans. Howard Eiland and Kevin McCoughlin (Cambridge, MA and London: The Belknap Press, 1999), pp. 203–11.

—— 'Unpacking My Library,' *Selected Writings, Vol 2: 1927–1934*, ed. by Michael W. Jennings, Howard Eiland, and Gary Smith, trans. Rodney Livingstone et al. (Cambridge, MA and London: The Belknap Press, 1999), pp. 486–93.

Berenson, Bernard, *The Italian Painters of the Renaissance* (Oxford: Clarendon Press, 1930).

—— *Seeing and Knowing* (London: Evelyn, Adams & Mackay, 1968).

Bergson, Henri, *Matter and Memory*, trans. Nancy Margaret Paul and W. Scott Palmer (New York: Zone Books, 1988).

Bloom, Harold, 'Visionary Cinema of Romantic Poetry', in *The Ringers in the Towers: Studies in Romantic Tradition* (Chicago and London: University of Chicago Press, 1971), pp. 37–52.

Brake, Laurel, 'Endgames: The Politics of *The Yellow Book* or, Decadence, Gender and the New Journalism', *Essays and Studies*, 48 (1995), 38–64.

—— *Print in Transition, 1850–1910: Studies in Media and Book History* (Basingstoke and New York: Palgrave – now Palgrave Macmillan, 2001).

—— and Ian Small, eds, *Pater in the '90s* (Greensboro, NC: ELT Press, University of North Carolina, 1991).

—— Lesley Higgins and Carolyn Williams, eds, *Walter Pater: Transparencies of Desire* (Greensboro, NC: ELT Press, 2002).

Briggs, Asa, *Victorian Things* (1988; Thrupp, Glos: Sutton, 2003).

Bristow, Joseph, 'Symonds's History, Ellis's Heredity: *Sexual Inversion*', in *Sexology and Culture: Labelling Bodies and Desires*, ed. by Lucy Bland and Laura Doan (Cambridge: Polity Press, 1998), pp. 79–99.

—— ed., *The Fin-de-Siècle Poem* (Athens, Ohio: Ohio University Press, 2005).

Brown, Bill, 'Thing Theory', *Critical Inquiry*, 28:1 (Autumn 2001), 1–22.

Bryson, Norman, *Tradition and Desire* (Cambridge: Cambridge University Press, 1984).

Burton, Richard, 'Terminal Essay', *The Book of the Thousand Nights and a Night*, vol. 10 (Benares: Kamashastra Society, 1885).

Burwick, Frederick, *Mimesis and its Romantic Reflections* (University Park, PA: Pennsylvania State University Press, 2001).

Buss, Helen M., David Lorne MacDonald, and Anne McWhir, *Mary Wollstonecraft and Mary Shelley: Writing Lives* (Windsor, Ontario: Wilfred Laurier University Press, 2001).

Carlyle, Thomas, 'The Dandiacal Body', *Sartor Resartus* (Oxford: Oxford University Press, 1999).

Cevasco, George A., *Breviary of the Decadence: J.K. Huysmans's A Rebours and English Literature* (New York: AMS Press, 2001).

Christ, Carol T. and John O. Jordan, eds, *Victorian Literature and the Victorian Visual Imagination* (Berkeley and London: University of California Press, 1995).

Classen, Constance, ed., *The Book of Touch* (London and New York: Berg, 2005).

Cleto, Fabio, ed., *Camp: Queer Aesthetics and the Performing Subject: a Reader* (Ann Arbor: The University of Michigan Press, 1999).

Codell, Julie F., 'Painting Keats: Pre-Raphaelite Artists between Social Transgression and Painterly Conventions', *Victorian Poetry*, 33:3/4 (1995), 341–70.

Colvin, Sidney, *Keats* (London: MacMillan, 1887).

Cook, Matt, *London and the Culture of Homosexuality 1885–1914* (Cambridge: Cambridge University Press, 2003).

Craft, Christopher, 'Come See About Me: Enchantment of the Double in *The Picture of Dorian Gray*', *Representations*, 91 (2005), 109–36.

Crary, Jonathan, *Techniques of the Observer: On Vision and Modernity in the Nineteenth Century* (Cambridge, MA and London: MIT Press, 1990).

—— *Suspensions of Perceptions: Attention, Spectacle, and Modern Culture* (Cambridge, MA, and London: MIT Press, 2000).

Curtis, Gerard, *Visual Words: Art and the Material Book in Victorian England* (Aldershot: Ashgate, 2002).

Davis, Whitney, 'Homoerotic Art Collection from 1750–1920, *Art History*, 24 (2001), 247–77.

de Man, Paul, *The Rhetoric of Romanticism* (New York: Columbia University Press, 1984).

Dellamora, Richard, *Masculine Desire: the Sexual Politics of Victorian Aestheticism* (Chapel Hill: University of North Carolina Press, 1990).

Derrida, Jacques, *Of Grammatology*, trans. Gayatri Chakravorty Spivak, 3rd edn (Baltimore: Johns Hopkins Press, 1974, repr. 1997).

—— *Memoirs of the Blind*, trans. Pascale-Anne Brault and Michael Naas (Chicago: University of Chicago Press, 1993).

Dollimore, Jonathan, *Sexual Dissidence* (Oxford: Clarendon Press, 1991).

Dowling, Linda, 'Letterpress and Picture in the Literary Periodicals of the 1890s', *Yearbook of English Studies*, 16 (1986), 117–31.

Edwards, Elizabeth and Janice Hart, eds, *Photographs, Objects, Histories* (London and New York: Routledge, 2004).

Edwards, Steve, *The Making of English Photography: Allegories* (University Park, PA: Pennsylvania State University Press, 2006).

Eliot, Simon, ' "Never Mind the Value, What about the Price?"; Or, How Much did "Marmion" Cost St. John Rivers?', *Nineteenth-Century Literature*, 56:2 (2001), 160–97.

Elsner, John and Roger Cardinal, eds, *The Cultures of Collecting* (London: Reaktion Books Ltd., 1994).

Feldman, Jessica R., *Gender on the Divide: the Dandy in Modernist Literature* (Ithaca: Cornell University Press, 1993).

Felski, Rita, *The Gender of Modernity* (Cambridge, MA: Harvard University Press, 1995).

Ferris, Ina, ed., 'Romantic Bibliomania', special issue of Romantic Circles in *Romantic Libraries*, http://www.rc.umd.edu/praxis/libraries/index.html, accessed 16 December 2008.

Fish, Stanley, *Self-Consuming Artifacts: The Experience of Seventeenth-Century Literature* (Berkeley: University of California Press, 1972).

Fitzgerald, Percy, *The Book Fancier, or The Romance of Book Collecting* (London: Sampson Low, Marston, Searle & Rivington, 1886).

Flint, Kate, *The Victorians and the Visual Imagination* (Cambridge: Cambridge University Press, 2000).

Foucault, Michel, *The Birth of the Clinic: An Archaeology of Medical Perception*, trans. A.M. Sheridan Smith (London: Tavistock, 1973; rpt. 1975).

Frederick, Burwick and Jürgen Klein, eds, *The Romantic Imagination: Literature and Art in England and Germany* (Amsterdam and Atlanta, GA: Rodopi, 1996).

Freud, Sigmund, 'Medusa's Head', *The Standard Edition of the Complete Psychological Works of Sigmund Freud*, 24 vols, trans. and ed. by James Strachey (London: The Hogarth Press, 1953–1974), XVIII, 273–4.

Fuss, Diana, *The Sense of an Interior: Four Writers and the Rooms that Shaped Them* (New York: Routledge, 2004).

Gagnier, Regenia, *Idylls of the Marketplace: Oscar Wilde and the Victorian Public* (Stanford: Stanford University Press, 1986).

Goethe, Johann Wolfgang von, *Italian Journey* (1786), trans. W.H. Auden and Elizabeth Mayer (London: Penguin, 1976).

—— *Roman Elegies and Other Poems*, ed. and trans. Michael Hamburger (London: Anvil Press Poetry, 1996).

Groth, Helen, *Victorian Photography and Literary Nostalgia* (Oxford and New York: Oxford University Press, 2004).

Halberstam, Judith, *Female Masculinity* (Durham and London: Duke University Press, 1998).

—— *In a Queer Time and Place: Transgender Bodies, Subcultural Lives* (New York and London: New York University Press, 2005).

Hatt, Michael, 'Near and Far: Homoeroticism, Labour, and Hamo Thornycroft's *Mower*', *Art History*, 26:1 (2003), 26–55.

Hawthorne, Nathaniel, *The Marble Faun: or, the Romance of Monte Beni*, The Centenary Edition of the Works of Nathaniel Hawthorne, IV (Columbus: Ohio State University Press, 1968).

Hawthorne, Sophia Peabody, *Notes on Italy 1853–1860* (London: Sampson Low, 1869).

Heffernan, James, 'Ekphrasis and Representation', *NLH*, 22 (1991), 301–2.

—— *Museum of Words* (Chicago: The University of Chicago Press, 1993).

Hemingway, Andrew, ed., *Marxism and the History of Art: from William Morris to the New Left* (London and Ann Arbor, MI: Pluto Press, 2006).

Horne, Peter, and Reina Lewis, eds, *Outlooks: Lesbian and Gay Sexualities and Visual Cultures* (London: Routledge, 1996).

Horne, Philip, 'Henry James at Work: The Question of Our Texts', in *The Cambridge Companion to Henry James*, ed. by Jonathan Freedman (Cambridge: Cambridge University Press, 1998), pp. 63–72.

Houfe, Simon, *Fin de Siècle: The Illustrators of the Nineties* (London: Barrie & Jenkins, 1992).

Howes, David, 'Charting the Sensorial Revolution', *Senses and Society*, 1 (2006), 113–28.

—— ed., *Empire of the Senses: The Sensual Culture Reader* (Oxford and New York: Berg, 2005).

Huysmans, Joris Karl, 'Modern Art', in Rosemary Lloyd, ed., *Revolutions in Writing: Readings in Nineteenth-Century French Prose* (Indiana University Press, 1996).

—— *Against Nature*, trans. Margaret Mauldon and ed. by Nicholas White (Oxford: Oxford University Press, 1998).

Jacobs, Carol, 'On Looking at Shelley's Medusa', *Yale French Studies*, 69 (1985), 163–79.

James, Henry, 'A Passionate Pilgrim', *The Atlantic Monthly*, 27 (March 1871), 352–71, and *The Atlantic Monthly* (April 1871), 478–99.

—— *Letters*, ed. by Leon Edel, 4 vols (Cambridge, MA: The Belknap Press of Harvard University Press, 1974).

—— *Italian Hours* (New York: Penguin Books, 1995).

—— *Henry James: Complete Stories 1898–1910* (New York: The Library of America, 1996).

—— *The Golden Bowl*, ed. by Virginia Llewellyn Smith (Oxford: Oxford University Press, 1999).

Jay, Martin, *Downcast Eyes: The Denigration of Vision in Twentieth-Century French Thought* (Berkeley, Los Angeles and London: University of California Press, 1993).

Keats, John, *The Letters of John Keats, 1814–1821*, ed. by Hyder Edward Rollins, 2 vols (Cambridge, MA and London: Harvard University Press, 1958).

—— *The Poetical Works and Other Writings of John Keats*, ed. by Henry Buxton Forman, 4 vols (London: Reeves and Turner, 1883).

Kooistra, Lorraine Janzen, *The Artist as Critic: Bitextuality in Fin-de-Siècle Illustrated Books* (Aldershot: Scolar, 1995).

—— 'Poetry and Illustration', in Richard Cronin, Alison Chapman and Antony H. Harrison, eds, *A Companion to Victorian Poetry* (Oxford: Blackwell, 2002), pp. 392–418.

Krauss, Rosalind, 'Notes on the Index: Part 1 and Part 2', in *The Originality of the Avant-Garde and Other Modernist Myths* (Cambridge, MA and London: MIT Press, 1986), pp. 196–219.

Krieger, Murray, *Ekphrasis: The Illusion of the Natural Sign* (Baltimore: Johns Hopkins University Press, 1991).

Kwint, Marius Christopher Breward and Jeremy Aynsley, eds, *Material Memories: Design and Evocation* (Oxford and New York: Berg, 1999).

Lacan, Jacques, *The Four Fundamental Concepts of Psychoanalysis*, trans. Alan Sheridan (London: Penguin, 1977).

Lamb, Charles, 'Detached Thoughts on Books and Reading', *The London Magazine* VI: xxxi (July 1822).

Larrissy, Edward, *The Blind and Blindness in Literature of the Romantic Period* (Edinburgh: Edinburgh University Press, 2007).

Lee, Vernon and Clementina Anstruther-Thomson, *Beauty and Ugliness and Other Studies in Psychological Aesthetics* (London: John Lane, The Bodley Head, 1912).

Lessing, Gotthold Ephraim, *Laocoon: an Essay on the Limits of Painting and Poetry*, trans. Edward Allen McCormick (Baltimore and London: Johns Hopkins University Press, 1984).

Levin, David Michael, ed., *Modernity and the Hegemony of Vision* (Berkeley: University of California Press, 1993).

—— ed., *Sites of Vision: The Discursive Construction of Sight in the History of Philosophy* (Cambridge, MA: MIT Press, 1996).

Lévinas, Emmanuel, *The Levinas Reader*, ed. by Seán Hand (Oxford: Basil Blackwell, 1989).

Lukács, Georg, 'Narrate or Describe?', in *Writer and Critic and Other Essays*, trans. and ed. by Arthur Kahn (London: Merlin Press, 1970), pp. 110–48.

Mannoni, Laurent, *The Great Art of Light and Shadow: Archaeology of the Cinema*, trans. and ed. by Richard Crangle (Exeter, UK: University of Exeter Press, 2000).

Marin, Louis, *To Destroy Painting*, trans. by Mette Hjort (Chicago and London: The University of Chicago Press, 1995).

Marjorie, Garber and Nancy J. Vickers, eds, *The Medusa Reader* (New York and London: Routledge, 2003).

Markiewicz, Henryk, 'Ut Pictura Poesis...A History of the Topos and the Problem', *New Literary History*, 18:3 (1987), 535–58.

Marx, Karl, *Capital Volume I*, trans. Ben Fowkes (London: Penguin, 1976).

—— *Economic and Philosophical Manuscripts of 1844*, trans. by Martin Milligan (Amherst, NY: Prometheus Books, 1988).

—— and Frederick Engels, *The German Ideology*, trans. C.J. Arthur (London: Lawrence, 1974).

Mason, Michael, 'The Way We Look Now: Millais' Illustrations to Trollope', *Art History*, 1:3 (1978), 309–40.

Maxwell, Richard, ed., *The Victorian Illustrated Book* (Charlottesville and London: University Press of Virginia, 2002).

McGann, Jerome J., *The Textual Condition* (Princeton: Princeton University Press, 1991).

McLuhan, Marshall, *Understanding Media: the Extensions of Man* (London: Routledge, 1964, repr. 2002).

Merleau-Ponty, Maurice, *The Primacy of Perception and Other Essays on Phenomenological Psychology, the Philosophy of Art, History and Politics*, ed. by James M. Edie (Chicago: North Western University Press, 1964).

—— *The Visible and the* Invisible, trans. Alphonso Lingis (Evanston, IL: Northwestern University Press, 1968).

—— *The Merleau-Ponty Aesthetics Reader: Philosophy and Painting*, ed. by Galen A. Johnson, trans. Michael B. Smith (Evanston, IL: Northwestern University Press, 1993).

Miller, Daniel, *The Comfort of Things* (Cambridge: Polity Press, 2008).

Mitchell, W.J.T., *Iconology: Image, Text, Ideology* (Chicago: University of Chicago Press, 1986).

—— *Picture Theory: Essays on Verbal and Visual Representation* (Chicago and London: University of Chicago Press, 1994).

—— *What Do Pictures Want? The Lives and Loves of Images* (Chicago and London: Chicago University Press, 2005).

Morris, William, *The Ideal Book. Essays and Lectures on the Arts of the Book by William Morris*, ed. by William S. Peterson (Berkeley and Los Angeles: University of California Press, 1982).

Najarian, James, *Victorian Keats: Manliness, Sexuality and Desire* (Basingstoke: Palgrave – now Palgrave Macmillan, 2002).

Nead, Lynda, *Victorian Babylon: People, Streets and Images in Nineteenth-Century London* (New Haven and London: Yale University Press, 2000).

—— *The Haunted Gallery: Painting, Photography, Film c.1900* (New Haven and London: Yale University Press, 2007).

Nelson, James G., *The Early Nineties: A View from the Bodley Head* (Cambridge: Harvard University Press, 1971).

—— *Publisher to the Decadents: Leonard Smithers in the Careers of Beardsley, Wilde, Dowson* (High Wycombe: Rivendale Press, 2000).

O'Dea, William T., *The Social History of Lighting* (London: Routledge, 1958).

Ovid, *Metamorphoses,* trans. A.D. Melville (Oxford: Oxford University Press, 1986).

Pascoe, Judith, *The Hummingbird Cabinet: a Rare and Curious History of Romantic Collectors* (Ithaca and London: Cornell University Press, 2006).

Pasztory, Esther, *Thinking with Things: Towards a New Vision of Art* (Austin: University of Texas Press, 2005).

Pater, Walter, *Plato and Platonism* (1893; London: Macmillan and Co., Ltd., 1910).

—— *The Renaissance* (1873; London: Macmillan, 1910).

Pearce, Susan M., ed., *Interpreting Objects and Collections* (London, Routledge, 1994).

Pemble, John, *The Mediterranean Passion* (Oxford: Clarendon Press, 1987).

—— *Venice Rediscovered* (Oxford and New York: Oxford University Press, 1996).

Potts, Alex, *Flesh and the Ideal: Winckelmann and the Origins of Art History* (New Haven and London: Yale University Press, 1994).

Poulet, Georges, 'The Phenomenology of Reading,' *New Literary History*, I:1 (1969), 53–68.

Powell, Cecilia, *Turner in the South: Rome, Naples, Florence* (New Haven and London, Yale University Press 1987).

Prettejohn, Elizabeth, ed., *After the Pre-Raphaelites: Art and Aestheticism in Victorian England* (Manchester: Manchester University Press, 1999).

Proust, Marcel, *Time Regained*, trans. by Andreas Mayor (London: Chatto & Windus, 1970).

—— *On Reading Ruskin*, trans. and ed. by Jean Autret, William Burford, and Phillip J. Wolf (New Haven and London: Yale University Press, 1987).

—— *In Search of Lost Time: Swann's Way*, trans. C.K. Scott Moncrieff and Terence Kilmartin, revised D.J. Enwright (London: Vintage, 1996).

Richardson, Alan, *British Romanticism and the Science of the Mind* (Cambridge: Cambridge University Press, 2001).

Riegl, Alois, *Late Roman Art Industry*, trans. Rolf Winkes (Rome: Bretschneider, 1985).

Rogers, Samuel, *The Italian Journal of Samuel Rogers*, ed. by John R. Hale (London: Faber and Faber 1956).

Rossetti, William Michael, *Life of John Keats* (London: Walter Scott, 1887).

Ruskin, John, *Ariadne Florentina: Six Lectures on Wood and Metal Engraving, with Appendix, Given before the University of Oxford in Michaelmas Term 1872* (London: George Allen, 1890).

—— *The Complete Works of John Ruskin*, ed. by E.T. Cook and A. Wedderburn, 39 vols (London: George Allen, 1903–12).

—— *Praeterita*, (London: George Allen, 1907).

—— *Sesame and Lilies*, ed. Deborah Epstein Nord (New Haven and London: Yale University Press, 2002).

Salecl, Renata and Slavoj Žižek, eds, *Gaze and Voice as Love Objects* (Durham and London: Duke University Press, 1996).

Saslow, James M., *Pictures and Passions: a History of Homosexuality in the Visual Arts* (New York and London: Viking Penguin, 1999).

Schivelbusch, Wolfgang, *Disenchanted Night; the Industrialisation of Light in the Nineteenth Century*, trans. Angela Davies (Berkeley: University of California Press, 1995).

Scott, Grant F., *The Sculpted Word: Keats, Ekphrasis and the Visual Arts* (Hanover, NH, and London: University Press of New England, 1994).

Sedgwick, Eve Kosofsky, *Between Men: English Literature and Male Homosocial Desire* (New York: Columbia University Press, 1985).

—— *Epistemology of the Closet* (Berkeley: University of California Press, 1990).

Shelley, Mary, *The Journals of Mary Shelley 1814–1844*, ed. by Paula R. Feldman and Diana Scott-Kilvert (Baltimore and London: Johns Hopkins University Press, 1995).

Shelley, Percy Bysshe, *Shelley's Prose Works*, 2 vols, ed. by R.H. Shepherd (London: Chatto & Windus, 1906).

—— *The Letters of Percy Bysshe Shelley*, 3 vols, ed. by Frederick L. Jones (Oxford: Clarendon Press, 1964).

Siegel, Jonah, *Haunted Museum: Longing, Travel, and the Art-Romance Tradition* (Princeton: Princeton University Press, 2005).

Sigel, Lisa Z., *Governing Pleasures: Pornography and Social Change in England, 1815–1914* (New Brunswick and London: Rutgers University Press, 2002).

Simmel, Georg, 'Adornment', *The Sociology of Georg Simmel*, trans. and ed. by Kurt H. Wolf (New York: Free Press, 1950), pp. 338–44.

Smith, Graham, *'Light that dances in the mind': Photographs and Memory in the Writings of E. M. Forster and his Contemporaries* (Oxford: Peter Lang, 2007).

Smith, Lindsay, *The Politics of Focus: Women, Children and Nineteenth Century Photography* (Manchester: Manchester University Press, 1998).

Solkin, David H. ed., *Art on the Line: The Royal Academy Exhibitions at Somerset House 1780–1836* (New Haven and London: Yale University Press, 2001).

Sontag, Susan, *On Photography* (1973; Harmondsworth, Middlesex: Penguin, 1979).

—— 'Notes on "Camp"', *Against Interpretation* (New York, Picador, 2001), pp. 275–93.

Starobinski, Jean, *The Invention of Liberty, 1700–1789*, trans. Bernard C. Swift (Geneva: Skira, 1964).

—— *1789 – The Emblems of Reason*, trans. Barbara Bray (Cambridge, MA and London: MIT Press, 1988).

Stebbins, Theodore E., *The Lure of Italy: American Artists and the Italian Experience 1760–1914* (Boston and New York: Museum of Fine Arts, Boston, and Abrams, 1992).

Stowe, William W., *Going Abroad: European Travel in Nineteenth-Century American Culture* (Princeton: Princeton University Press, 1994).

Sussman, Herbert, *Victorian Masculinities: Manhood and Masculine Poetics in Early Victorian Literature and Art* (Cambridge: Cambridge University Press, 1995).

Symonds, John Addington, *Studies of the Greek Poets* (London: Smith, Elder, & Co., 1873).

—— *Sketches in Italy and Greece* (London: Smith, Elder, & Co., 1874).

—— *Italian Byways* (London: Smith, Elder, & Co., 1883).

—— *The Letters of John Addington Symonds*, 3 vols, ed. by Herbert M. Schueller and Robert L. Peters (Detroit: Wayne State University Press, 1967–69).

—— *The Memoirs of John Addington Symonds*, ed. by Phyllis Grosskurth (New York: Random House, 1984).

Symons, A.J.A., 'An Unacknowledged Movement in Fine Printing: The Typography of the Eighteen-Nineties', *Fleuron* (1930), 83–119.

Szegedy-Maszak, Andrew, 'A Perfect Ruin: Nineteenth-Century Views of the Colosseum', *Arion: A Journal of Humanities and the Classics*, 2:1 (1992), 115–42.
Thomas, Julia, *Pictorial Victorians: the Inscription of Values in Word and Image* (Athens, Ohio: Ohio University Press, 2004).
Twyman, Michael, *Printing 1770–1970: An Illustrated History of its Development and Uses in England* (1970; London: The British Library, 1998).
Vance, William L., *America's Rome*, 2 vols (New Haven and London: Yale University Press, 1989).
Watson, Janell, *Literature and Material Culture from Balzac to Proust* (Cambridge: Cambridge University Press, 1999).
Wellek, René, 'Vernon Lee, Bernard Berenson and Aesthetics', in *Friendship's Garland: Essays Presented to Mario Praz*, ed. by Vittorio Gabrieli, 2 vols (Rome: Edizioni di Storia e Letteratura, 1966), II, 233–51.
Wilde, Oscar, *An Ideal Husband* (Oxford: Oxford University Press, 1998).
—— *Oscar Wilde: The Importance of Being Earnest and Other Plays*, ed. by Peter Raby (Oxford: Oxford University Press, 1998).
—— *The House of Pomegranates, Oscar Wilde: Complete Shorter Fiction*, ed. by Isobel Murray (Oxford: Oxford University Press, 1998).
—— *The Picture of Dorian Gray: The 1890 and 1891 Texts*, ed. by Joseph Bristow (Oxford: Oxford University Press, 2005).
Winckelmann, Johann, *History of the Art of Antiquity*, ed. by Alex Potts and trans. Harry Francis Mallgrave (Los Angeles: Getty Publications, 2006).
Wolf, Bryan, 'Confessions of a Closet Ekphrastic: Literature, Painting and other Unnatural Relations', *Yale Journal of Criticism*, 3 (1990), 181–203.
Wordsworth, William, *The Prelude: The Four Texts (1798, 1799, 1805, 1850)*, ed. by Jonathan Wordsworth (Harmondsworth: Penguin, 1995).
—— and Dorothy, *The Letters of William and Dorothy Wordsworth: The Early Years: 1787–1805*, ed. by E.D. Selincourt, revsd by Chester L. Shaver, 2nd edn (Oxford: Clarendon Press, 1967).
—— *The Letters of William and Dorothy Wordsworth*, 8 vols, ed. by Ernest de Selincourt, revsd by Alan G. Hill, 2nd edn (Oxford: Oxford University Press, 1979).

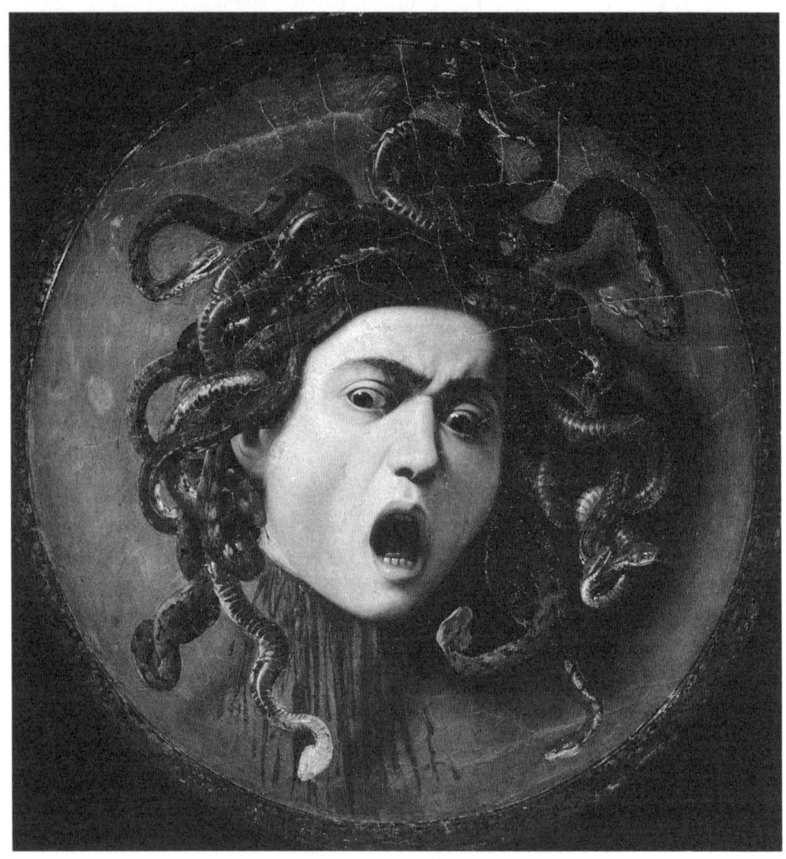

Plate 1   Michelangelo Merisi da Caravaggio, *Medusa Painted on a Leather Joust-ing Shield*, *c.*1596–98 (oil on canvas attached to wood) © Galleria degli Uffizi, Florence, Italy / The Bridgeman Art Library

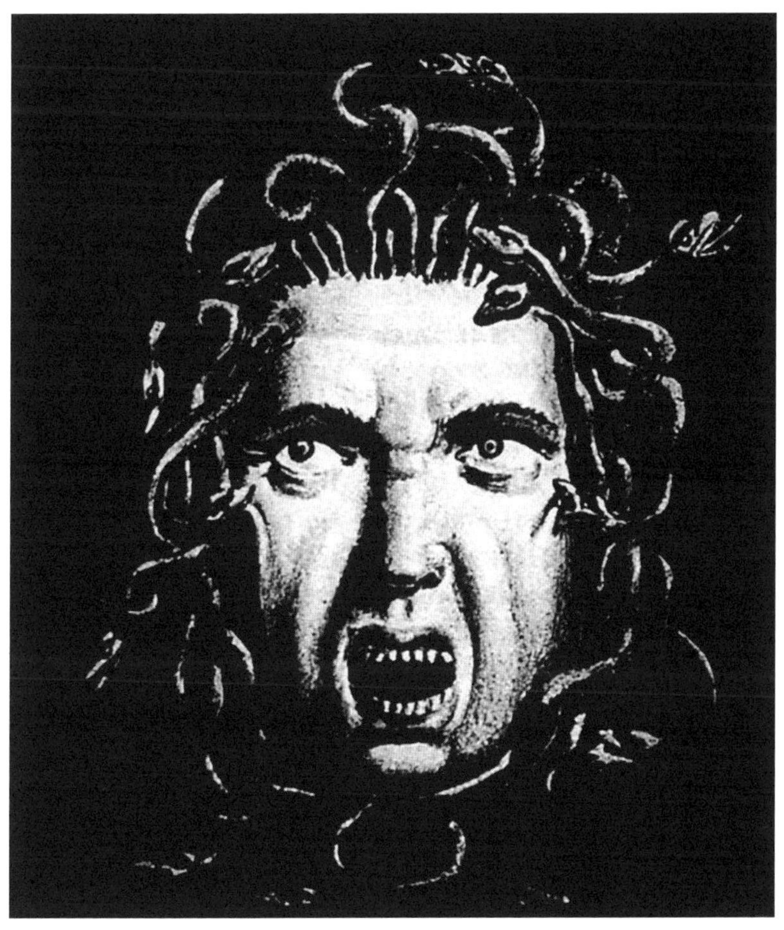

Plate 2 Medusa Head, hand painted animated lantern slide, France, *c*.1800;
courtesy of the collection of Laurent Mannoni

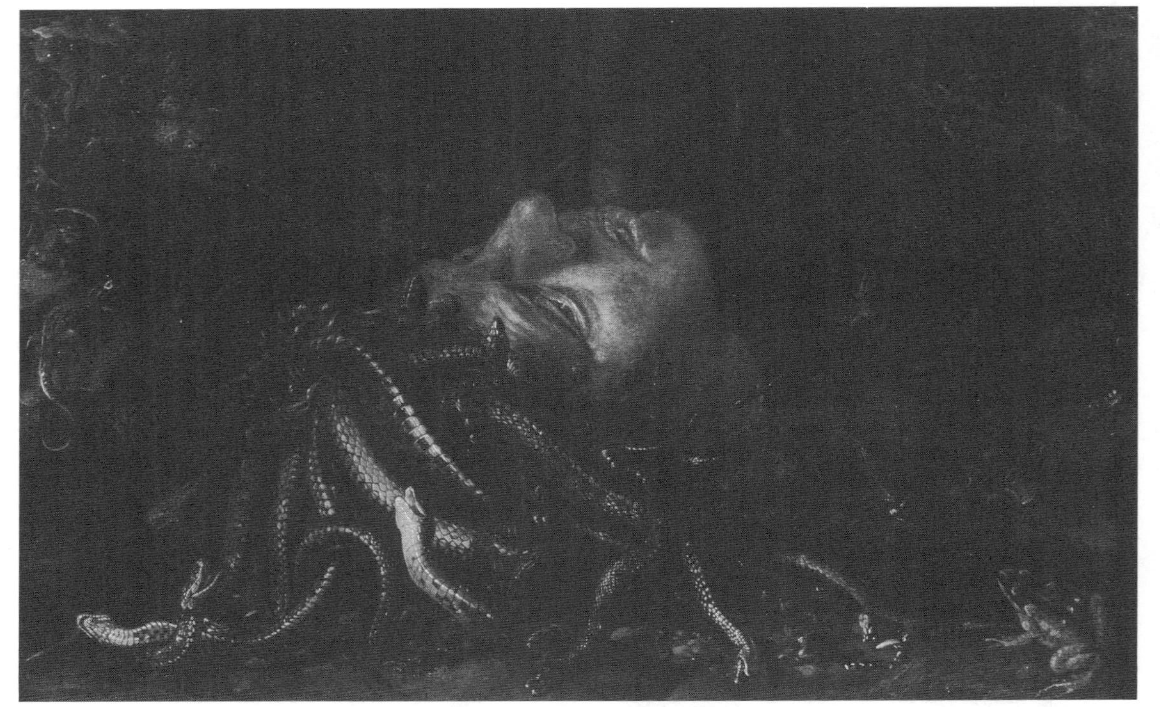

Plate 3 Flemish School, *Head of Medusa* (oil on wood) 16th century © Galleria degli Uffizi, Florence, Italy / The Bridgeman Art Library

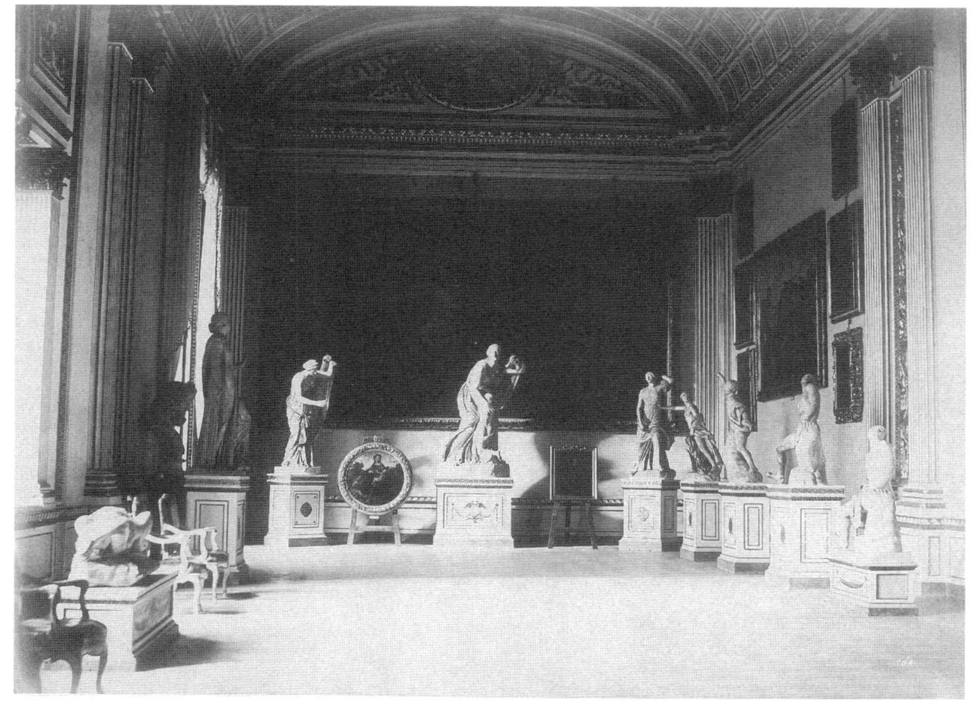

Plate 4   Alinari Archives – Florence: Gaspare Maria Paoletti, 'Sala della Niobe nella Galleria degli Uffizi di Firenze' (Gallery of Niobe in the Uffizi, Florence) (1856–57), albumen print

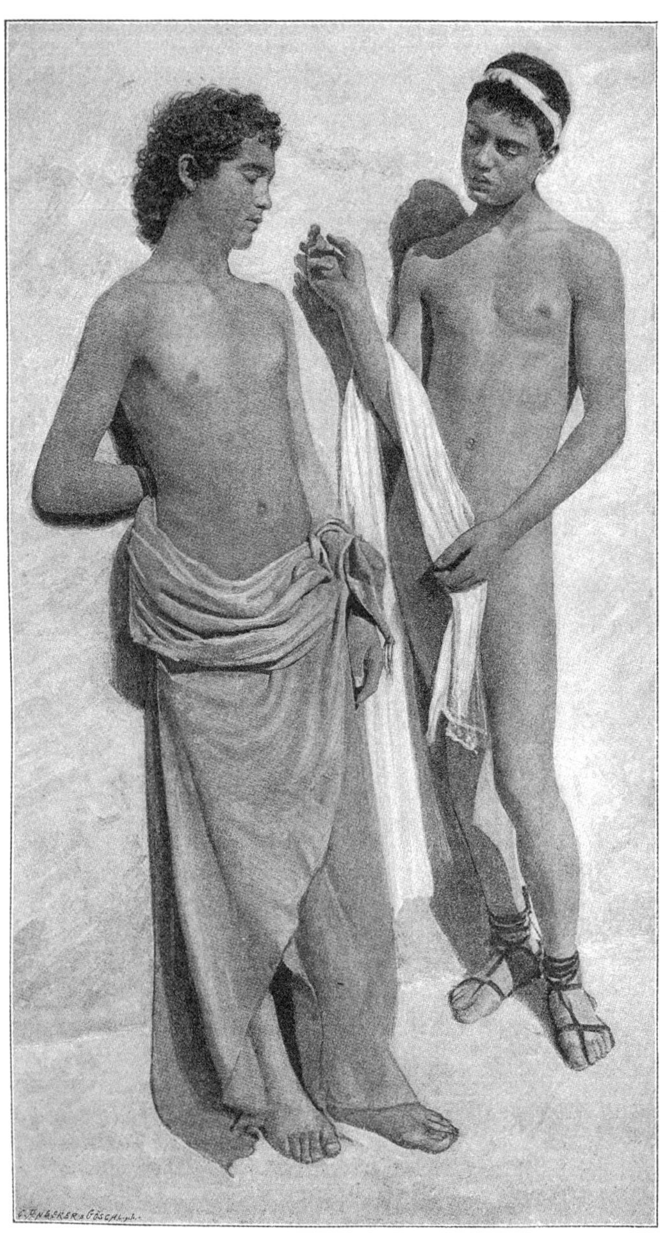

Plate 5 'Sicilian Youths: from a Photograph by W. Gloëden', *The Studio* (June 1893), p. 103, courtesy of The Bodleian Library, University of Oxford, Per. 17006 *c*.29

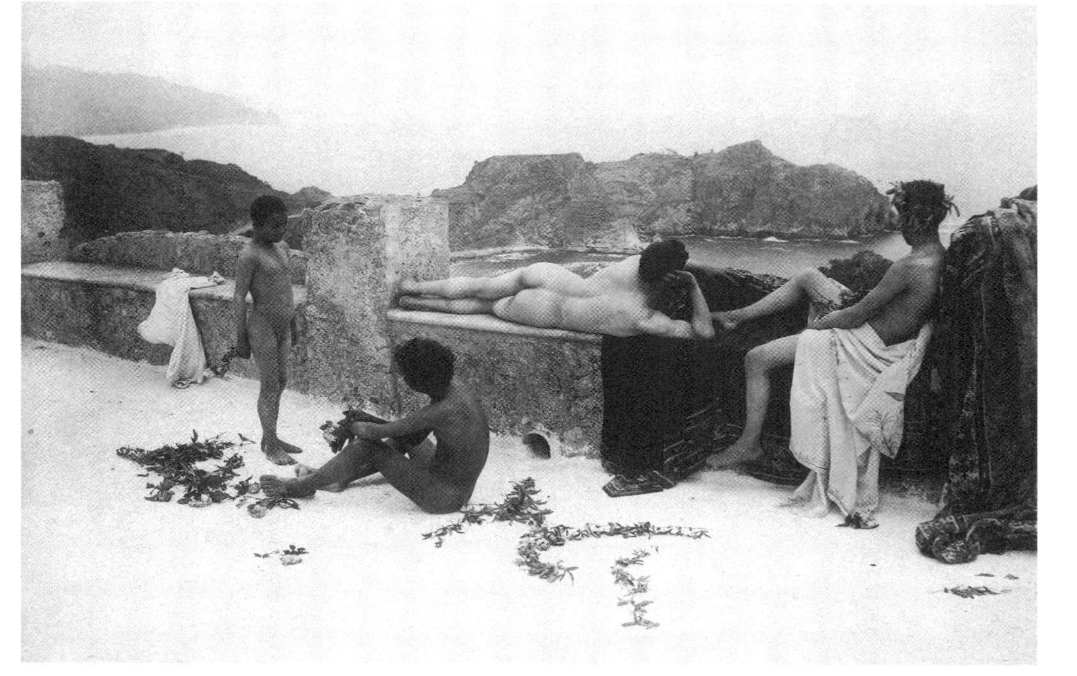

Plate 6   Alinari Archives – Florence: Wilhelm Von Gloeden, 'Giovani nudi su una terrazza panoramica' (Naked youths on a panoramic terrace (*c*.1900))

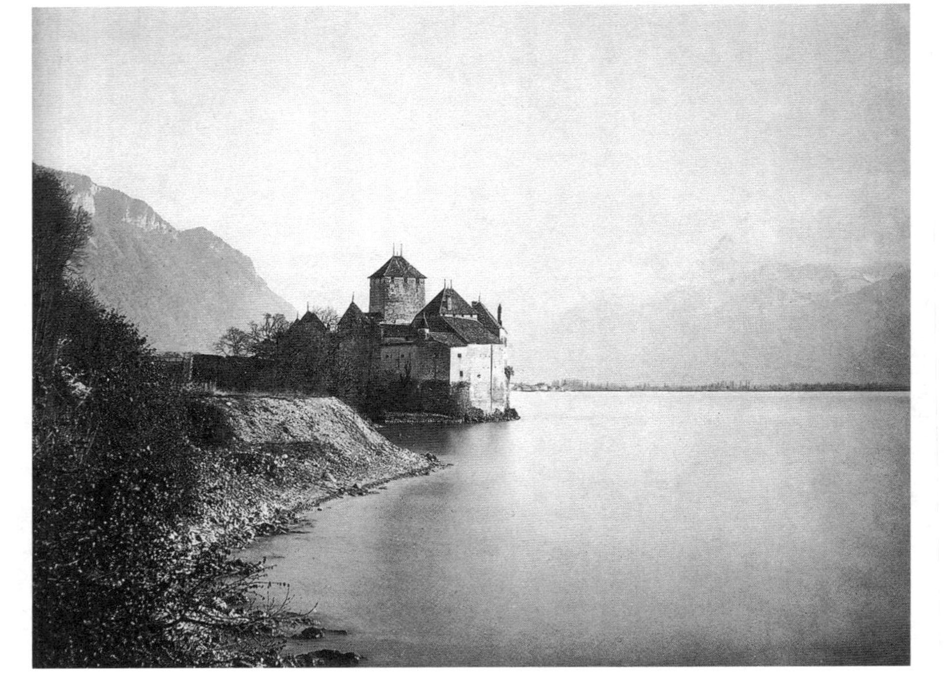

Plate 7 Adolphe Braun, 'The Castle of Chillon', Lake Geneva (*c*.1867), albumen print, Museum of Fine Arts, Boston, Lucy Dalbiac Luard Fund, 1982.322, photograph © 2009 Museum of Fine Arts, Boston

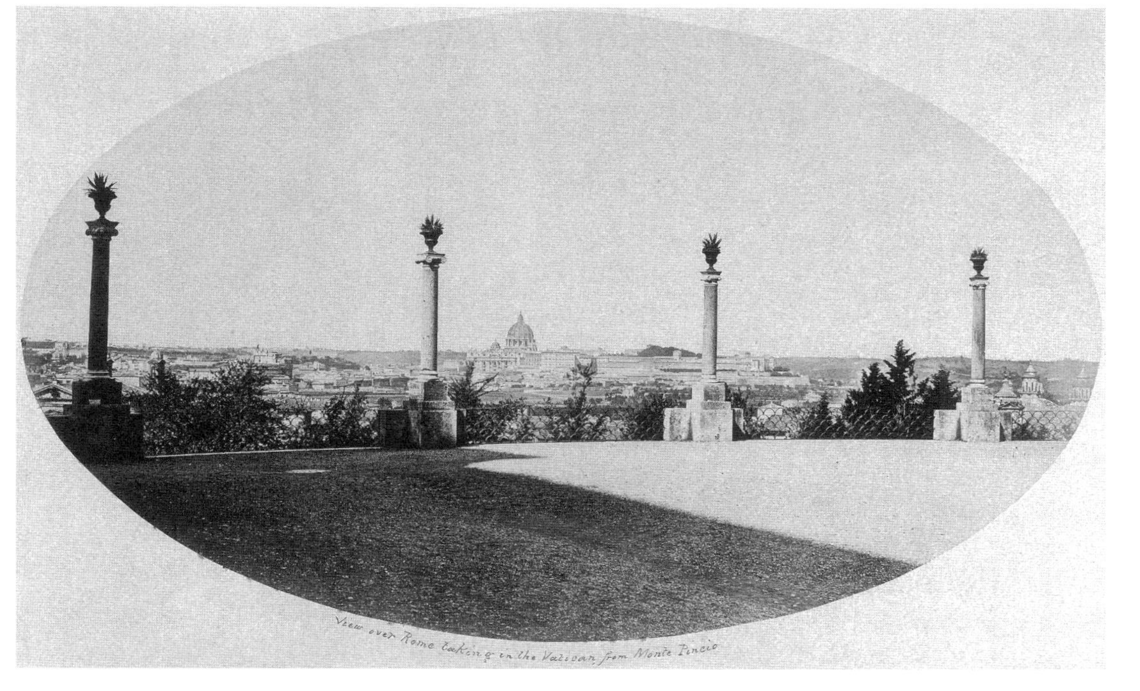

Plate 8   Alinari Archives – Florence: Robert Macpherson, 'Photographic Pictures of Rome: Veduta di Roma dal Monte Pincio' (View of Rome from the Pincio hill) (*c*.1860), albumen print

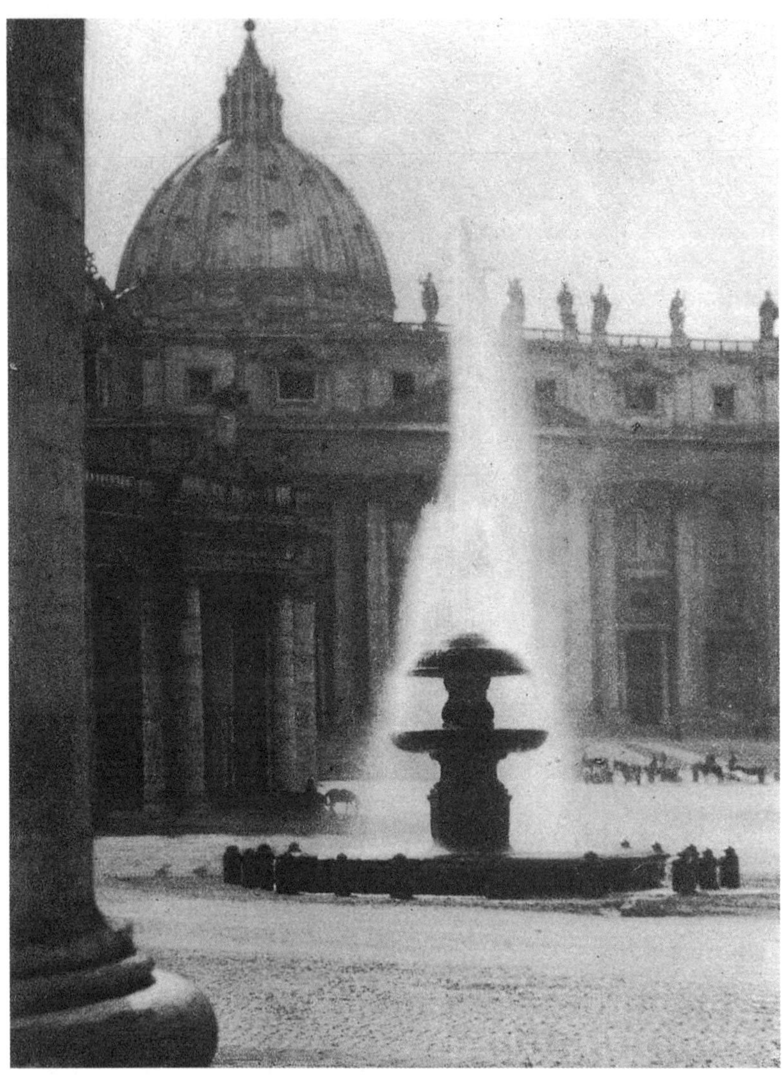

Plate 9 Alvin Langdon Coburn, *By St Peter's*, 1906, photogravure used as frontispiece to 'Daisy Miller', *The Novels and Tales of Henry James*, Volume 18 (New York: Charles Scribner's Sons, 1908), private collection

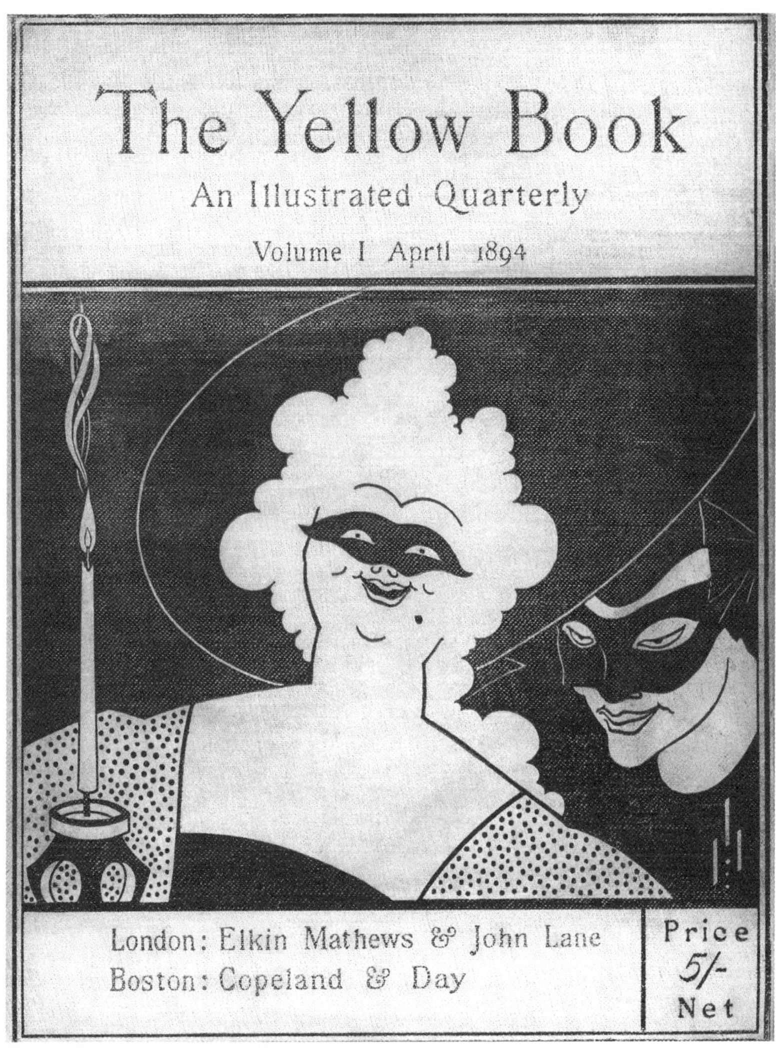

Plate 10 Front cover of *The Yellow Book* 1 (1894), designed by Aubrey Beardsley, private collection

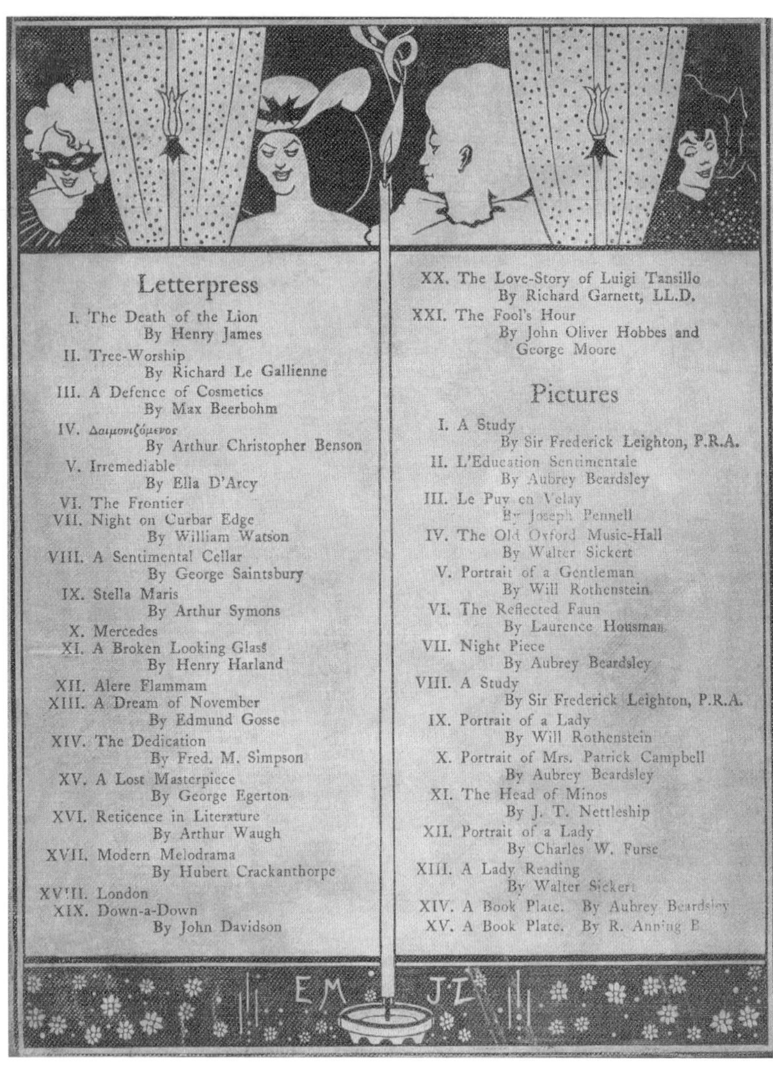

Plate 11   Back cover of *The Yellow Book* 1 (1894), designed by Aubrey Beardsley, private collection

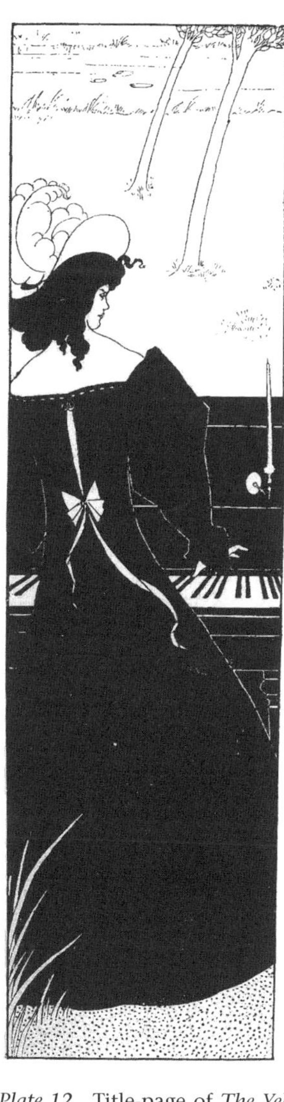

The Yellow Book

An Illustrated Quarterly

Volume I   April 1894

London : Elkin Mathews
          & John Lane
Boston : Copeland &
          Dav

Plate 12   Title-page of *The Yellow Book* 1 (1894), designed by Aubrey Beardsley, private collection

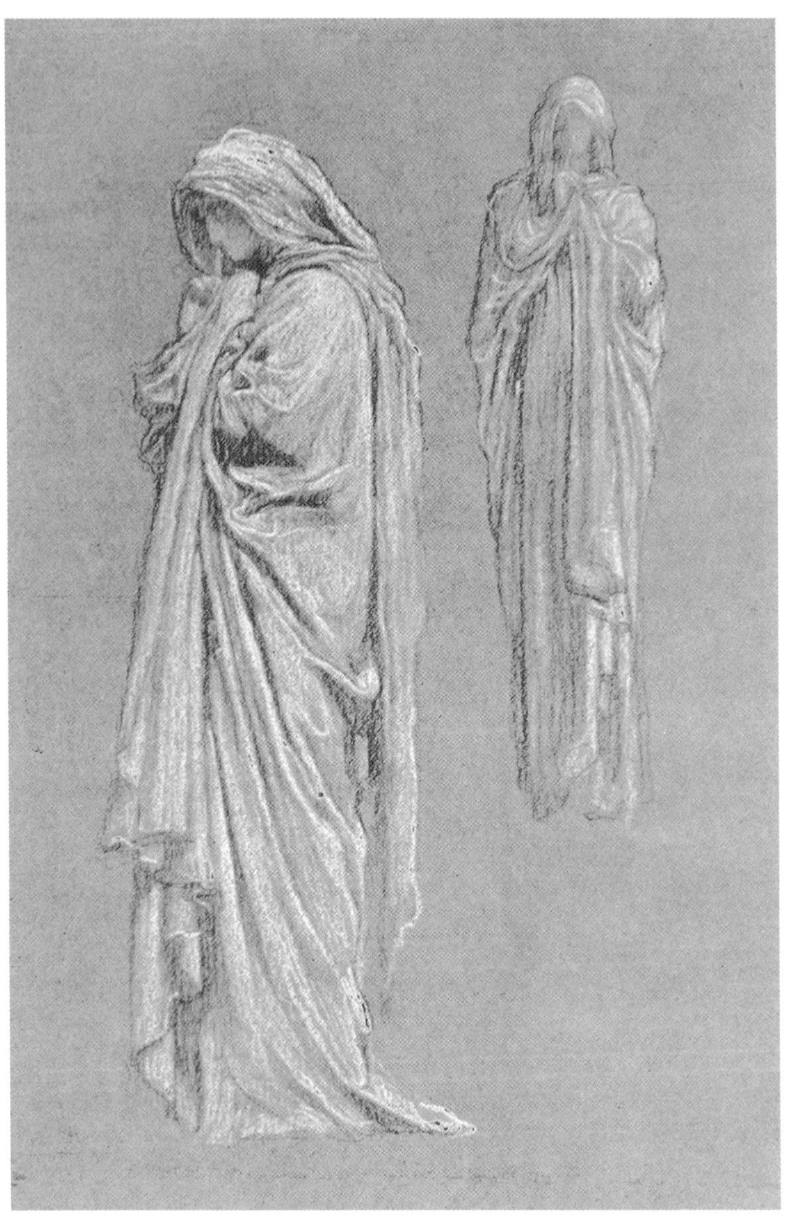

Plate 13 Frontispiece of *The Yellow Book* 1 (1894), with 'A Study' by Frederic Leighton, private collection

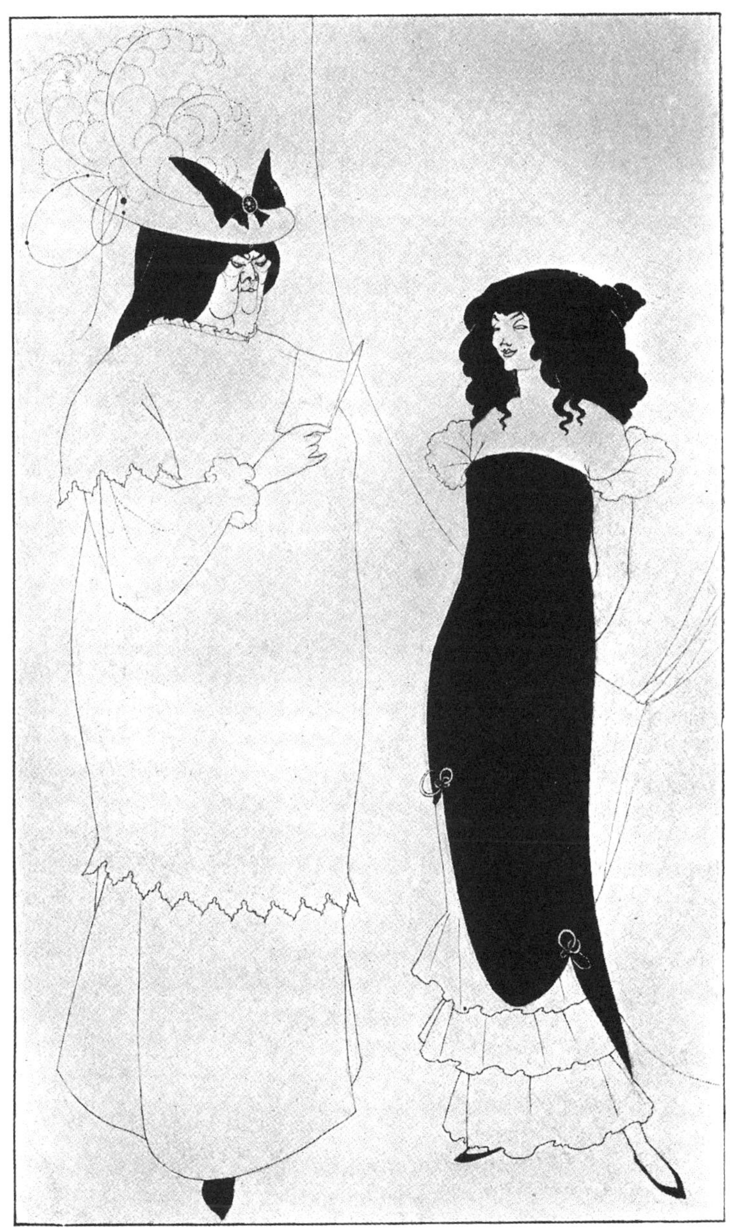

Plate 14   Plate II of *The Yellow Book* 1 (1894), with 'L'Education Sentimentale' by Aubrey Beardsley, private collection

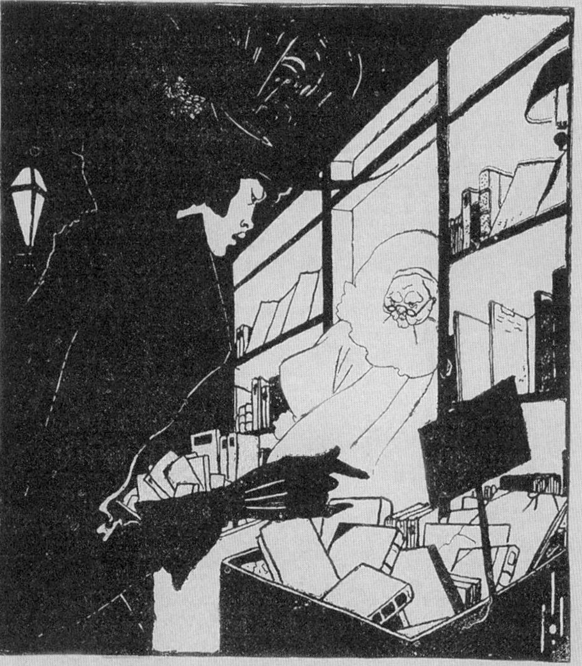

Plate 15 Cover of the prospectus to Volume 1 of *The Yellow Book* (1894), designed by Aubrey Beardsley, private collection

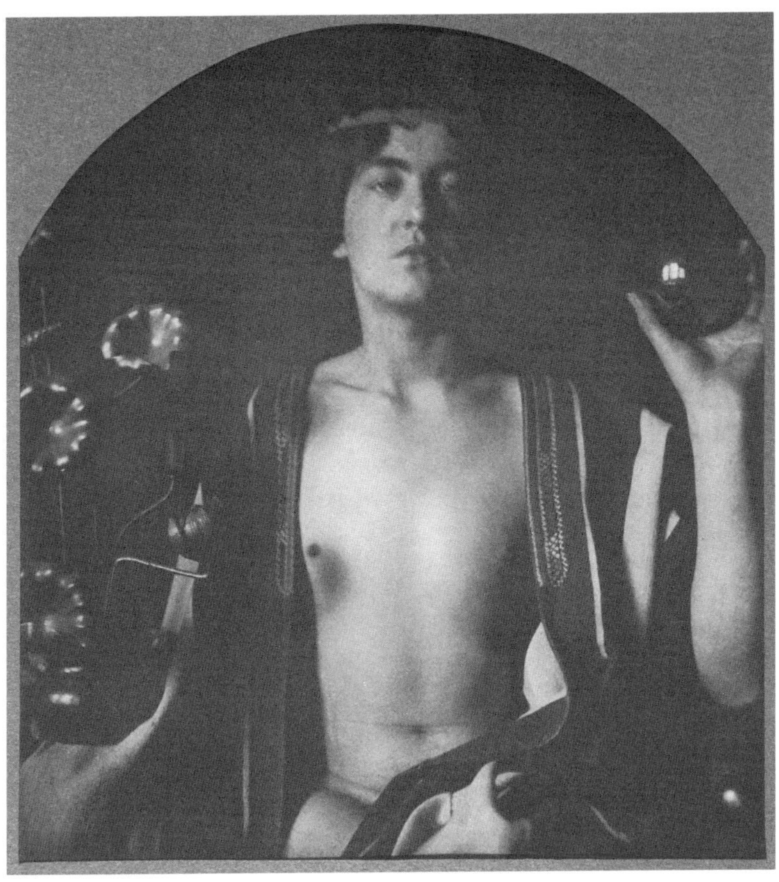

Plate 16 Fred Holland Day, 'Beauty is Truth, Truth is Beauty' (1896); photogravure from *American Pictorial Photography*, Series One, 1899, courtesy of Mark Katzman, Photogravure.com

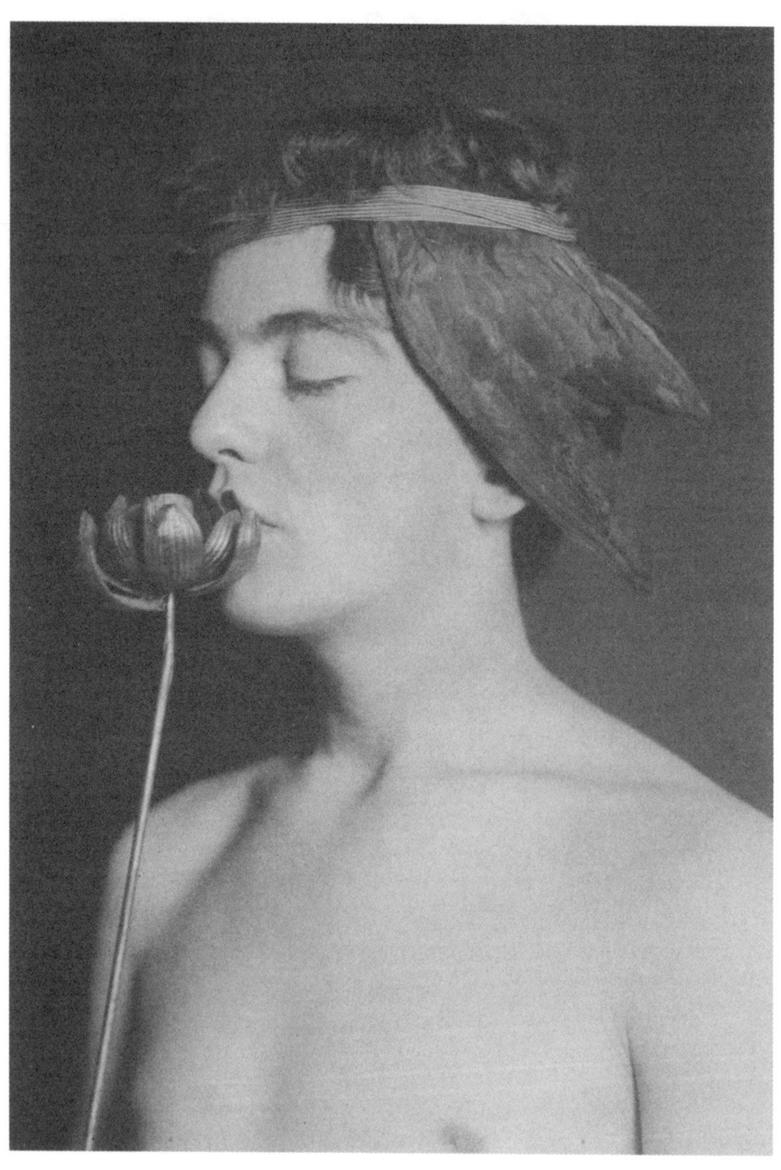

Plate 17 Fred Holland Day, 'Hypnos' (*c*.1896), Royal Photographic Society, Science and Society Picture Library

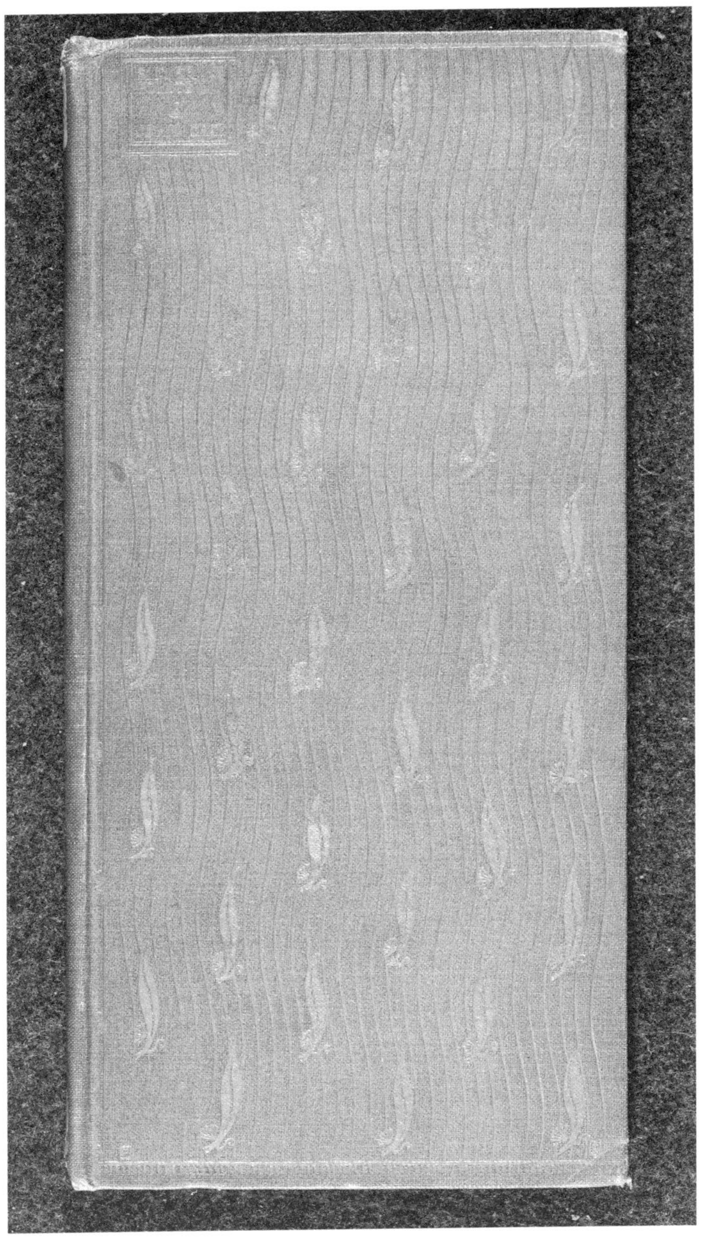

Plate 18   John Gray, *Silverpoints* (London: Elkin Mathews and John Lane, 1893), designed by Charles Ricketts © The British Library Board (C.134.C.14)

SENSATION

I WALK *the alleys trampled through the wheat,*
Through whole blue summer eves, on velvet grass.
Dreaming, I feel the dampness at my feet;
The breezes bathe my naked head and pass.

I do not think a single thought, nor say
A word; but in my soul the mists upcurl
Of infinite love.   I will go far away
With nature, happily, as with a girl.

XXXII

Plate 19   Page xxxii from John Gray, *Silverpoints* (London: Elkin Mathews and John Lane, 1893), designed by Charles Ricketts © The British Library Board (C.134.C.14)

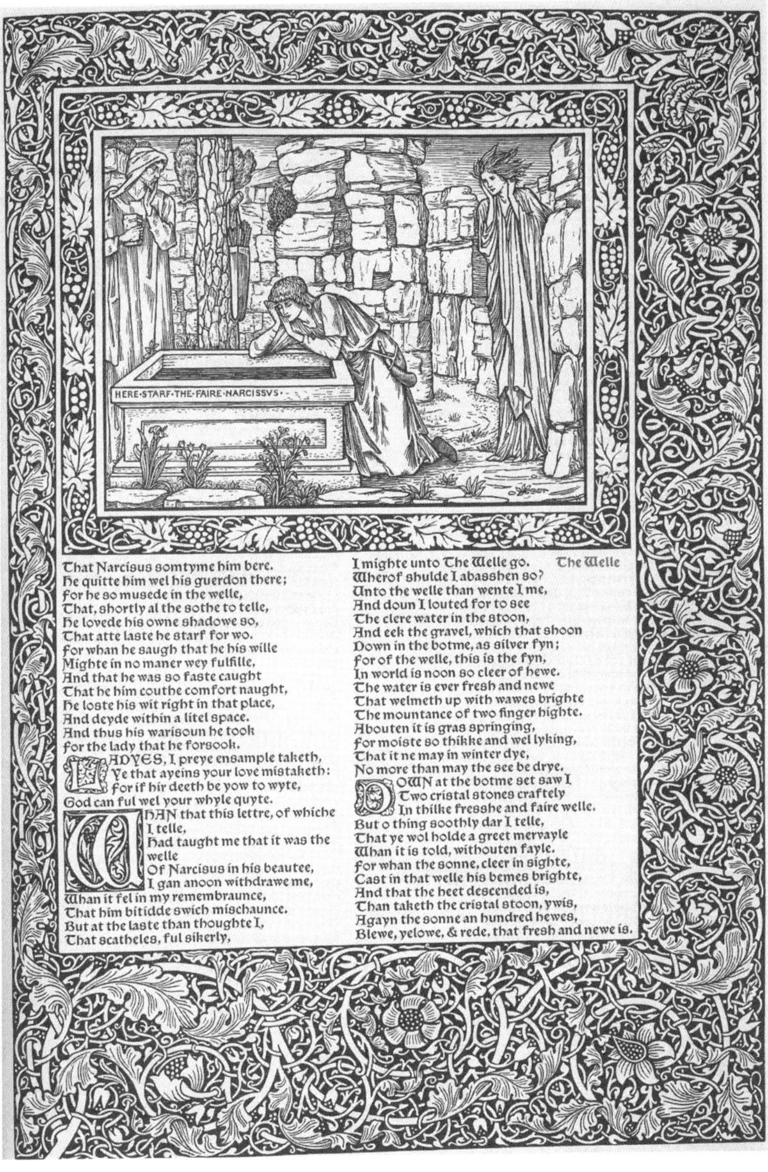

Plate 20 'Narcissus' from *The Works of Geoffrey Chaucer*, 'now newly imprinted, edited by F.S. Ellis, ornamented with pictures designed by Sir Edward Burne-Jones, and engraved on wood by W.H. Hooper' (Hammersmith, London: Kelmscott Press, 1896) © The British Library Board (076956)

Index